Communist Strategy
and Tactics in
Czechoslovakia, 1918–48

Communist Strategy and Tactics in Czechoslovakia, 1918–48

PAUL E. ZINNER

GREENWOOD PRESS, PUBLISHERS
WESTPORT, CONNECTICUT

Library of Congress Cataloging in Publication Data
Zinner, Paul E
    Communist strategy and tactics in Czechoslovakia, 1918-
48.

    Reprint of the ed. published by Praeger, New York,
which was issued as no. 129 of Praeger publications in
Russian history and world communism.
    Includes bibliographical references and index.
    1. Czechoslovak Republic--Politics and government.
2. Komunistická strana Ceskoslovenska. 3. Czechoslovak
Republic--History--Coup d'état, 1948. I. Title.
[DB215.Z55 1975   943.7'03   75-32464
ISBN 0-8371-8550-5

Originally published in 1963 by Frederick A. Praeger,
Publisher, New York

Reprinted with the permission of Praeger Publishers, Inc.

Reprinted in 1975 by Greenwood Press,
a division of Williamhouse-Regency Inc.

Library of Congress Catalog Card Number 75-32464

ISBN 0-8371-8550-5

Printed in the United States of America

943.903
Z78c
1975

PREFACE

THE COMMUNIST seizure of power in February, 1948, in the country created by Masaryk and Benes provoked a revulsion of feeling throughout the Western world not far short of what was felt when Hitler violated Czechoslovakia a decade earlier. Even before the new Communist-dictated government had been sworn in, the United States, Great Britain, and France declared in a joint statement that "the events which have just taken place in Czechoslovakia place in jeopardy the very existence of the principles of liberty to which all democratic nations are attached." Only a veto of the Soviet Union prevented the Security Council of the United Nations from adopting a resolution, offered by Chile, to set up a subcommittee to hear witnesses and obtain information about the coup d'état.

The impact of the coup was intensified by its unexpectedness. In the opinion of political observers with no particular ax to grind, no less than of those who favored collaboration with Communism, the Czechoslovak experiment of combining political democracy with a large degree of socialism had seemed to be succeeding almost until the moment it collapsed. The seizure of power was regarded as an act of supreme perfidy, for in this case neither the Communist Party nor the Soviet Union had even the remotest justification for the overthrow of the existing social and political order.

Czechoslovakia was genuinely friendly to the Soviet Union and placed itself voluntarily under Russia's tutelage in international affairs. Internally, the distribution of forces favored the Communist Party and assured it of a respectable if not always a dominating position in the government. There was no danger of social and economic retrogression. Thus the application of methods

v

used to subjugate other East European states, less friendly to the Soviet Union and less favorably inclined to espouse progressive social and economic policies, served as convincing proof of Communist disingenuousness and put the Western powers on their guard as never before.

The coup gave strong impetus to the creation of a Western defense alliance. On the tenth anniversary of the North Atlantic Treaty Organization, its Secretary-General, Paul Henri Spaak, recalled: "In 1948 the Prague coup d'état dissipated the last illusions and forced us to look facts in the face: The Soviet Union was out to conquer the remainder of Europe." In the popular mind, the coup epitomizes Communist betrayal just as Munich connotes diplomatic appeasement. Actually, the events of February, 1948, were merely the logical conclusion of a process begun much earlier. The foundations of the conquest were laid during World War II. The coup was in many respects an anticlimax; the decisive phase of the struggle had already taken place.

This study attempts to analyze Communist strategy and tactics in context, taking into account the continuous interaction between the Party and the social, political, and economic environment in which it operates, from which it cannot extricate itself, and which it seeks to control, and bearing in mind the influence of outside forces that mold the character of the Party and impinge on its immediate, national environment.

This is not a history either of the Communist Party or of Czechoslovakia, but a case study of power seizure that draws upon data, sets up categories of analysis, defines problems, and illustrates procedures as these appear relevant to an understanding of the complex social processes under investigation.

A historical section on the nature of the First Czechoslovak Republic and the origin and development of the Communist Party from 1918 to 1938 provides indispensable background information. A section on World War II delineates the beginnings of the Communist strategy of conquest in conjunction with the destruction of the political and legal fabric of Czechoslovakia at the hands of the Germans and the ground swell of sentiment in favor of a drastic reorientation of domestic and foreign policies. A final section on the national and democratic revolution deals with the events from the liberation of the country to the coup d'état.

I am grateful to the Russian Research Center at Harvard University for the generous assistance that made it possible to devote myself to research, reflection, and writing, free of other cares, and to Merle Fainsod for his unfailing patience, understanding, and confidence. My wife gave invaluable aid in preparing the manuscript for publication.

My thanks to the editors of *Foreign Affairs* for permission to quote extensively from my article "Marxism in Action: The Seizure of Power in Czechoslovakia," which appeared in the July, 1950, issue of that quarterly.

PAUL E. ZINNER

Davis, California,
March 4, 1962

CONTENTS

*Communist Strategy
and Tactics in
Czechoslovakia, 1918–48*

PART ONE

*Origin and History of the Communist Party
of Czechoslovakia, 1918–38*

1. THE POLITICAL CHARACTER OF CZECHOSLOVAKIA[1]

THOMAS G. MASARYK, the true founder and first President of Czechoslovakia, explaining his choice of a republican form of government, drew attention to a number of similarities between the social structure of his country and that of the United States. In Czechoslovakia, as in America, said Masaryk, there had been "no dynasty, no national aristocracy, no old militarist tradition in the army, and no church politically recognized in the way the older . . . absolutist, Caesarist, theocratic states [recognized it]."[2]

Neither the validity of these sociological observations nor their far-reaching effect on the democratic orientation of both the United States and Czechoslovakia can be doubted. The similarities cited by Masaryk probably go a long way toward explaining the widespread feeling on this side of the Atlantic that somehow Czechoslovakia was more "American" in its ways than most other Continental countries. In this context it may be worth elaborating on one of Masaryk's points, the full implications of which he did not spell out. Czechoslovakia, despite a strong numerical majority of Catholics, was essentially a Protestant country. As such, it was spiritually closely akin to the great Anglo-Saxon democracies. The influence of what may be roughly identified as the Protestant ethic was pervasive, and Protestants wielded disproportionate power in the country's political life. Reinforced with a strong fiber of nationalism stemming from the inextricable

NOTE: This chapter is not to be construed as a substitute for an exhaustive history or detailed study of government and politics in Czechoslovakia between the two world wars. It is no more than a sketch of the salient features and influences that gave Czechoslovakia its distinctive character and were relevant to the development of the Communist Party.

combination of religious and nationalistic elements in the legacy of Hussitism, this Protestant influence extended over the great number—perhaps even the majority—of Czech Catholics who were only nominal members of the Church. The case of Slovakia was somewhat different, but even though the Catholic Church retained a strong spiritual influence, the primacy of Protestants in affairs of state was apparent.

The traits cited by Masaryk were important in shaping the character of Czech democracy. Their easy and unqualified acceptance as the sole determinants of Czechoslovak politics, however, could hardly be justified. Nor did Masaryk intend them to be. Had he sought to analyze more profoundly his country's functioning as a social system, he would have also found it necessary to reveal the significant differences in the historical experience, political heritage, and social composition (despite some striking similarities) between the American and the Czech nations and the vastly dissimilar circumstances in which Czech democracy, once established, developed. Certain differences were the result of Europe-wide social, political, economic, and cultural trends in the maelstrom of which the Czechs were caught up. Others were wholly *sui generis*. What then were the major influences shaping the character of Czechoslovakia?

Concepts of Freedom

Freedom was the birthright of Americans who fought to prevent the loss of what they considered to be their natural rights. It came to the Czechs after 300 years of foreign rule. During these centuries of subjugation, the Czechs almost lost their national identity. It was not until the beginning of the nineteenth century—when nationalistic feeling swept over the Continent in a series of revolutionary waves—that national consciousness was revived.

Among the Czechs, romantic nationalism was limited to the glorification of past revolutionary and cultural achievements. The leaders of the awakening—Jan Kollar, Karel Havlicek Borovsky (better known as Havlicek), and Frantisek Palacky (the "Father of the Nation" and, until Masaryk, the outstanding Czech patriot*) —invariably invoked the example of the Hussite movement,

---

*Palacky was once identified by Marx as a "German gone mad."

which had combined ardent fighting for freedom of conscience with toleration and strict allegiance to the laws of morality. For the present, revolutionary means of attaining freedom were soft-pedaled. The fulfillment of Czech national destiny was seen in the closest possible identification with panhuman aspirations. (For example, in Kollar's famous poem *Slavy Dcera,* the identification of "Slav" with "human" is complete.) As a matter of practical attitude, caution was advocated. Havlicek, perhaps the most celebrated revolutionary of his time, reportedly said: "Elsewhere men have died for the honor and welfare of their fatherland; the same reasons impel us to live for it."[3] Palacky, in turn, is credited with the famous statement: "We were here before Austria and will be here after it is gone." The implication of outlasting the oppressor rather than overthrowing him is clear.

It is perhaps unimportant to search for the causes that might account for the absence of revolutionary zeal among the Czechs in the nineteenth and twentieth centuries. It is also unnecessary to label this quality a permanent national character.[4] For our purposes, it is sufficient to note that the Czech national reawakening proceeded under the aegis of strong moral overtones and in the absence of any propensity for forceful self-assertion. This is not meant to disparage the personal courage of individual members of the society, or to deprecate the fighting qualities of the Czech soldier in uniform, but merely to assert that in a given period of time, the Czechs were loath to rise in arms for whatever purpose. The very culmination of the long period of national rebirth, the creation of an independent Czechoslovak state, was itself devoid of violence. Similarly, on subsequent critical occasions when the nation might well have chosen to fight, alone if necessary, it invariably chose the bloodless course.

Social Structure

Czechoslovakia came of age long after the industrial revolution was over in Western Europe and the Czechs themselves had attained considerable industrial maturity. Industrialization had a profound impact on the social composition of the Czech people, who had absorbed the social and political ideas of the late nineteenth and early twentieth centuries.

The backbone of the people, unlike the thirteen American colonies at the time of their revolution, was not a class of independent farmers or individualist entrepreneurs, but a proletarian working class (which accounted for one-third of the population), an urban petty bourgeoisie (including a large number of salaried civil servants), and a peasantry. The robust individualism of the United States was nowhere in sight. Czech individualism was at best a tender garden variety of the species, requiring great care and protection to blossom. It is not inaccurate to describe the social and political orientation of the Czechs as strongly collectivist. Individually, and as a nation, they looked for a sheltering environment. Implicit in their political philosophy was the concept of strong—but just and benign—government which "encourages the free development of individuals with varying natural and physical endowments."

It was not accidental that Social Democrats organized the first Czech political party and that this party commanded a sizable following. The trade-union movement was also well developed, and the proportion of workers with membership in the unions was unusually high. The Social Democrats emerged as the most numerous group in 1918. Their primacy was short-lived, but the political orientation of the Czechs, judged in terms of the usual left-right spectrum, remained considerably to the left of the normal spread in Western Europe. The extreme right (i.e., the fascists) never attained prominence, whereas on the left there were a number of socialist parties with democratic orientation. The Catholic People's Party—center by Czech standards—was definitely leftist compared with Western European Christian Social movements. The most prominent conservative party, the Agrarian, could be more appropriately designated as a center rather than a rightist party, despite some obvious (and in the end predominant) reactionary tendencies in its leadership.[5] All politics moved in an atmosphere of social reformism. Although the vision of economic and social democracy, much in evidence immediately after 1918, remained substantially unfulfilled and tended to recede into the ever more distant future, some economic reforms (e.g., land reform) were carried out, and a high degree of social justice was attained. The social-security system was among the more comprehensive in the world. In sharp contrast to the

United States, where socialism has never taken hold, the concept and practice of democracy had a distinctive "welfare" character in Czechoslovakia.

Masaryk and Benes

No appraisal of Czechoslovakia, however sketchy, could be complete without due consideration of the influence of Thomas G. Masaryk. In him, the Czechs found an ideal leader. Learned, wise, kind, deeply religious and moral, he fitted perfectly the role of the charismatic, benevolent philosopher-king (President) whom the Czechs seemed to want and need. His contribution to the making of the state was enormous. In addition, he supplied the philosophical premises on which Czechoslovakia was founded and guided the destiny of his country with a firm but kindly hand for almost two decades.

Masaryk's home-grown type of humanism embodied elements of the Hussite legacy, which had figured prominently in the recapture of national consciousness, and included tenets of more recent Western philosophical thought (the influence of Kant and Hume was especially discernible). Finally, it reflected the growing social awareness of the late nineteenth and the twentieth centuries.[6]

Masaryk's philosophy provided both an ideal to be upheld and a practical guide for everyday politics and living. Its main supporting pillars were moral obligation, self-discipline, and ethical sympathy. Reduced to its fundamentals, it could be expressed in three slogans: "Truth prevails"; "Jesus, not Caesar"; and "Do unto others as you would have them do unto you." The first of these slogans was the official "motto" of the Republic. Humanism, to Masaryk, essentially meant "ethical sympathy, men's respect for their fellow men, a recognition of the worth of human personality. Politically and socially, these principles imply equality between all citizens of a state and the bringing together of nations and states in a closer community of interest on the basis of common humanity."[7] Democracy and internationalism (of the League of Nations type) followed naturally from these premises.

The impact of Masaryk's ideas was enhanced by the spontaneous harmony which they achieved with popular value orientations among the Czechs. Their influence was the more enduring because they were shared by Eduard Benes, his closest friend and protégé, who succeeded him in the Presidency.

Benes even more than Masaryk was concerned with the relation between the individual and society, and it was no secret that he was a self-styled socialist. The problem of democracy, as he saw it, and this was of overriding concern to him, was "to find the right compromise between individualism and socialism."[8] Surely this was no startling discovery, but few statesmen in the twentieth century have striven more earnestly to find a practical solution to this problem.

The good name of Czechoslovakia abroad was due largely to the air of morality Masaryk and Benes imparted to it and to the high degree of identification of the country with the personal attributes of these popular and well-known leaders. Within the country, the moral standards postulated by them served as a yardstick by which the people generally measured their conduct—public and private. Masaryk's spell over all the people, regardless of social class and age, was truly remarkable. The younger generation who grew up under the Republic embraced "Masarykism" still more enthusiastically than their elders.

But it would be utopian to believe that the realities of political life corresponded to the exalted precepts of Masarykist morality. No society could abide consistently by these standards. Czechoslovakia was not devoid of its share of deficiencies.

It was a new democracy, and while the moderate disposition of the Czech people safeguarded them from the misfortunes of adventurism and extremism, there was a pronounced tendency toward political irresponsibility. Furthermore, Czechoslovakia lacked the cohesiveness that might have ensured its stability. Social homogeneity, as well as most of the other traits to which Masaryk had alluded, was properly applicable only to the Czechs —who constituted the largest single national element in the state and played a dominant part in its government, but accounted for no more than half the total population.

The rest of the population was made up of Slovaks and Ruthenians* (who, together with the Czechs, represented the

---

*The Ruthenian problem, although very intricate and not without significance, will not be discussed here, for it has only marginal bearing on the main theme of the study.

majority Slavic component), Germans, Hungarians, and a scattering of other national minorities. All of them differed significantly from the Czechs in regard to social composition, political orientation, and intensity of religious association. In varying degrees, all national groups except the Czechs harbored feelings inimical to the best interests of the Republic. In the final analysis, the political evolution of Czechoslovakia was influenced as much by its ethnic fractionization as by the character and disposition of the Czech people and Masaryk.

Czechs and Slovaks

The Czech-Slovak dichotomy deeply affected the political balance and evolution of the young republic. It had its roots in the dissimilar historical circumstances in which the two nations—the Czechs under Austrian rule, the Slovaks under Hungarian overlordship—had developed for centuries before attaining independence. The basic factors underlying the conflict were: (a) fundamental differences between the Czech and Slovak economies, (b) unequal political and cultural development, and (c) divergence in the intensity of religious affiliation with the Catholic Church. Superimposed on these factors were the frictions and political tensions almost inevitably generated in the course of adjusting to the conditions of independence and self-rule.[9]

The Czechs in 1918 were a modern industrial nation—with all that implies. The Slovaks were just emerging from a feudal stage. Their province was primarily an agricultural area and for the most part a poor one. It was economically backward and socially retarded. Whereas in the Czech lands less than 35 per cent of the population were engaged in agriculture and close to 40 per cent in industrial pursuits, the figures for Slovakia were 60 and 19 per cent respectively. The difficulties of reconciling the interests of two regions so sharply divergent in their economic and social development are not unfamiliar to Americans. Indeed, in some respects, the Czech-Slovak conflict closely paralleled that of the North and South in the United States. There were other problems as well.

The lack of Slovak national consciousness in 1918 and the absence of an educated middle class were responsible for much of the political friction that developed between the Czechs and Slovaks. The latter had been subjected to a harsh policy of Magyarization during the half-century preceding their liberation. As a result, they had all but lost their national identity. The conditions of social success were so rigidly controlled by the Hungarian authorities that the middle class in Slovakia consisted almost entirely of Magyars or Magyarized Slovaks who had given up their ethnic identity for the sake of a more highly respected place in society. According to the eminent British historian R. W. Seton-Watson, only a small nucleus of a few hundred Slovaks possessed the qualities necessary for building the state—sincere nationalism and an education.[10]

The urgent need to protect Slovakia from actual Hungarian military onslaught and to establish a viable administration loyal to the Republic led to the rapid centralization of power in Prague and the establishment of Czech dominance over Slovakia. Between 1918 and 1920, more than 70,000 Czechs were dispatched to Slovakia. Although the acute threat to the safety of Slovakia subsided rapidly, the influx of Czech personnel continued, at a somewhat reduced rate, throughout the 1920's. By 1930, there were 120,000 Czechs in Slovakia.[11] Of these, 20,000 were military personnel, and 50,000 were gainfully employed—20,000 of them in the public services and the rest in private enterprise, especially in the armament industry, which was expanding its operations eastward; the remaining 50,000 were family dependents. Whatever the justification might have been for centralizing power in Prague and dispatching Czech civil servants to Slovakia during the formative years of the Republic, the need decreased as an indigenous Slovak intelligentsia was trained. The Czechs in Slovakia, however, had acquired vested interests and resisted any efforts to transfer them. In this manner, they contributed to unemployment among Slovak intellectuals and technicians and caused ill-feeling in an articulate and active group. The nature of the functions they performed—police, tax collection, law enforcement in general—further increased the grievances of the local population and fanned the fires of Slovak "autonomism," which had become the main issue of political opposition to the Czechs.

The leaders of these two nations, who had joined in good faith in the formation of a common state, failed to settle matters relating to the division of power and the actual internal structure of the Republic. The question of the constitutional position of Slovakia, the degree of influence that the Slovaks were to have in affairs of state, and the measure of self-rule they were to enjoy in their province quickly became subjects of dispute. As the issues became aggravated, both sides tended to take extreme positions. Slovaks charged that they were being deprived of rights that had been agreed to before independence. They based that charge on a declaration signed at Pittsburgh (the famous "Pittsburgh Agreement") by Slovak-Americans and Masaryk when the latter was visiting the United States in the spring of 1918. The declaration indeed did refer to the principle of autonomous status for Slovakia. Whether or not it was meant to serve as a guide for future action or could be considered binding on the President, who affixed his name before he had any official title, is subject to debate. At any rate, Masaryk denied that he ever construed the Pittsburgh declaration as having any bearing on the organization of Czechoslovakia. If the Slovaks somewhat irrationally harped on the unfulfilled promise of the Pittsburgh declaration, overzealous Czechs countered by denying the existence of a separate Slovak nation. They also sought to suppress the Slovak language, which, though very closely related to Czech, is nevertheless morphologically distinct from it. All this did not make for amicable relations.

Religion was another factor that consistently blighted relations between the two peoples. The Catholic Church, which retained predominant influence in Slovakia, was disturbed by the secular, not to say anticlerical, orientation of the central authorities in Prague. It objected to the government's efforts to secularize the school system and undermine the economic support of the Church by subjecting its land holdings to the limitations set by the land-reform decrees. The government in turn suspected, not without reason, that large numbers of the Catholic hierarchy harbored pro-Magyar feelings. Concern over the political allegiance of the clergy caused the government to seek a voice in the appointment of bishops. This issue and others, relating to diocesan jurisdiction between Hungarian and Slovak districts and to the commemoration of Jan Hus Day as a religious and national holiday, led to bitter controversy not only with the local clergy, but also with the Vatican. The controversy with the Vatican was resolved by a *modus vivendi* in 1928. Accordingly, diocesan frontiers were redrawn to terminate Hungarian ecclesiastic jurisdiction over Slovak administrative districts, and while the Vatican retained the right to appoint bishops, it could do so only with the prior approval of the Czechoslovak Government.

The formal settlement of these questions failed to mollify the Slovak Catholic hierarchy, which had become the focal point of anti-Czech political agitation. Clergymen had been instrumental in founding the Slovak People's Party, better known as the Hlinka Party (after its leader, Father Andrej Hlinka). This party was the standard-bearer of autonomist aspirations. It polled one-third of the votes cast in Slovakia, and was by far the strongest party there. (Its closest competitor, the Agrarian Party, obtained less than 20 per cent of the vote.) This was no more than a plurality, but in appraising the significance of these figures, one must remember that, with the exception of the Communists in Ruthenia, no political party in Czechoslovakia (on either a nationwide or a provincial basis) attracted a comparable percentage of votes, and the remainder of the votes in Slovakia was by no means cast for parties supporting the central government. The Communists, with 13 per cent, and the Hungarian and German minority parties, with 16 per cent, rounded out the opposition. All told, the parties of the government coalition were in a minority by an uncomfortable margin. Nor was the electoral support received by these parties an unequivocal index of popular sentiment favoring centralization of power in Prague. The Agrarian Party, for example, attracted a large number of voters favoring decentralization. Their voices were muted because of their anomalous position. They could not afford to undermine their party's appeal in the Czech lands—and that would have been the effect of a strong stand on Slovak autonomism. Moreover, being for the most part Protestants, they were mindful of their rivalry with the Hlinka Party, and worried that under conditions of self-rule they might lose the influence they enjoyed by virtue of their association with fellow Agrarians from Bohemia and Moravia.

The unresolved issue of Slovak autonomy had a deleterious effect on political stability and development. This is not to say that the Republic was continually on the verge of splitting into its component parts. Many of the leaders of the Slovak People's Party, including Father Hlinka, who was its Chairman until his death in the summer of 1938, pursued limited objectives. Although they were predisposed to be authoritarian, they favored constitutional, legal methods for settling their differences with the Czechs. For a short period—from October, 1926, until December, 1929—the party even joined the government coalition. But there were other, more reckless leaders, like Bela Tuka, who either flirted with or actually were in the pay of foreign governments. In the end, the less temperate faction gained the upper hand, and, in 1939, at Hitler's direct instigation, it contributed to the dismemberment of Czechoslovakia.

Germans and Hungarians

The influence of the ethnic minorities on Czechoslovak politics requires no more than brief mention. Their story has been much publicized and is well known.[12] Despite an honest effort by the Czechoslovak Government to live up to the letter of the extensive obligations it had incurred by signing international treaties that guaranteed the protection of minorities, the integration of diverse ethnic groups into the body politic of the Republic was an arduous undertaking that had only temporary and partial success. While obstruction on the part of the minorities was responsible for most of the difficulties, the Czechs, for all their efforts, did not always act felicitously in matters concerning ethnic problems and helped to aggravate tensions.

Following the very difficult years immediately after the establishment of Czechoslovak independence, when nationalist agitation among the minorities was still at a high pitch and their allegiance to the Republic was tenuous, some headway was made toward cooperation. "Masarykism" seemed to be gaining among minorities as well. Of the two large ethnic blocs living in contiguous areas, the Germans were conciliated more rapidly than the Hungarians.

Representatives of two moderate German parties, the Agrarian and the Christian Social, entered the government in 1926. Three years later, the Social Democrats joined the governing coalition, so that one or another moderate German party retained membership in the government until September, 1938; but after 1935, they no longer could claim to speak for the German constituency.

The conciliatory attitude of the Germans during the late 1920's and the first year or two of the 1930's reflected the absence of nationalist agitation by the Weimar Republic. The rise of Nazism, coupled with the adverse repercussions of the depression, which affected the heavily industrialized Sudeten area more severely than some other regions, helped to revive German irredentism. By 1935, the great majority of Germans voted for the Sudeten German Party, organized and led by Konrad Henlein. As a result, it emerged from the general elections that year numerically stronger than any other party. It received 14.3 per cent of the total popular vote—a fraction of a percentage more than the Agrarians, the largest party of the government coalition. Totalitarian in its ideological and organizational make-up, opposed to the best interests of the Republic, and supported from abroad by the growing power of Hitler's Germany, the Sudeten German Party constituted a fifth column that threatened the very existence of Czechoslovakia.

The Hungarian minority was consistently less willing to cooperate than the German. This was in part due to the vigor and the persistence of the Hungarian Government's irredentist agitation throughout the 1920's, as well as the 1930's. However, given the limited strength of Admiral Horthy's government, the Magyar minority, once contained, was not a serious menace until the fall of 1938, when the fabric of the state was weakened and the Hungarians also could have their way.

The external threat to Czechoslovakia was, if not at all times actual, potentially ever-present. In combination with the attitudes of the ethnic minorities, it put a high premium on protecting the sovereign independence of the Republic.

To meet the external threat, Czechoslovakia clung closely to policies of collective security based on the League of Nations. Supplementing this security system was a network of bilateral and multilateral agreements with states other than its immediate neighbors (except Rumania, with whom Czechoslovakia both shared a frontier and had an alliance). The cornerstone of the Czechoslovak system of alliances was a mutual-assistance and friendship treaty with France, which was supplemented in 1935 by a similar treaty with the U.S.S.R. Finally, there was the Little Entente, a tripartite alliance with Rumania and Yugoslavia, aimed particularly at containing Hungary.[13]

This impressive network of treaties had serious structural defects. Eventually, it failed Czechoslovakia completely. To honor their commitments, Czechoslovakia's allies needed to be impelled by an exceptionally strong sense of obligation. They could give assistance by attacking the foe from the rear, and thus court involvement in a war that otherwise seemed avoidable. Alternatively, they could bolster the defensive capacity of Czechoslovakia directly by offering men and arms. To this end, they would have to surmount grave diplomatic and technical difficulties interposed by countries whose territory they would have to cross.

At the critical moment, Czechoslovakia's friends lacked the fortitude to brave these dangers and to overcome these obstacles. Left to its own devices, Czechoslovakia stood little chance of defending itself successfully, although it had a large and well-trained army. It did not have the cohesiveness that would have enabled the government to choose to fight even against heavy odds. The presence of disaffected nationalities robbed the country of the moral unity and fervor needed to meet crises heroically. It also had other curious effects, giving rise to intense chauvinism among Czechs and patriotic Slovaks. The panhumanism in which they believed was reserved for distant nations, whereas their chauvinism was directed at individuals and groups with whom they lived in daily contact.

Political Parties

The ethnic fractionization of the country contributed to a formidable proliferation of political parties. At election time, from twenty to thirty parties made their appearance. Although many of them did not attract sufficient support to gain a seat in parliament, no fewer than thirteen and often more parties were represented in the Senate and the National Assembly. More important, however, were the limitations imposed on the scope and meaning of politics. The peculiar ethnic composition of the country and its exposed international situation had contradictory effects, inhibiting political irresponsibility in certain respects and increasing it in others. Knowledge of the potential dangers of extremism which might upset the delicate equilibrium restrained centrifugal tendencies among Czech and Slovak political parties, causing several of them to coalesce—an accomplishment of which they would have been incapable under different circumstances. At the same time, the threat to national security was invoked as a convenient excuse whenever one or another of the coalition parties wanted to forestall the enactment of legislation it opposed. This condition made for political impotence and stagnation, and accounted for the lack of discernible progress along political, social, and economic lines after the initial impetus supplied by independence had spent itself.

The existence of many parties reflected the national composition of the state and the usual class and ideological divisions which made coalition government necessary. As a rule, the government consisted of ministers from four to seven parties and one or two nonparty experts (technicians). Given the divergent interests of the parties, a dynamic program was hardly possible. In the absence of an alternative, the government carried on, substantially unchanged, with the Agrarian, National Socialist, Social Democratic, and Czech People's parties as its core. (The National Socialists and Social Democrats did not participate between 1926 and 1929.) When the cabinet encountered an unusually vexatious issue, it resigned, more or less as a gesture of futility. It was then re-formed in virtually the same composition. Thus, while the average life of a cabinet was only fourteen months (two months longer than the average life of French cabinets in the interwar period), not a single one was removed from office by a vote of nonconfidence.[14] Moreover, the relative constancy of the electoral support of the major parties ensured comparable continuity in the number of cabinet posts assigned to them. For example, the Agrarians—who after 1920 were consistently the strongest party (they outstripped their nearest competitor by 2–3 per cent of the total vote)—held the Premiership and the Ministries of the Interior, Defense, and Agriculture. The Social Democrats alternated between the Ministries of Justice, Social Welfare, and Education, and the National Socialists held the portfolio of Foreign Affairs in perpetuity.

Underneath this artificial façade of serenity, however, an atmosphere of inflamed party relations permeated the entire life of the country. The reasons for this are not fully known. Perhaps the frustrations of the political leaders, stemming from the limitations mentioned above, caused them to release aggression in other directions. Be that as it may, the personal element in Czechoslovak politics supplied the fuel for much political strife. Each party was the instrument of a tightly knit group of men who jealously guarded their prerogatives. Opposition within the parties was ruthlessly stifled and could assert itself only by splitting away from the parent organization. To protect their unity and to maintain discipline, the parties exercised strict control over their parliamentary deputies.

According to Czechoslovak law, each candidate for election, as a precondition to nomination, had to place himself totally at the disposal of his party, acquiescing in his own recall at the pleasure of the party executive. This prerogative was invoked freely at the slightest sign of recalcitrance by a deputy. Appeals against recall were never successful. The electoral court invariably backed the party executive.[15] The parties also kept a tight rein on their cabinet representatives. In 1921, when the first government of non-party "technicians" came into office, a council composed of the chairmen of the five largest parties was formed to act as liaison between the cabinet and the parties. The government of experts soon resigned, but the so-called Council of Five remained in existence, gaining in power until at last it became the major policy-making body in the state.

The tendency toward oligarchic organization in the parties stunted the development of a new generation of talented politicians. The dominating personalities were relics of the nineteenth century. Their failure to groom a young political elite deprived Czechoslovak democracy of much-needed vitality. The lack of greater popular control over party affairs was also detrimental to the vigor of democracy. It reduced the vast mass of the people to passivity as spectators rather than participants in politics.

The swing of the political pendulum, allegedly characteristic of parliamentary democracies, was not perceptible in Czechoslovakia. Over the years, the electoral strength of the left tended to decrease slightly, while that of the right rose commensurately. The slow but steady numerical gains of the right were accompanied by a faster and more pronounced growth in its political power. The splintering of the leftist, socialist, or socialist-tinged vote among the several parties, who were unable to make common cause for ideological reasons, deprived this large segment of public opinion of a unified and effective voice in the affairs of state. The right did not suffer similar diffusion. Its strongest spokesman, the Agrarian Party, was able to preserve a slight numerical edge over all others. This infinitesimal advantage over its individual competitors (the combined votes of Social Democrats, National Socialists, and Communists outnumbered the Agrarian vote by almost three to one) gave the Agrarian Party disproportionate influence in the executive and legislative branches of the government. The benefits that accrued to the Agrarians as a result of the strangle hold they had on key institutions are readily apparent. The Ministry of the Interior entailed control of the police and of the vast bureaucratic apparatus of local government; with it went enormous powers of patronage. The Ministry of Agriculture in turn had strong influence over the peasantry in fiscal and other affairs. No wonder that prior to 1938 many Czech and Slovak politicians plaintively referred to the "dictatorship" of the Agrarian Party.

During the late 1930's, when totalitarian forces were in ascendance all around Czechoslovakia, authoritarian trends within the country also gained momentum. The crumbling of the international order established at Versailles and the simultaneous retreat from glory of democratic government everywhere on the Continent could not be without repercussions in Czechoslovakia. The leaders of the Agrarian Party had never been friendly toward Benes and his brand of internationalism. These leaders were also perhaps the least addicted to the ideals of Masaryk. As the viability of the Republic was ever more seriously questioned and threatened, they advocated a *rapprochement* with Hitler's Germany as an alternative to Benes' system of paper alliances. Despite the existence of such tendencies in its strongest coalition party, Czechoslovakia, in sharp contrast with its immediate neighbors, preserved a functioning parliamentary order until it was destroyed from outside.

The Breakup of the Republic

The Munich agreement of September, 1938, which gave the Reich all German-inhabited territories in Czechoslovakia, and the Vienna award of November of the same year, which gave Hungary the Magyar-inhabited parts of Slovakia, caused Benes to abdicate from the Presidency and to leave the country. It also spurred the growth of authoritarian trends in the truncated, so-called Second Republic.[16]

In Bohemia and Moravia, the political structure was simplified by the coordination of the various parties into two political blocs. The Party of National Solidarity (Narodni Sourucenstvi) included elements from all the former "bourgeois" parties. But it was in fact dominated by the conservative leaders of the Agrarian Party, who quickly developed a taste for dictatorial practices. The "opposition," concentrated in the National Labor Party (Narodni Strana Prace), was composed of former members of the socialist parties. It was rendered almost powerless by its stronger adversary, the National Solidarity, which passed laws enabling itself to rule with a free hand. In Slovakia, where developments were marked by a rapid proliferation of secessionist aims, all parties except one were abolished. The Slovak People's Party seized a monopoly of power.

After the German occupation of the Czech lands in March, 1939, political life was reduced to a minimum. The Party of National Solidarity was slated to become a Czech counterpart of the Nazi Party, but, after two years of faltering efforts, it disappeared from public view. It was revived in the spring of 1945, by Emil Hacha, the Czech puppet President of the Protectorate, in a last desperate lunge for political vitality. Vlajka, a German-sponsored fascist group, took up where the Party of National Solidarity left off in 1941. Its appeal to the population was negligible, however, and its only claim to fame lay in the rowdyism of its members. It was disbanded in 1943.

In Slovakia, which became an independent republic under German tutelage, the People's Party followed the totalitarian pattern of the Nazi governmental organization. "Masaryk's democracy" ceased to exist.

The circumstances of Czechoslovakia's development prior to 1938 tended to relegate incipient social strife and class conflict to a secondary place. Because of the large degree of social homogeneity among the Czechs, who in 1918 lacked not only an aristocracy but a well-developed class of capitalist exploiters as well, social conflict was not of primary import. Moreover, the workers were exhilarated by their newly won national independence. In time, social differentiation inevitably took place. Its effects, however, were mitigated by the fact that the class of exploiters included fewer Czechs and Slovaks (relatively speaking) than Germans and Hungarians, so that a process which under different circumstances might have led to increasing social friction was subsumed under the broader aspect of national strife. The Czech workers by and large felt a real sense of belonging to their country and had a stake in its survival. The absence of a revolutionary tradition, the deeply rooted preferences for gradual and peaceful change, the socialist bias of prevailing political ideas, and, finally, the acceptance of Masaryk's humanism as a suitable code of collective and individual conduct also molded the character of the Communist Party and affected its strategy and tactics.

This is not to say that Communism and the Communist Party were rejected in Czechoslovakia. On the contrary, the Communists were permitted to operate in the open with very little interference from the police, and the political climate was hospitable to them. Soviet Communism seemed less formidable in Czechoslovakia than in neighboring countries, which had suffered disastrous experiences with Imperial Russia and had also come into bruising contact with Bolshevik violence, military invasion (in Poland), and massive internal subversion (in Hungary). The Czechs and the Slovaks had no similar experiences either with Russia under the Czars or with the Soviet regime.

Some groups, such as conservative industrialists centered in the National Democratic Party and legionnaires (veterans who had fought against the Communist revolutionaries in Russia), harbored vigorous anti-Bolshevik sentiments. Majority public opinion, however, took a dispassionate view of Bolshevism, regarding it not as an unmitigated evil to be exorcised from all those suspected of being under its spell, but as a monumental social, economic, and political experiment, which, though hardly applicable to Czechoslovakia, had a capacity for internal growth and had to be judged from a very broad historical perspective. Many groups, including the Social Democrats, soberly exposed the terroristic and antihumanitarian practices of Bolshevism and condemned them, without creating a mood of national hysteria.

The policies of the government toward the Soviet regime were cautiously ambiguous. The Communist government in Moscow was not considered a menace to the integrity of the Czechoslovak Republic, and Benes, the architect of Czechoslovak foreign policy, maintained that the participation of the Soviet Union in European affairs was essential to assure a stable peace. But he refrained from leading a movement to give diplomatic recognition to the Bolsheviks or from developing close political relations with them. The Czechoslovak authorities were receptive to the idea of trade relations with Soviet Russia. At the same time, they granted asylum to a very large number of refugees from Bolshevik terror, and Prague became an important White Russian political and intellectual center.

De jure recognition was withheld from the Soviet Government until 1934. By this time, Germany had withdrawn from and Soviet Russia had joined the League of Nations; it did not seem incongruous to exchange diplomatic representatives with a country that had established formal relations with the leading powers of the world, including the United States. The conclusion of a mutual-assistance treaty with the U.S.S.R. in 1935 represented, from Benes' point of view, a practical arrangement between states whose self-interest coincided. Both were mindful of the growing threat from Nazi Germany. Even so, the alliance with Russia incurred the displeasure of some influential politicians, including the leaders of the Agrarian Party. Benes himself was under no illusion concerning the repercussions that would follow the implementation of the terms of the treaty, and he categorically rejected the possibility of inviting Soviet aid without concomitant Western assistance to balance the forces brought into play in the defense of the *status quo* in Central Europe. He did not want to be responsible for opening the door to a Bolshevik invasion of Europe.

The government's attitude toward the Czechoslovak Communist Party was correct within the letter of the law. The Party was allowed the privileges guaranteed to all political groups. But the authorities showed no inclination to tolerate sedition. Communist journals were frequently censored, and many Communists—including parliamentary deputies, whose immunity was readily lifted when necessary—were jailed for brief periods because they violated legal regulations. Free of the restrictions that hampered their activities in many countries, the Communists in Czechoslovakia fared well in electoral contests and had a large roster of registered members. The premises underlying the appeal of Communism, however, must be carefully examined in order to determine whether they enhanced or retarded the development of a militant, revolutionary party such as the Comintern sought to create.

2. THE ORIGINS OF THE COMMUNIST PARTY

THE COMMUNIST PARTY of Czechoslovakia, like so many other European Communist parties, came into being as a result of a split in social democratic ranks after World War I. The Social Democratic Party was the oldest and largest Czech political party. It had been founded in 1878, as a branch of the Austrian Social Democrats. Although it established a separate identity in 1906, it continued to cooperate closely with the Austrian Socialists. During World War I, Czech Social Democrats were subjected to severe strain. Their socialist orientation tended to conflict with growing national emancipatory tendencies among the population, and a differentiation in their ranks along nationalist and socialist lines took place. Ultimately, nationalism carried the day. When the Republic was created, the majority of Social Democratic leaders instinctively knew their place. They immediately joined the cabinet, although it meant collaborating with the bourgeoisie. A decision of such importance—marking a radical departure from the party line—obviously required the sanction of the membership. A Congress was called for December 27, 1918, to assess the role of the party in the newly created Republic.

The Congress marked the beginning of a struggle between "right" and "left" tendencies for the "workers' soul"[1] which led, two years later, to the creation of a separate Communist Party. Meanwhile, it seriously undermined the capacity for political action of the most powerful party in the country and profoundly affected the course of the young Republic.

The issue over which the Social Democratic "right" and "left" differed was cooperation with the bourgeoisie. The platform of the "right" was simple, aiming primarily at "safeguarding the

Republic" and "evolving toward socialism through democracy."[2] It thought that "hasty expropriation would meet with great difficulties and would not benefit even the working class." The "left" was less encumbered with nationalist sentiments. Essentially, it adhered to the traditional, orthodox Social Democratic oppositional viewpoint, and its spokesmen, among them Antonin Zapotocky, urged the party to abandon its "all-national policy" and to turn to a "socialist proletarian policy."[3]

The Impact of the Russian Revolution

The impact of the Russian Revolution was clearly felt, and demands were made to "become true Bolsheviks."[4] Those who clamored for "true Bolshevism," however, displayed little, if any, acquaintance with its precepts. They also lacked the necessary will to carry out a revolutionary policy. One of them, when asked what Bolshevism was, replied as follows: "The Communists want . . . the dictatorship of the working class . . . we strive to capture political power in the National Assembly, to emerge victorious from our electoral struggle, to break through the phalanx of the bourgeoisie and the capitalist world, so that we may . . . dictate our demands [in the legislative assembly]."[5]

The impetus for the radicalization of the Social Democratic "left" and for outright Communist agitation did not come from the Social Democratic Party, but from Russia, where in May, 1918, a "Czechoslovak Communist Party" was formed by a small group of Czech prisoners of war, who, unlike the overwhelming majority of their compatriots, developed sympathies for the Bolshevik cause.[6] At the head of this "party" stood Alois Muna, a former tailor and Social Democrat. He received hasty revolutionary schooling and then, after being instructed by Lenin on November 10 and 12, 1918, was dispatched to Czechoslovakia to agitate for the organization of a Communist Party and propagate the glory of the Bolshevik Revolution.[7]

Muna's return to Czechoslovakia exacerbated the conflict within the Social Democratic Party as well as its conflict with other political groups. The Czech legionnaires issued warrants against him and several of his colleagues—Hais, Knoflicek, Benes (not Eduard), and Ruzicka—branding them as traitors and asking that they be delivered to the field courts of the legion for trial.

Failing that, a group of legionnaires vowed to capture Muna and kill him.[8] The authorities opposed Muna's "persecution," on grounds that events that had taken place in Russia were outside the competence of the state. Nevertheless, Muna became a martyr to the workers, who identified themselves with him. Overnight he became a symbol of the workers' own grievances and of the achievements of the Russian Revolution. The mine and metal workers of Kladno, a Communist stronghold comparable to Kronstadt in Russia, invited Muna into their midst, and he set up headquarters among them.

Angered by the challenge of the legionnaires, forty-six Social Democratic functionaries—headed by Bohumir Smeral and Josef Stivin—formed a "committee to guard against the White terror" and warned that Muna's violent death would be "the signal for a great revolution in the Czech nation."[9] Subsequently, the legionnaires carried out part of their threat, in that a group of them caught up with Muna and gave him a thorough thrashing. But the incident passed without additional consequence. On the contrary, the Social Democratic "left," while welcoming Muna's presence for reasons of its own, appealed to the Czech Communists returning from Russia not to precipitate disturbances. The appeal stressed the innocence of the Czech bourgeoisie in World War I and emphasized that:

> The situation of the Socialists in Czechoslovakia is basically different from that in Russia and Germany. . . . It is a situation without parallel throughout the world . . . making it our duty to arrange our affairs accordingly. . . .
>
> The government of the Czechoslovak Republic . . . announced its program in which [our] minimal demands are discussed. The working class regards this program as a partial political success and wants now calmly to wait and see how fast the program will be implemented. For that reason our Party remains on the chosen, peaceful road of democracy.[10]

Essentially, the Social Democratic "left," pointing to the uniqueness of the Czechoslovak situation, argued against class warfare and justified an evolutionary, constitutional approach to the fulfillment of workers' demands.

Muna's disturbing influence and his open references to himself as a Communist caused the Social Democratic executive to expel him from the party in January, 1919. At the same time, the party dissociated itself from the "tactics of Russian Bolsheviks and German Spartacists, who lead the state and the working class only to ruin and catastrophe, and cause the spilling of the workers' blood in fratricidal struggles."[11] The resolution ordering Muna's expulsion was adopted by a narrow margin of twenty-five votes against twenty, the "left" being in the opposition. But the "left" was able to sabotage the resolution, for though it was in a minority in the executive, it controlled a majority of the responsible posts in the party apparatus. Muna remained in the party, undermining the authority of the "right" from within and contributing to the strategy devised by Bohumir Smeral, the leading figure of the "left," who shunned challenging the party openly by setting up a rival organization but strove instead to capture it from inside.

The Leadership of Smeral

Smeral was no parvenu on the Czech political scene, but an elder statesman, a one-time vice-president of the Social Democratic Party, and chairman of the Czech parliamentary club in Vienna. He was one of the more brilliant Czech politicians—a cool, calculating man, not given to romantic fancies.[12] In 1918, he was at the nadir of his career. Throughout the war, he had stubbornly upheld an "Austro-Slavist" orientation, seeking a solution of the Czech question within the Austrian monarchy. This view was not unique with Smeral. Frantisek Palacky held it in the nineteenth century, as, initially, did Thomas G. Masaryk. Smeral, however, persisted in this view at a time when the overwhelming majority of his compatriots demanded emancipation from foreign domination. Thus he became one of the more hated men in Czechoslovakia.

He clashed with the "right" over the nationalist orientation of the latter, rather than over its lack of social radicalism. Unlike the "right," which hoped to solve social problems within the context of the Czechoslovak state, Smeral continued to search for an international constellation within which to implement socialist aims. This constellation presently appeared in the form of the Third International. (The fact that Smeral's internationalist outlook was not accompanied by radical socialist and revolutionary strivings was the root cause of his serious disagreement with the Comintern, which affected the development of the Czechoslovak Communist Party.)

Although the Social Democratic "left" harbored more radical spokesmen than Smeral, they bowed to his tactical direction, which sought to prevent a "leap into Communism" and to act as a midwife, instead, to a gradual transformation to Communism. When the "left" attacked the "right," it did so in the name of Social Democratic orthodoxy, not under the banner of revolutionary Bolshevism. It avoided the Communist label and vigorously resisted insinuations that it was Moscow's servant. For a time it even moderated its slogans, and when it finally resorted to the use of bolder terminology, it continued to hold out the prospect of nonviolent revolution. Ivan Olbracht, one of several Czech literati who espoused the cause of Communism, declared that a revolution without bloodshed was quite possible in Bohemia. Smeral in turn asserted that the "left" did not "for a minute consider civil war justified."[13]

For two years, the "right" hesitated to expel the "left," which, in turn, refrained from forcibly splitting the party. The "left" called no political strikes and staged no street demonstrations. In Smeral's words, it acted as "the scientific observer of the course of the stars." It kept in close touch with the working class but did not hurry its radicalization. This policy was successful, for when the two factions separated, the majority of the Social Democratic rank and file—variously estimated at two-thirds or four-fifths—went with the "left." Thus, Smeral's tactics made for a mass party dedicated to the implementation of traditional social democratic aims, but weak in revolutionary fervor. The very size of the party was a liability for the type of operation the Third International required.

The dangers inherent in Smeral's policy were quickly recognized by the Comintern, which, in 1920, grew impatient and began pressing the Czechs to identify themselves clearly with the Third International and to adopt a more openly revolutionary policy. Smeral was guilty of *"khvostism"* ("tailism")—lagging behind the workers rather than leading them—which the Comintern could not be expected to condone. As a latter-day Communist

critic put it: "The left did not regard itself as the leader and or-
ganizer of the revolution, but as the observer of developments
. . . It wanted to leave the revolution to a spontaneous outburst
of the masses."[14]

On August 26, 1920, the Executive Committee of the Comintern (ECCI) criticized the "left" for excessive enthusiasm in implementing the slogan "everything for the unity of the Party,"
and cited the approval given by the Social Democratic parliamentary faction to a government proclamation as too high a price
for unity. The ECCI urged the speedy establishment of a "united,
international, centralized Communist Party embracing all nations living in Czechoslovakia," and expressed the hope that the
party would soon join the Third International.[15]

Despite urging from the ECCI, Smeral temporized and the impetus for an open break actually came from the "right." The regular Congress of the party had been scheduled for September 25,
1920. Alarmed by growing leftist influence, the "right" moved to
forestall the capture of the party by the Communists. At a meeting of the executive committee on September 14, the "right"
forced the adoption of a resolution embodying the principle of
incompatibility between belief in Communism and membership in the Social Democratic Party. The resolution declared,
among other things, that "due to the basic differences between
the principles of social democracy and Communism as it is propa-
gated from Moscow, the followers of the Communist orientation
can no longer remain members of the [Social Democratic]
Party."[16]

The executive committee also voted to postpone the scheduled
Congress for three months, in order to re-examine the creden-
tials of the delegates who had already been selected, and to dis-
qualify all Communists among them. In May, the executive had
declared that only members of at least three years' standing in
the party could be designated as delegates. This was intended to
reduce the strength of the "left," for the party's ranks swelled
rapidly after the establishment of the Republic, and the majority
of the newcomers were of a radical orientation. Now even more
drastic measures were taken. Delegates were required to pledge,
in writing, that they did not support the Third International.

The "Left" Breaks Away

Challenged in this manner, the "left" chose to defy the executive and announced that the Congress would be held on the appointed date. A majority of the delegates, 338 out of 527, heeded the call of the "left," and the Congress opened on time exclusively under "left" auspices.

The main address was delivered by Smeral. Although he now, for the first time, openly called himself a Communist, he continued to equate Communism with "honest social democracy." Refuting accusations that the Social Democratic "left" was Moscow's agent, he said:

> It is interesting that while we are told that we are under Moscow's command, we are the only ones [of the European "left" Social Democrats] who have not followed the Russian example. . . . I felt from the beginning that this tactic would not work here . . . and we worked out our own tactic . . . When I went to Russia [in the spring of 1920] I told [Lenin] that although we pursue revolutionary aims, we cannot follow the tactic worked out by Russian theory . . . and we think that our tactics are more successful than those pursued in Vienna and Budapest. Our viewpoint was not immediately understood, but in the end—I think—the Russian comrades acknowledged the correctness of our policy at least for the time being.

Smeral ignored the demand of the Comintern to form a united, centralized, multinational Communist Party, and asserted that the distrust which even the workers of the various nationalities included in the Czechoslovak state felt toward each other could not be overcome at once. Under these circumstances, it would be unwise to create a single party. He urged patience in bringing about a gradual rapprochement between the workers of diverse national backgrounds. He also refused to declare openly for the Third International and stated that formal association with it was not necessary in order to adhere to its principles.[17]

The Congress took no vote on founding a united, centralized, multinational party, and avoided a decision to join the International. The new party eschewed the Communist label and called itself the "Marxian left" of Social Democracy. Furthermore, Smeral, while announcing the break with the "right," disavowed any intention of pursuing a negative policy toward Parliament. He declared that "we go into Parliament as an opposition party; who would dare to refuse us this constitutionally guaranteed right?"

As a result of the breakup of the Social Democratic Party, its parliamentary club also split, with eighteen of the seventy-four deputies elected on the Social Democratic ticket opting for the "left."

The struggle between Social Democratic factions led to the first serious clash between the workers and the police. In September, when the "left" withdrew, it seized the party headquarters and the printing plant of the Social Democratic daily, *Pravo Lidu,* on grounds that it represented the majority of the membership and was, therefore, entitled to control this valuable real estate. The "right" naturally objected to this illegal seizure, claiming that the "left" had excluded itself from the party. Unable to dislodge the "left," the "right" took its case to the state authorities, who declared in its favor. On December 9, police were dispatched to Social Democratic headquarters to evict its occupants. As word of the government's action spread, workers from several factories in and around Prague marched on the party headquarters, where they tangled with the police. In the scuffle, several workers were wounded.

On the following day, the Central Committee of the "left" met at the parliamentary club, for want of a better meeting place, and issued a call for a general strike. The government responded by declaring martial law and calling out the police and army. The strike was far from general, however, and no serious attempt was made by the "left" leadership to transform it into an assault on state power. Only in a few isolated areas, such as Kladno, did the strike assume an insurrectionary character. On December 14, a delegation of the "left," headed by Skalak and Vanek, sought President Masaryk's intercession to stop the struggle. The President refused to negotiate with them. On the following day, the Central Committee called off the strike.[18]

The failure of the strike brought mixed reactions from the

Comintern. The boldness and daring of the workers were warmly praised and, for propaganda purposes, vastly overestimated. On the other hand, the indecision of the leadership and its obvious organizational and political backwardness were sharply condemned and used as a springboard for renewed demands for a united, multinational party with true revolutionary content.

Although the strike was unsuccessful, it stirred the "left" to increased activity. A number of regional and district conferences followed, at which the burning issues of the day—the demands of the Comintern—were discussed. At a district conference at Reichenberg (Liberec), on January 9 and 10, 1921, the "left" of the German Social Democratic Party called for the convocation of an extraordinary Congress. The leadership responded by expelling the leftist-controlled Reichenberg district organization on January 17. Less than two months later, on March 12, the "left" held its Congress, at which it unanimously voted to adopt the name "Communist Party of Czechoslovakia, German Section."[19]

Similarly, in Slovakia, where conditions were unsettled, the Social Democratic "left" acted radically. In the summer of 1919, under the influence of developments in Hungary, where Bela Kun's Red regime held power at that time, a Soviet Government was proclaimed at Presov, one of the larger towns in the easternmost part of the province.[20] In January, 1921, the Social Democratic "left" of Slovakia called a Congress in Lubochna, a small resort in the interior of the province. The Congress was presided over by Marek Culen. Altogether, 149 delegates attended, including 88 Slovaks, 36 Hungarians, 15 Germans, 6 Ruthenians and 4 representatives of Jewish groups. Ivan Olbracht and Karl Kreibich represented Czech and German Communists respectively. The Congress accepted all but the seventeenth of the Communist International's Twenty-one Conditions. The question of a name for the Party was left open for future consideration.[21]

Meanwhile, the Czech and German youth groups joined the Youth International, and on May 14, the Czech Social Democratic "left" also gathered for a Congress. The Communist International, grown tired of Smeral's "hesitating tactics," exerted extreme pressure to overpower his obdurate resistance. Zinoviev, reporting to the Tenth Congress of the Communist Party of Russia in March, 1921, attacked Smeral and declared that a Communist

Party must be founded in Czechoslovakia even without him.[22]
The ECCI also intervened with a "letter" to the Czech comrades:

> Two and a half years have passed since Czechoslovakia be-
> came independent. . . . The Czech workers viewed independ-
> ent Bohemia with great hope and confidence . . . Freed of
> the overlordship of a foreign bureaucracy, they regarded
> themselves as masters in their house. . . . The working masses
> —under the influence of nationalist sentiments—looked on
> Communists as agents of Russia.
>
> The December strike showed not only the daring and en-
> ergy of the Czecho-Slovak revolutionary workers, but also the
> organizational and political shortcomings that became
> rooted in the Social Democratic left . . . elements of which,
> isolated at the top, knowingly or unknowingly sabotaged the
> Communist rising.
>
> If these elements to date have had insufficient daring
> openly to join the Third International—excusing their ac-
> tion by the nationalist sentiments of the workers: if they did
> not dare to join openly with the German workers, then it is
> clear that they are unfit to lead the struggle against the
> Czech bourgeoisie. . . .
>
> We hope that the Congress will adopt the name of Com-
> munist Party not only to distinguish itself outwardly from
> the Social Democrats, but also to accept the tactics and prin-
> ciples of the Third International.
>
> The Executive Committee of the Comintern does not
> overlook the need for cautious measures if these help to
> gain a majority, but whoever does not understand that ille-
> gal organization in the period of world revolution is a neces-
> sary prerequisite for the struggle against the bourgeoisie is
> not a Communist but a centrist.
>
> The time for half-measures has passed, whoever hesitates
> . . . is counterrevolutionary. . . . Only those who are ready to
> unite all Communists in one party for a life and death
> struggle for the dictatorship of the proletariat . . . in a party
> of determined, conscious, revolutionary workers, can . . . be-
> long to the Communist International. Only within these
> limits is it possible to make concessions to individuals and
> traditions.[23]

The Congress voted overwhelmingly (562 to 7) to accept the Twenty-one Conditions of the Communist International, but took no action to implement them.

Consequently, invitations to the Third Congress of the Comintern in June and July, 1921, were still addressed to a motley group of organizations such as the "Communist Party of German-Bohemia," the "Marxist left of Czech Socialists," the "Socialist Party of Slovakia" and the "International Socialist Party of the Ruthenian Population."[24] Altogether, twenty-nine delegates from Czechoslovakia attended.[25]

The Congress again urged the Communists in Czechoslovakia to unite in a single Party, and Zinoviev, Chairman of the ECCI, criticized the "soft" leadership and "centrist" tendencies in the Party.[26]

While the mass basis of the Czechoslovak Party (actually parties) was noted with satisfaction—as it well might have been, for the Czech and German Communists together were estimated to be 420,000 strong—the quality of its work was found wanting.[27] Zinoviev accused the Party of passivity, lack of revolutionary zeal, and backwardness in the education and indoctrination of its members. He pointed out that, by Comintern standards, mere quantity without revolutionary quality was not sufficient.[28] And Lenin took exception to the great desire of the Czechs to avoid sacrifices and entirely to abstain from revolutionary practices.[29]

The Czech delegates, incensed at so much criticism, retorted through their spokesman, Burian, who denied the passivity of the Party and stressed its complete unity. He also refuted allegations concerning a rift between intellectuals such as Smeral and "the best imprisoned [proletarian] comrades such as Muna, Hula, and Zapotocky," and rebuked the Comintern for its lack of patience and understanding.[30]

If Comintern criticism was not well taken by the Czechs, Lenin's personal intervention melted their resistance to a united, multinational Party. In October, 1921, a Unification Congress was held, at which the Communist Party of Czechoslovakia (Section of the International)—including Czechs, Slovaks, Germans, Hungarians, Poles, and Ukrainians—finally came into being.

3. THE BOLSHEVIZATION OF THE COMMUNIST PARTY

THE UNCERTAIN beginnings of the Communist Party had lasting effects on its development. The struggle for its Bolshevization was difficult and drawn out, and while the problems that arose were similar to or identical with those experienced in other, especially West European, Communist parties, "reformist, social democratic" tendencies—as the Comintern called them—hung on more tenaciously in Czechoslovakia than elsewhere. The Party had to undergo complete metamorphosis before even its top leadership could be considered Bolshevik. As for the membership, the task of transforming it into a revolutionary striking force was not really accomplished before 1938.

The history of the Party, from its Unification Congress in 1921, until December, 1938, when it was disbanded, can be divided into two distinct periods, with the Fifth Congress in February, 1929, as the watershed. Before 1929, the policy of the Party was singularly un-Bolshevik, and it was torn by factional struggles, numerous changes in leadership, and frequent interference by the Comintern. Party policy conformed to the program of the Third International in words, if not always in fact.

The Problem of Nationalities

Of the many problems that plagued the Czechoslovak Communist Party during the first years of its existence, the national-minority issue was the most troublesome. Despite formal unification, the Communist Party continued to reflect national antagonisms as they existed in the Czechoslovak state. As one Comintern official put it, "the Party was constantly menaced by dispersal into its national joints." Nationalism broke through at all levels.

Comintern policy tended to inflame conflicts. In Moscow's view, the proletariat of the oppressed minorities (especially the German proletariat), due to the objective conditions of their existence, displayed a far more consistent revolutionary attitude than did the Czechs. Stalin, speaking in the Czech Commission of the Fifth Enlarged Plenum of the ECCI in March, 1925, analyzed the situation in the following terms:

The Czech workers are not badly off, the idea of the national state holds everything under its spell. . . . All this creates an illusion associated with national peace. . . . This accounts for the division between right and left [in the Communist Party] along national lines. . . . Slovaks and Germans [oppressed nations] have drifted to the left while the Czechs have gone in the opposite direction.[1]

Stalin's main point was that in Czechoslovakia the danger of rightist deviation was by far the greater. He supported this assertion with three arguments: first, in a period of revolutionary stagnation such as the middle 1920's, the rightist danger—discouragement and apathy in the performance of revolutionary tasks—is always greater; second, the Czechoslovak Party was under the spell of a strong social democratic tradition; and third, the national victory of the Czechs placed the Czech working class in a privileged position and made it complacent toward class struggle. Stalin's judgment was supported by D. Z. Manuilsky, who revealed that in the past the Politbureau of the Czechoslovak Party had included five Czechs and four Hungarians, Slovaks, and Germans, whereas now it was composed of seven Czechs and two Germans with the other nationalities not represented at all. This intolerable situation required immediate correction.[2] As a result, the Germans and other minorities were given what to the Czechs appeared to be unduly large influence.

Social Democratic Survivals

But the "incorrect," "social patriotic" idea of a "national community of interest," which, of course, entailed an insufficient appreciation of the class struggle, remained the hallmark of the Czechoslovak Party at least until 1929.[3] For this it was severely and continuously criticized by the Comintern and by its own emerging "left wing." Under the influence of "social patriotism," the Party engaged in little if any revolutionary activity. It seldom appealed to the masses, for, as Antonin Zapotocky explained at the Third Enlarged Plenum of the ECCI, in June, 1923, "the masses cannot be incited to a final struggle" under highly "nonrevolutionary" conditions.[4]

The chief activity of Communists centered in Parliament, but even there they failed to carry out a "revolutionary policy," which would have consisted of using Parliament as a propaganda forum. They were content merely to play the part of "an opposition party."[5]

The Party continued to be excessively preoccupied with the quantity of its supporters and abstained from educating its members in a revolutionary spirit for revolutionary battles. It also avoided open discussions—then a favored method of the Comintern to bring about the necessary switch to policies desired by it —purportedly for fear of losing members. When, under Comintern prodding, such discussions were held, and membership concomitantly decreased, Zapotocky, reflecting the opinion of the leadership, bitterly exclaimed, "we paid for the discussion with 40,000 organized members."[6]

When united front tactics were called for, the Czech Communists tended to view them as a genuine coalition with the Social Democrats. When the slogan of "Workers' and Peasants' Government" was put forth, they interpreted it as a means to a "peaceful transition to the dictatorship of the proletariat."[7] When the Comintern ordered its sections to reorganize on the basis of factory units (nuclei) instead of the prevailing system of local units, the Czech Party balked, because of "resistance from the rank and file and the functionaries." Zapotocky, again acting as his Party's spokesman, explained that the workers objected to the organization of factory units for fear that it would increase "the persecution of Communists" and endanger their job security.[8]

The Party resisted the rough-and-ready ways recommended by the Comintern, because of a realistic appraisal of the environment in which it operated. It was well aware of the mood of the Czech working class and refrained from imposing on the workers opinions, views, and especially actions with which they did not spontaneously agree. Zapotocky, for example, considered it a mistake to give factory nuclei too many big tasks: "They must be grad-ually trained to deal with bigger tasks, and that must be done in such a manner that it will give pleasure to the workers and func-tionaries in the nucleus."[9]

The consensus of the Czech Party about the methods of the Comintern was aptly expressed by Karl Kreibich, the first leader of the German Communists in Czechoslovakia, who had moved from an "ultra-left" position (in 1921) to the "right," and in the process had become an astute observer of the Czech political scene:

> Bolshevization should be carried out not only from above . . . it requires grasping the situation in each country and adapting our methods to it. . . .
>
> The Czech worker grew up in national struggle against the authority of the state and any authority at all. . . . The path to the Czech worker . . . does not lead through assertion of authority and discipline from the outside. . . . He needs to be convinced and won over. . . . The method of command will not win him.[10]

Leninism does not oppose persuasion as a means of winning the workers. It does, however, resolutely oppose catering to the mistaken moods of the workers and doing no more than keeping in step with the spontaneous radicalization of the workers' move-ment. Leninist theory holds that a spontaneous workers' move-ment cannot exceed trade union consciousness, and this is not enough to win the revolution. In the opinion of the Comintern, which was correct, the Czech Party did not combat the mis-taken moods of the masses. On the contrary, it "systematically promoted" them.[11]

The Comintern attributed these shortcomings to "the tradi-tion, training, and orientation of many of the members and an even greater proportion of the leaders," which caused "this Party to be burdened more heavily than other parties with the rem-nants of social democratic ideology."[12] An estimated three-fourths of the Party's cadres were Social Democratic holdovers. To rem-edy his situation, the Comintern recommended a drastic reorgan-ization of the Central Committee by admitting to membership in it "a large number of workers," and asked for "greater activity" and "unconditional acceptance of the line of the International."[13]

The Party in Travail

The ECCI undertook to implement reorganization and to this end dispatched D. Z. Manuilsky to the Second Congress of the Party, in October, 1924. An account of what happened was given by Josef Bubnik, political secretary of the Prague region and a member of the "right" before his expulsion shortly thereafter:

> In the election committee which had to put forward candidates, the majority were in favor of the old leadership. The representative of the Third International, Comrade Manuilsky, supported by Comrade Katz from Germany, demanded, however, that the new Central Committee consist of a majority of left-wingers. . . . The representative of the Third International threatened that in the event the majority did not submit, the discussion would be prolonged and an extraordinary Congress would be convened within three months, at the command of the International.[14]

The Central Committee elected at this Congress included fourteen "rightists" and eighteen "leftists," but power was still in the hands of the "right." The representatives of the "left" were young and inexperienced, and they had no following. In fact, of the regional organizations of the Party at that time, only districts with large ethnic minorities and two Czech districts—Prague and Moravska Ostrava—had strong "leftist" nuclei. In Prague, the "left" included Jan Sverma, Rudolf Slansky, Jan Vodicka, and Josef Guttmann; in Moravska Ostrava, it was headed by Klement Gottwald and Vaclav Kopecky.[15] Alois Neurath and Jeno Fried were the most vocal representatives of the German and Hungarian "left," respectively.

Intervention by the Comintern did not immediately solve the Party's problems.

The "left," conscious of its power in the Central Committee and anxious to give a good account of itself to its sponsors, almost immediately called for a political demonstration against inflationary price increases. On this issue it came into conflict with Josef Bubnik, political secretary at Prague, where the demonstra-

tion was to take place. Bubnik allegedly sabotaged the demonstration by making arrangements to avoid a clash with the police. As
a result, he was expelled from the Party, in February, 1925. The
Central Committee vote for expulsion stood at eighteen to eleven
—all of the "left" in favor and the majority of the "right" in opposition.[16] Among those who voted against Bubnik's expulsion
were Smeral and Zapotocky. They sought to smooth over matters
by holding a conference of functionaries. The Comintern also
entered the controversy and invited workers' delegations from
three key trouble spots—Prague, Kladno, and Brno (where the
majority of the district executive fell into line behind Bubnik)—
to attend the forthcoming meeting of the ECCI in Moscow, "in
order to arrive at an agreement regarding the liquidation of inner
party difficulties."[17]

The Party crisis was now in full swing. It received thorough
airing at the Fifth Enlarged Plenum of the ECCI in March, 1925.
There, the Czechoslovak question "assumed great international
importance," not only because of its specific interest, but because
—as Manuilsky explained it—"the most important question before the Plenum, the stabilization of capitalism, mainly centered
around the Czech question. . . . The Czech comrades think that
their position is unique; this is not so; these are pangs of growth
and are inevitable in the Bolshevization of Parties."[18]

At the conclusion of the plenum, the ECCI once again appealed to the Czechs to combat the "rightist" danger by the combined efforts of "all revolutionary elements in the Party," the
developing "left," and the "center." The ECCI also ordered the
convocation of a new Party Congress within four months.

The Congress convened in September, 1925, and installed a new
leadership. Smeral was relieved of his post and dispatched by the
Comintern to Outer Mongolia. In his place, Josef Haken—a
schoolteacher of proletarian background—who, though an old-
timer, had displayed the proper understanding of the Moscow
line, became chairman of the Party executive (the Central Committee), while Bohumir Jilek, a "leftist" intermittently critical of
Smeral, became leading secretary and head of the organization department.[19] The position of the younger leftists was strengthened,
but they were not yet numerous enough, nor sufficiently sea-
soned, to take over the direction of the Party.

In 1926, at the Sixth Enlarged Plenum of the ECCI, Zinoviev expressed great satisfaction with the Party's progress and asserted that it had become a "real proletarian Party and a loyal section of the International."[20] Zinoviev's appraisal proved optimistic, for two years later, at the Sixth Congress of the Comintern, the Czech Party was identified as the worst section of the International, and a complete purge of the leadership was ordered. So thorough was the ensuing house cleaning, that only one member of the old leadership, the durable Antonin Zapotocky, retained his post.[21]

The tempo of the struggle for power in the Party now quickened. Every additional demonstration of weakness on the part of the "right" hastened its eventual liquidation by the Comintern, and the years 1927 and 1928 provided ample opportunity for revealing weaknesses that stemmed from an "inadequate grasp of the development of the class struggle." Meanwhile, the young leftists supported by the Comintern were increasing in numbers and gaining in influence in the lower echelons of the Party. Selected young Communists (for example Bruno Kohler and Jan Sverma) received schooling in the Soviet Union and returned to Czechoslovakia as faithful servants of the International. When the time came—as it did after the Sixth Congress of the Comintern, in August, 1928—the number of reliable young Communists on hand was sufficient to staff the key posts in the Central Committee.

In 1927 and 1928, as the stabilization of capitalism continued and prospects for an early social revolution became more and more unlikely, the Czechoslovak Party—as was to be expected —became ever more lackadaisical in the performance of any kind of revolutionary activity. Its attitude was diametrically opposed to that of the Comintern, which perceived the stabilization of capitalism and the concomitant, growing danger of a new imperialist war as sources of "intensified class contradictions" requiring ever greater revolutionary activity.[22] The Czechs revealed a "mechanistic concept of the stabilization of capitalism"; that is, while they recognized a leftward movement of the masses, they interpreted it to be of a defensive rather than offensive nature. Moreover, Jilek maintained that objective conditions were not as important in determining strategy and tactics as the Comintern claimed:

We have already lived through a period which objectively was revolutionary. We had the possibility of overthrowing capitalist rule. Why did we not do it? . . . For one simple reason: because the necessary subjective conditions were not fulfilled (the masses were passive).[23]

The Comintern condemned this attitude, and a small group of Czech Communists, together with the "left wing" of the German Communists in Czechoslovakia, became more vocal in high Party councils, attacking the leadership and seeking to force it to adopt the Comintern line. A new crisis developed and came to a head as a result of the utter failure of Red Day, in July, 1928. The occasion was a Communist sport festival, a "Spartakiade," which was to be accompanied by a mass demonstration. However, Party and Communist trade-union leaders were unable to summon enough courage to lead the Czech working class in such a demonstration, and the affair ended in a complete fiasco.[24] This lack of backbone gave rise to a heated discussion of the Czech situation at the Sixth Congress of the Comintern a short time later. In these deliberations, Klement Gottwald—who had been elected to the Politbureau of the Czechoslovak Party in 1925—played a prominent part. Sometimes referred to as Comrade Graham (a pseudonym he used intermittently during this period), Gottwald did the Comintern's bidding, and at the conclusion of the Congress he was elected to its Executive Committee.

Gottwald in Command

The debates in Moscow were followed by an open letter from the ECCI to the Czechoslovak Communists, in which all the shortcomings of their Party were laid bare and the "recruitment of young revolutionary cadres" was ordered.[25] The ECCI approved the letter on September 3, 1928, and its contents were discussed by the Czechoslovak Communist Party at the end of the same month. The struggle between the incumbent leadership (Jilek and his supporters) and the radical elements clustered around Gottwald entered the decisive phase. In the fierce strife that raged throughout the fall and winter of 1928–29, Gottwald was steadily gathering strength. He had a slim majority in the Central Committee, and in the course of Party conferences held in preparation for a forthcoming Congress, he managed to enlist the support of four important regions—Prague, Kladno, Moravska Ostrava, and Hradec Kralove—"a highly significant fact" according to the ECCI, "since the right wing was strong in purely Czech areas."

Coincidentally with the opening of the Congress, a second open letter from the ECCI arrived. It noted that "the Party still has not entirely renounced its inaccurate view that the Social Democrats represent the working class equally with the Communists. . . . The Party continues to . . . share with the reformists the leadership of the insurgent masses."

At the same time, however, the ECCI also recorded a hopeful, positive development:

> During the course [of the Party discussion] an opposition, with Comrade Gottwald at its head, emerged, took on a definite formation and consolidated its position, embracing the leading sections of the Party, and not only acknowledging the Open Letter, but insistently struggling for the realization of the tasks set by it.[26]

The Congress—the Czechoslovak Communist Party's Fifth and perhaps most celebrated one—met from February 18 to 23. Gottwald, with the unmistakable approval of the ECCI, indeed carried the day. He and Jilek had been designated to give political reports. But Jilek, outmaneuvered (no material was made available to him) by the Central Committee, which by then favored Gottwald, was unable to give his address. Gottwald spoke for five hours in true Bolshevik fashion. At the end of the Congress, he was unanimously elected Secretary-General of the Party. Sharing honors with him were Rudolf Slansky, Vaclav Kopecky, Paul Reimann, and Otto Synek, all representatives of the younger generation. Also present, in somewhat minor roles, were Vaclav Nosek, Marie Svermova (then known by her maiden name Svabova), Bruno Kohler, Josef Krosnar, Viliam Siroky, Jaromir Dolansky, and Anezka Hodinova, all of whom later rose to prominence in the Party. The Congress was packed with "workers from the bench": Ninety per cent of the delegates present were workers, the majority of them metalworkers. The new Central Committee of fifty-two members included seventeen party functionaries and thirty-two factory workers. By nationality, thirty-two members of the Central Committee were Czechs, eleven Germans, four Slovaks, two Ukrainians, two Hungarians, and one a Pole.

The new Politbureau included Klement Gottwald, Cenek Hruska, Jan Sverma, Josef Haken, Hruby, Stulik, Rudolf Slansky, Josef Guttmann, Paul Reimann, Melzer, Jeno Fried, and Antonin Zapotocky. The Secretariat included Gottwald, Sverma, Melzer, and Fried. Both Jilek and Smeral were recalled from the ECCI, but while Jilek was stripped of all functions, Smeral was retained in the service of the Comintern and gradually regained prestige in the Party, as an honored elder statesman.

The victory of the "left" was total. The Comintern observers, Paul and Ziegler, were of the opinion that "perhaps no Party had ever been faced with such organizational and political problems as those now confronting the Communist Party of Czechoslovakia."* They nevertheless agreed that the Gottwald leadership possessed the necessary qualities to overcome the difficulties.[27]

To sum up, prior to Gottwald's installation in power, the Communist Party had given little indication of being a revolutionary party.

Ideologically, it made scant effort to acquaint the mass of members with Marxist-Leninist revolutionary theory. The Czech Social Democratic Party traditionally had been backward in its theoretical repertoire, and this characteristic carried over into the Communist Party. Systematic agitation and propaganda were at a minimum and were carried out in a mechanical manner, with almost complete disregard for personal agitation, which was urged on the parties by the Comintern.[28]

The ideological shortcomings of the leadership included an incorrect appreciation of the nature of a revolutionary party, underestimation of the class struggle, an erroneous attitude toward the Czechoslovak state, insufficient attention to the manipulation of revolutionary reserves, the exploitation of the national aspirations of ethnic minorities, the peasant problem, and the trade-union question. The Czechoslovak Party continued to regard the Social Democrats as "another proletarian party," a cardinal sin by Bolshevik standards, according to which "it is impossible to conquer capitalism without eliminating social democratism from the

---

*According to a later Communist account, the Comintern was represented by G. Henrikovsky (Ziegler), J. Lensky, and D. Z. Manuilsky. Ustav Dejin KSC, *Dejiny KSC* (History of the Communist Party of Czechoslovakia; Prague: SNPL, 1961), p. 258.

labor movement."[29] As to the state, the Communist leadership on the whole approved the creation of the Czechoslovak Republic and did not aim at its overthrow. The imperialist nature of the Czechoslovak Republic eluded the comprehension of Czechoslovak Communists, who tended to view the country as a vassal of Western imperialism. In the late 1920's, when the Comintern saw a "consolidation of the bourgeoisie" in Czechoslovakia—as it did elsewhere—with a resulting rapprochement between "finance capital which directs the Agrarian Party" and President Masaryk, the Czech Communists saw a differentiation in the camp of the bourgeoisie "which will lead to a coup d'état of the right wing of the bourgeoisie against the left wing led by Masaryk."[30] The resulting tendency to support Masaryk *in extremis* was, of course, strongly censured by Moscow.

Trotskyism raised its ugly head in the Czechoslovak Party as in all Communist parties in the middle 1920's. But whereas Trotskyite deviation constituted a major menace in most parties, it was never more than a side issue in Czechoslovakia. Among the Czech Communists, Trotskyism was limited to a small group of intellectuals led by Professor Pollak in Prague. Militant "left" slogans met with more sympathetic reception in German nationality districts and the German Trotskyite faction led by Alois Neurath* grew to be quite influential.[31] However, by 1928 the ECCI felt justified in proclaiming that the Czechoslovak Party "has most decidedly overcome the Trotskyite tendencies in its midst."[32] The "right" danger at that time continued rampant.

The ideological shortcomings of the Party reflected both on its political and organizational work. The Party did not exhaust all forms of activity, parliamentary and nonparliamentary, legal and

---

*The Trotskyite label has been known to cover a multitude of sins. Although Neurath is recorded as Trotskyite in the annals of the Czechoslovak Communist Party, for which the Gottwald leadership was responsible, the designation in his case, and in other cases as well, perhaps requires qualification. Neurath himself appeared to be a follower of Zinoviev. An allusion to the "sympathies" which some Czechoslovak Trotskyites had for the "Leningrad opposition" in Russia (i.e., Zinoviev and his group) can be found in P. Reimann's *Geschichte,* p. 256. Thus it is possible that the Trotskyite label fits Neurath only to the extent to which it was applicable to Zinoviev too. Whatever the case may be, Neurath the "Trotskyite" was expelled from the Czechoslovak Communist Party in June, 1929, after the victory of Gottwald. See K. Gottwald, *Spisy* (Prague, 1951), 1, 335.

illegal, but satisfied itself primarily with legal parliamentary activity. It did not carry the class struggle relentlessly into every walk of life. It did not maintain continuous revolutionary vigilance and fitness, working toward revolutionary aims regardless of the remoteness of actual revolutionary possibilities. It worked spasmodically, primarily as an election apparatus. As one Comintern official expressed it, "on elections there is a revival; when it is finished they go to sleep again."[33] In organization, the Party was far from monolithic. It did not exercise strict control over its parliamentary faction, the Red Trade Unions, or the Young Communist League. Its regional and local centers were not secretariats, functioning around the clock. For example, the Prague district organization, with 12,000 members—one of the largest and most important of the Party—had only one permanent, paid functionary.[34]

In its relation to the Comintern, the old leadership was either unable or unwilling to show unquestioning obedience. On the contrary, it stubbornly resisted the Comintern's intrusions into everyday activities. Smeral voiced the opinion that "freedom and elasticity of tactics in the various phases of development . . . is absolutely necessary."[35] Zapotocky expressed a similar view in referring to the experience the Party had had with an instructor sent by the ECCI to introduce proper organizational methods in trade-union work:

> We came into conflict with the instructor because he insisted on issuing a plan with wholly mechanical dates, which we considered impracticable, for the completion of work. Nevertheless, the plan was published, but it remained absolutely without effect. In organization work, dates . . . can be set, but the mechanical setting of dates from week to week for a long period is impossible.[36]

The greatest and most persistent difficulties facing the Party were in the trade-union field. Comintern policy called for incessant struggle against splitting the unions. A united trade-union movement was one of the foremost aims set by the International, for as Zinoviev asserted at the Fifth Congress of the Comintern, "in spite of the treachery of the Social Democrats, the trade-union movement is the historically inevitable form for uniting the entire proletariat . . . Leninism in the trade-union movement means the struggle against splitting the unions."[37] The Czechoslovak Communists were unable to keep the union movement united. The political rift between Social Democrats and Communists was perpetuated in the union movement, which after 1918 grew into a mighty mass organization embracing close to 900,000 workers. At a national trade-union Congress in January, 1922, the majority of the delegates voted in favor of the Amsterdam (Socialist) International. Shortly thereafter the reformist unions in Czechoslovakia expelled the Communists, forcing them to establish their own trade-union center. With a split in the trade-union movement factional work in the reformist unions became the most important task of Communists. In this endeavor, the Czechs proved singularly inept. Their work was complicated by excessive splintering in the union movement along political lines. Every party had its own unions. This presented an almost insurmountable obstacle to amalgamating the diverse elements of the labor movement into one organization.[38]

An apathetic attitude toward factional work, however, was not the only shortcoming of the Communist union movement.[39] The unions suffered from excessive legalist and economist tendencies. They shied away from political strikes, and misinterpreted the Bolshevik concept of "partial economic struggles" by imputing an aim of finality to them, instead of using them merely as stepping-stones to more decisive political struggles. The Communist unions had considerable difficulty in attracting adherents, and in deference to the desires of the ordinary members, who were afraid of retaliation against them, i.e., of being fired, the leadership refrained from unnecessarily exposing the unions. In the late 1920's, when the Communist unions were ordered to put forth their own slate in factory council elections, they balked for fear of arousing open hostility among other workers and in the management. Simultaneously, the number of Communist-instigated strikes dropped off sharply.[40] The standard explanation offered by Communist trade-union leaders was that the numerical inferiority of the Communist unions—they then encompassed only about 12 to 13 per cent of the organized workers—made it impossible for them to operate more boldly and with greater success.[41] This situation prevailed under the leadership of Josef Hais—who broke with the movement in 1929—as well as under the collective leadership headed by Antonin Zapotocky.

In organization, the Communist union leaders favored a highly centralized bureaucratic structure instead of a decentralized system of factory units. The reason they gave for their preference was that, under a centralized system, Communist union members would be less directly exposed at their place of work. By and large, Communist union leaders failed to understand the compatibility between a struggle for trade-union unity and against social democratism in the labor movement. The most plausible means of unification appeared to be some sort of amalgamation with the reformist unions, and where unifying efforts succeeded— as they did in some cases—they took on the aspect of organizational unification from above rather than from below. This placed the Communists in an inferior position to the reformist unions, which were better organized and had a much larger membership.

The Bolshevik concept of the dialectic, which frequently entails the simultaneous pursuit of two apparently—and often actually—contradictory aims without becoming confused as to the real goal, continually eluded the Czech Communist trade-union leadership, as it did the rest of the Communist old guard.

Under New Leadership

With Gottwald in control, a vigorous effort was made to remedy ideological, political, and organizational weaknesses. Gottwald himself, in his inaugural speech, showed that he had at least properly mastered Bolshevik terminology. He condemned the previously dominant false view of the character of the Czechoslovak state and described it as an "imperialist state . . . under the rule of the financial bourgeoisie." He also characterized "the Castle" (the President's office) as "an instrument of finance capital" and declared war on the bourgeois-democratic state apparatus.[42] He emphasized the need for improving the social composition of the Party (what he really meant was its age composition) by attracting "young revolutionary workers and young blood into the whole cadre of Party functionaries." The slogan "through fights for partial demands to the decisive fight for the dictatorship of the proletariat" was to serve as a guide to the Party's immediate tasks.[43]

After his election to Parliament, in October, 1929, Gottwald also initiated new tactics in that body, utilizing it as a propaganda platform and a forum for attacking the government coalition unmercifully. The trend of the parliamentary behavior of Communist deputies after 1929 was set by Gottwald's maiden speech, in which he boasted of "going to Moscow to learn . . . how to wring the neck" of bourgeois and reformist representatives.

Rebuilding the Party was, however, a complicated task. The Party discussion of 1928–29, which led to a complete change in leadership and the adoption of an entirely new, much tougher policy, cost the Party its mass character. Its membership, which at the outset of the showdown hovered around the 100,000 mark, dwindled to about 24,000. Among the defectors were a considerable number of its more prominent adherents. The majority of the Party's senators—fourteen out of twenty—and fifteen out of forty-one parliamentary deputies deserted the Communist camp.[44] A number of intellectuals—among them several stalwarts of socialism, such as Ivan Olbracht, Marie Majerova, Josef Hora, Helena Malirova, and Josef Seifert—either withdrew or were expelled.[45] The Communist trade unions split, and one section, led by Josef Hais, joined forces with the Social Democrats. Several founding members, including Alois Muna, also left the Party.

From the point of view of the new leadership the departure of dissident elements was not a total loss for it left the Party with a small nucleus of relatively like-minded members who served as a good matrix for Bolshevizing the entire apparatus. But the Party could not extricate itself overnight from previously dominant opportunistic tendencies. Correct policy formulation did not automatically ensure equally correct implementation on the operational level, and at no time before 1938 did the subjective abilities of the Party measure up to the objective tasks set for it.

As its Comintern critics pointed out, the Party continued "to hide its revolutionary face" and did not go all out to "inculcate the masses with the notion of revolutionary socialism." It also failed to combat with sufficient vigor the very strong "constitutional illusions among the masses of the Czechoslovak proletariat and even within the Communist Party itself."[46] As the Comintern critic put it:

The question is not one of concentrating the attention of the

Czechoslovak proletariat on the absence, for the moment, of an open fascist dictatorship (which is true in itself and should be discussed), but of making clear to every worker . . . that a speedy process of fascistization is already developing and must be combated.[47]

Trade-union work continued to display the symptoms of previous shortcomings. Failures were consistently explained by the numerical weakness of the Communist unions, and, more often than not, Communists interpreted united front tactics as a "bloc [with the] Social Democrats," ignoring the crucial question of "Communist leadership" in this endeavor.[48] Nevertheless, there was an increase in the number of strikes initiated and led by Communists, although in most cases the Communists were unable to attract the support of workers organized in other unions and thus could not accomplish their major objective.

In general, the Party continued to overlook class antagonism as the moving force of Communism. It developed theories of class cooperation with the peasantry, and failed to rid itself of the concept of a national community of interest. For example, Jan Sverma, writing on the "Czechoslovak question" in 1934, was able to formulate things in the following terms:

The question what role Marxism is to play in the Czech nation and in the struggle of the Czech nation for emancipation is becoming more and more acute. The Czech nation is at a historical crossing of ways.[49]

Ideological deviations also persisted; every turn in Comintern policy brought new ones to light. At times it appeared as if Gottwald alone were capable of consistently following the approved Leninist line. But the manifestations of deviationist attitudes no longer seriously threatened the Party's close adherence to the Comintern, and with Gottwald's unerring instinct for the correct policy, they were invariably remedied without serious repercussions.

No sooner had Gottwald come to power than an "ultra-left" deviation asserted itself. The cause of this ultra-left deviation was a virtual repetition, in 1929, of the previous year's Red Day fiasco. Despite a change in leadership, the Party was unable to mobilize the masses for a large-scale political demonstration for the defense of the Soviet Union against imperialist aggression. Demonstrations were particularly anemic in the great industrial centers—Prague, Kladno, Plzen, and Moravska Ostrava.[50] Moreover, to arouse interest for the demonstration among the workers, the Communist Party, on Gottwald's directives, combined the political aspects of its call for a twenty-four-hour strike with "partial economic demands" for the workers. Both the method used and the over-all failure of the test of strength contributed to ultra-left attacks on the leadership. However, the Comintern, standing solidly behind Gottwald, assisted him in combating this deviation, by pointing out that this time the failure had not been due to the incorrect policy of the leadership, but rather to the continuing weakness of the Party apparatus, which was unable to implement objectively correct policies. Jeno Fried (a Hungarian) and Paul Reimann (a German), the leaders of the ultra-left, recanted and—after a year's disgrace, during which they were barred from the central secretariat—were reinstated.[51] (Reimann continued to work in the Czechoslovak Party. Fried was later sent to France as an agent of the Comintern, under the name of Clement. He was killed by the Nazis in Belgium during World War II.)

In 1933, as a result of the disastrous policy of the German Communist Party, another—this time a rightist—deviation made its appearance. The culprit was none other than Josef Guttmann, then one of the more influential leaders of the Party and editor of its central organ, *Rude Pravo*. Guttmann was unwilling to give unqualified approval—even if only overtly—to the strategy and tactics of the German Communist Party and to hail it as the very model of revolutionary parties. For this heresy, and for openly advocating a "defense of democracy" slogan even if it entailed an alliance with the Social Democrats (an attitude at the time still somewhat premature), he was expelled from the Party.[52] Gottwald, of course, hastened to affirm his unrestrained admiration for the German Party. But Guttmann insinuated that the majority of the Czechoslovak Communist leaders really shared his views.[53] This might well have been the case. The German question was a delicate one then, as at all times in the history of the Czech Party, and few of the leading Czech Communists sympathized with their German comrades.

Finally, in 1936, still another rightist deviation required attention. This time, the heretics were Jan Sverma and Rudolf Slansky —both then members of the secretariat of the Central Committee. Their mistakes apparently consisted in overinterpreting the new line calling for a positive attitude toward the defense of the Republic. Sverma and Slansky recanted their mistakes, but were temporarily relieved of their functions.[54] At about the same time, coincidentally with the great purges in the Soviet Union, a number of Trotskyites were expelled from the Party. Among them was Stanislav Budin, chief editor of *Rude Pravo*.[55]

Despite the difficulties encountered along the path of Bolshevization, steady progress was made toward consolidating the Party around its new leadership. By the time of the Sixth Congress in 1931, the younger element was in preponderance throughout the Party apparatus. While 60 per cent of the Party's members were over forty-five years of age, the same proportion of the delegates attending the Congress were under thirty-five years of age. Of thirty-two "workers from the bench" elected to the Central Committee in 1929, twenty had become permanent Party functionaries and in 1931 eighteen still held their jobs. The new Central Committee of sixty members included fifty-one workers and only nine intellectuals: thirty-two new members were again elevated to their positions from the factory bench. The nationality composition of the Central Committee was not appreciably altered. It included thirty-seven Czechs, ten Germans, eight representatives from Slovakia (these included both Slovaks and Hungarians), four Ruthenians, and one Pole. The leading members of the Central Committee were Klement Gottwald, Bruno Kohler, Rudolf Slansky, Cenek Hruska, Antonin Zapotocky, Jeno Fried, Josef Haken, Jan Harus, Vaclav Kopecky, Paul Reimann, Alexander Bubenicek, Rudolf Appelt, and Josef Krosnar.[56]

The Sixth Congress also witnessed, for the first time in the Party's history, the correct formulation of a policy toward the national minority problem and the peasant question. The Party at last brought itself to recognize the existence of Czech imperialism (vis-à-vis the national minorities) within the country and firmly espoused the cause of "self-determination of nations even to the point of secession." It also gave theoretical recognition to the necessity of dealing seriously with the peasant problem, especially in areas inhabited by national minorities where—in the view of the Comintern—the combination of agrarian and national problems provided fertile ground for revolutionary agitation.[57]

Early in 1933, steps were taken to establish a systematic control of cadres and, later in the year, preparations were begun for illegal work—a phase of activity which the Party had until then neglected. Rudolf Slansky was put in charge of this endeavor, for which few Communists had any enthusiasm. One sure sign of Bolshevization was the growth in the number of "aparatchiki." By 1934, the Party had a large staff of paid officials working full or part time. Party schools were educating about 2,000 functionaries yearly. In 1935, two new central schools were opened, which, according to one of the graduates, taught young Communists "to hate capitalism and how to fight it" and "to love the Soviet Union."[58]

The stability of the top leadership was not seriously threatened. Changes were relatively few, and what was more important, Gottwald seemed to enjoy the confidence of the Comintern. Opposition to the Comintern was now a rare manifestation of personal differences rather than a mass phenomenon. At the Sixth Congress, in 1931, Gottwald was able to report that the "debates and the unanimous election of the new Central Committee showed the complete unity of the whole Party."[59] The Seventh Congress, in April, 1936, was characterized as the "living expression of the unshakable unity of the Party . . . of the confidence and love felt by the whole Party for its leader, Comrade Gottwald."[60] Consolidation had progressed so far that Smeral and Kreibich were invited to address the Congress in order to herald the solidarity of the old and new generations.[61]

Like the problem of generations, the nationality question also ceased to be controversial. The ratio of Czechs to Germans in the Central Committee was stabilized at approximately three to one. Moreover, the significant losses suffered in the German areas after 1935 were compensated for by the increase in the Party's stature among Czechs. Gottwald's ascent to power and the confidence he enjoyed in the Comintern also contributed to the rise of the Czech element. Individual Germans, however, retained strong influence. Bruno Kohler headed the organization department of the Party, and served with Gottwald on the Presidium of the ECCI (although Gottwald, then a member of the Secretariat as well, was a step ahead of him). Paul Reimann was active in the agitation and propaganda department—which he headed for some time—and edited the Party's ideological journal.

Patriotism as the Password

Before further progress could be made toward Bolshevization, the Party was compelled to embark on a policy eminently conducive to wholesale opportunism. Within the general context of the united front approach it was ordered, in 1935, to adopt a positive attitude toward the defense of the Republic. The theoretical and practical justification of this *volte face* was the mutual-defense agreement which Czechoslovakia concluded with the Soviet Union in May, 1935. The defense of Czechoslovakia against fascism now became in effect a defense of the Soviet Union, and hence was placed in the realm of a just war.

The correct interpretation of the new Communist line supplied by Gottwald in 1936 was, of course, that "the defense of the state should be supported, but class struggle against the bourgeoisie does not cease, bourgeois armament policy is not to be supported."[62] Many of Gottwald's Party colleagues, however, were unable to follow this dialectical reasoning and their behavior was correspondingly incorrect. They emphasized the defense of the state and neglected the class struggle. In Gottwald's absence, in the winter of 1935—an absence that was due in part to the duties he had to perform in Moscow as a member of the ECCI Secretariat, and in part to the fact that a warrant for his arrest had been issued—the Party, led by Jan Sverma, made some tentative steps toward genuine rapprochement with the Czechoslovak Government. It voted for two items on the state budget—the Ministry of Foreign Affairs and of Social Welfare—and not only gave its approval to the government's armament policy, but called for more arms production. At the same time, the Communists supported Benes for the Presidency against Agrarian opposition, although only a year before they had opposed Masaryk's re-election.[63] This dangerous trend caused Gottwald to return from Moscow (happily a political amnesty had removed the threat of his arrest) in order to set matters straight. This was duly done, and, much to the regret of democratic public opinion, the brief but promising honeymoon of the Communists and the government came to an end.[64] However, from 1936 until the Munich agreement in 1938, even Gottwald was compelled to make increasingly frequent references to the defense of the state, and no matter how obliquely he stated his case, the effect was invariably a greater emphasis on the immediate necessity of defending Czechoslovakia than on the class struggle.

Although he stated that the Communists favored Soviet democracy and the Socialist Soviet Republic, and were against the suppression of national minorities, he asserted that despite this, the Communists would defend bourgeois democracy and the bourgeois Republic against fascism and would not surrender "a single village to Hitler, Horthy, or the Polish fascists."[65]

His parliamentary speeches after 1936 contained an increasing number of references to historic symbols of national greatness—such as the Hussite wars. The Communists were aligning themselves ever more closely with the defense of the historic rights of the Czechs.

Communist attempts to promote common action through a united front with the Social Democratic and National Socialist parties also gained impetus. In order to overcome the understandable reluctance of the leadership of the other two socialist parties, the Communists softened the conditions for cooperation and put forth a broad minimum program devoid of offensive and excessive economic and political demands.[66] Formal cooperation between the Communists on the one hand and the Social Democrats and National Socialists on the other, however, did not develop on the national level, although on the local level several promising starts were made.

Toward 1938, the Communists became the most vocal defenders of the Republic. They were the only political group consistently to expose Hitler's nefarious designs on Czechoslovakia, and mercilessly to attack the "Czech reaction"—especially the Agrarian Party—accusing it not only of planning a "rightist coup" but of playing directly and willfully into Hitler's hands and "wanting to sell out to him."[67]

Class war gave way to slogans of national solidarity and affirmations of national interest, which the Communists claimed to represent best. Attacks on the bourgeoisie were couched not so much in general terms as in the guise of assaults on a small group of reactionary politicians, the bureaucracy, and some generals who were identified as the real enemies of the people.

In May, 1938, when the government ordered a partial mobilization, the Communist Central Committee "approving and supporting all measures for the safety, unity, and independence of the Republic" issued a call to its members to be "in the first ranks of the defenders of the Republic."[68]

The Communist Party agitated against capitulation at the time of the Munich agreement. Immediately before Benes' acceptance of the humiliating terms of the Great Powers, the Communists led a workers' demonstration in Prague which contributed to the fall of the wavering government and brought about the creation of a new, apparently more resolute, cabinet with General Syrovy at its head. The gain, however, was purely illusory. Communists exhorted the population to fight even if abandoned by its Western Allies.

Gottwald, reportedly acting as Stalin's emissary, discussed the possibility of Soviet aid to Czechoslovakia with Benes, and allegedly urged the President to hold firm. Even if his intervention took place as reported, the choice of Gottwald instead of an accredited Soviet diplomat for the purpose of transmitting from Stalin as important a message as that concerning Soviet aid to embattled Czechoslovakia, cast the whole undertaking in a spurious light.

In any event, the Communists' protestations against the violence committed on Czechoslovakia at Munich did not cease. Theirs was certainly the loudest and least equivocal voice. Gottwald's forthright speech in the National Assembly, on October 11, 1938, although not then reported in the press, nevertheless became public knowledge. It was one of the strongest calls for open resistance to Nazism,[69] and is worth quoting at some length, not only because it summarizes the Communists' avowed position at that time, but also because it was later used by them as proof of their patriotism:

We have a right to protest against the violence of the aggressor.

We have a right to denounce the treason of the capitalist governments who called themselves our "friends" and "allies."

But we also have a right to assert that a nation so united and determined to defend its country, possessing such magnificent means of defense, such a splendid mobilized army, did not have to [submit] and should not have been led to the dishonor of capitulation, did not have to be and should not have been surrendered to the mercy of the harsh enemy.

The people, the nation, and the Republic now pay dearly for this capitulation, not only through a loss of strength, territory, population, and natural wealth, but also through a loss of honor. Do not deceive yourselves! The enemy who was yesterday afraid of us, today treats us with contempt . . . And democratic public opinion throughout the world is already asking a question, which it cannot explain to itself:

The Ethiopians fought, the Chinese fought, why did the Czechoslovaks, who had everything for their own defense, capitulate? Believe me: As a Communist, I was proud of being a Czech, [proud] of the nation of Hussites to which I belong. I know that the Czech people continue to be a nation of Hussites. But neither as a Czech nor as a Communist can I be proud of the government's deeds, which brought the nation . . . to these consequences. For that, all who have but a particle of honor left to them must be ashamed.[70]

Gratuitous as these words may have been, and insincere as the policies of the Communist Party may have been in this period, they had a powerful effect on the Czechoslovak people. They brought sympathy and support for the Communists,[71] and amassed for them political capital for future use.

In the immediate aftermath of Munich, many Czechs were inclined to regard the Communists as the left wing of the democratic, antifascist movement. This view—though tarnished during the Nazi-Soviet honeymoon—persisted, and colored appraisals of the Czech Communists at later stages of political negotiation.

Communist policy at the time of Munich may well have fostered opportunism in the Party's ranks, by arousing genuine patriotism among its followers. At the same time, it promoted good feeling between the Party and the people. The latter achievement more than offset the undesirable effects of opportunistic trends, and in the long run was unquestionably beneficial to the Communists in their quest for power.

4. THE PARTY AND THE MASSES

THE CZECHOSLOVAK COMMUNIST PARTY enjoyed greater popular favor than most of its European sister parties. However, the nature of its support requires careful scrutiny in order to determine its effectiveness.

In Czechoslovakia, as in other countries where Communist parties were permitted to operate legally, there was great disparity between the number of people who voted Communist and the number willing to identify themselves with the Party by joining its ranks. While Communist electoral support never dropped below three-quarters of a million votes, claimed membership, which was not necessarily identical with actual membership, at no time exceeded one-third of a million, and did not stay at that level for very long. What is more, while the number of Communist voters remained relatively stable (the biggest variation in Communist electoral strength was a 20 per cent drop between the general elections of 1925 and those of 1929), Communist membership fluctuated wildly. At its highest, it was approximately ten times greater than at its lowest. Although these extremes were reached only once, Party membership was in continuous flux over a very wide range.

Thus the Party, which always made a good showing\in the elections, could not boast of impressive organized strength. Communist trade unions were insignificant compared with Social Democratic unions, and especially with total trade-union membership in the country. Finally, the Communist youth organization (Komsomol) never had a membership of more than 12,000. In the 1930's, when the Komsomol was outlawed by the government, though the Party was not, it did not attract half that number of followers. Despite this, the Communist Party had a more

extensive mass basis in Czechoslovakia than anywhere in Europe
—except in Germany before 1932.

Membership

Paucity of reliable information, conflicting and inaccurate figures, and great gaps in data preclude a satisfactory, detailed ex-
amination of the changes in the numerical strength, the geographic distribution, nationality, and social composition of the
Communist membership. Only crude generalizations in this regard are possible.

When the Party was founded, it claimed that a majority of Social Democrats transferred allegiance to it. This might well have
been true, for the influence of the "left" exceeded that of the
"right" at the grass roots. However, in less than a year, membership decreased from 350,000 (a figure that seemed to represent an
inflated estimate) to 170,000. In 1925–26, as an aftermath of the
first serious internal Party crisis, membership dropped below
100,000. It staged a brief recovery in the succeeding two years,
only to fall off catastrophically as a result of the showdown between the "right" and the "left," from which Gottwald emerged
victorious. By the time the storm raised by the intense interne-
cine strife subsided, the Party was left with only 24,000 members.
As the new leadership consolidated its position, the Party once
again began to attract supporters. But Communist membership
in the 1930's never rose above 75,000 and for the most part fluctuated well below that figure. (Table 1.)

While it is highly improbable that the numerical changes in
Communist membership were affected by a single cause, ideological considerations attendant upon the forcible Bolshevization of
the Party appeared to be the most important factor influencing
its size and character.

Many old-time Social Democrats who had joined the Communist Party at its inception gradually withdrew from it, so that by
1928 they comprised only one-third of the Communist membership.[1] This proportion decreased sharply after the crisis of 1928–
29 when the new Communist leadership itself began emphasizing
the recruitment of younger, unskilled workers who were not
steeped in the tradition of social democracy and trade union-
ism. The degree of success with which these endeavors met

could not be ascertained. Judging by the amount of criticism and self-criticism voiced on this subject, the going could not have been easy. If, on the one hand, rising unemployment in the early 1930's was grist for the Communist mill, the workers' fear of losing jobs effectively stifled the desire they might have had to make common cause with the Communists. This is not to say that the Communist Party lost touch with the workers, but its proletarian base, once very substantial indeed, tended to shrink. Concomitantly, the influx of intellectuals, who were for the most part of middle-class origin, increased.

In Czechoslovakia, as elsewhere, the Communist Party appealed to deviant groups in the society. This included the Jewish ethnic-religious minority, which was more severely handicapped in its means of self-expression and self-fulfillment than other groups. But as the Party was not driven underground, it could tap a broader reservoir of potential supporters than, say, its East European sister parties, which were forced to operate in a conspiratorial atmosphere that favored a greater concentration of deviant elements.

All told, the Czechoslovak Communist Party included representatives from every stratum of the population. The number of peasants, however, was always very small (only 4,000 in 1928), despite the fact that the Communists did well in rural districts at election time.[2] Similarly, only a negligible number of women were organized in the Communist Party.

One thing which the Czechoslovak Communists had in common with other legally functioning Communist parties was a tremendous turnover in membership. In this respect, published membership figures do not begin to tell the story, for they say nothing about the constancy or length of membership. Nevertheless, it seemed that in any given period, the number of members who left the Party was likely to be as great as the number who joined. The rate of turnover might well have varied from 10 to 30 per cent or even more.[3] This, of course, was an undesirable phenomenon that constituted a major source of concern for the leadership.

Regionally, Party membership varied greatly. There were far more dues-paying Communists in the Czech lands than in Slovakia, where organized activity was chronically lagging. This contrasted with a higher percentage of Communist voting strength in Slovakia.

In terms of nationality, the greatest concentration of Communists was among the Magyar minority. Czechs, Germans, and Slovaks followed in that order, although it is possible that the proportion of Germans was higher, especially in the earlier period.

Communist Trade Unions

The trade unions affiliated with the Communist Party showed similar fluctuation in membership. In the 1920's, Communist trade-union strength varied from 160,000 to 210,000, while in the 1930's, it oscillated between 113,000 and 180,000. At no time did Communist trade unions comprise more than 12 per cent of all organized workers, and at their low point in the late 1930's less than 6 per cent of organized labor was in Communist unions. (Table 2.) Communist trade-union support was concentrated in the building trades, the textile and mining industries, and among metal and agricultural workers. But even in these fields Communist strength was far inferior to the Social Democrats. (Table 3.)

Social Democrats outnumbered Communists by a ratio of two to one among miners, and five to one among metalworkers. There were ten times as many Social Democratic union members as Communists among transportation workers, and the ratio was twenty to one in favor of the Social Democrats among white-collar employees. In the building trades, however, the ratio was only four to three, and in the textile, glass, and ceramic industries, the Communists had a slight edge in absolute numbers.

As a rule, Communist unions were weakest in large factories and in the mines. Only 1 per cent of all Communist trade-union members worked in enterprises employing more than 1,000 workers. In the larger and better known plants—such as the Skoda works in Plzen, the Vitkovice iron works, the Zbrojovka in Brno, and the CKD plant in Prague—Communist trade-union membership was counted in the two-figure bracket. Communist unions attracted most (67 per cent) of their support from medium-size plants employing from fifty to one hundred workers.[4] The weakness of Communist unions in large enterprises suggested difficulties in competing with well established Social Democratic unions, and fear on the part of the workers that open association with the

Communists would lead to discrimination against them. Membership in Communist unions in larger plants could not be concealed, and the pressure was great on Communist trade unionists to join factory nuclei of the Party. The relative success of Communist unions in smaller plants might have been due to a less developed network of reformist unions in these enterprises, and possibly to a tendency toward greater radicalism among employees—not for ideological reasons, but because of more direct exposure to the personal whims of the management. Still another reason for less reluctance to join Communist unions in the smaller plants, where there was less organized trade-union activity, might have been the fact that membership in Communist organizations could be concealed with greater ease.

Communist unions attracted workers of all nationalities. The ratio of Germans and Hungarians in the Communist unions, however, far exceeded that of Czechs and Slovaks. In 1937, only 4.1 per cent of Czech and Slovak union members associated themselves with Communist unions, whereas the corresponding figure for Germans was 7.4 per cent and for Hungarians 46.9 per cent. (Table 4.)

In absolute numbers, Czechs and Slovaks constituted only a small majority (52.5 per cent) of the membership of Communist trade unions. The large percentage of Hungarian workers in Communist unions, as well as the high proportion of Communist votes (24 per cent) in electoral districts inhabited preponderantly by Hungarians, could be explained by a combination of unfulfilled social, economic, and national strivings. The Hungarian proletariat lived under more desolate conditions than did the German. Moreover, many Hungarians were unable to find adequate outlets for their national aspirations through a minority party or identification with the regime of Admiral Horthy, whereas the Nazi movement, when it took root, really stirred the emotions of the Germans. The Communist Party and Communist trade unions, therefore, became repositories of the social as well as the national aspirations of a disproportionately high number of Hungarians living in Slovakia.

The Party at the Polls

At the polls, the Communist Party generally fared well. In the first general elections held in Czechoslovakia, in 1920, the Social

Democratic Party—then still united—won an overwhelming victory. It received 1,590,000 of a total of 6,200,302 votes. Of the Czech and Slovak votes cast in this election, the Social Democrats received 37.34 per cent. They were strongest in Slovakia, with 50.16 per cent of the vote, and weakest in Moravia with 31.59 per cent, while in Bohemia they polled 34.15 per cent.[5] No other party duplicated or even approached this feat during the First Republic.

Social Democratic strength in the Czech lands was not surprising, for it was approximately equal to that attained in the last prewar elections, in 1911. Social Democratic strength in Slovakia, however, was unexpected and was interpreted as a success of the Party's radical and down-to-earth election campaign, stressing material rather than ideological issues. The Party had campaigned largely with leftist slogans, and its most effective speakers were members of the "left."[6]

After the establishment of an independent Communist Party, the two Marxist parties vied for the support of about the same constituency. In the Czech lands, the combined Social Democratic and Communist vote corresponded closely to the initial support the Social Democrats had received. In absolute figures, their support rose approximately in proportion to the increase in the size of the electorate. In Slovakia, the Marxist parties lost a large portion of their support in 1925, but from then on, they showed a moderate rising tendency.

The greater oscillation in electoral support in Slovakia was probably due to the relative political immaturity of the Slovak population, and to considerably more unsettled conditions there than in the Czech lands.

In the second general election, held in 1925, which the Communists entered for the first time as an independent party, they received 933,711 votes (close to 12 per cent of the total) and trailed the strongest party—the Agrarian—by only 36,000 votes. In these elections, the Communists outdistanced the Social Democrats by a wide margin. The latter attracted only 630,894 votes. Communist support was proportionately strongest in Slovakia and weakest in Moravia-Silesia. A breakdown of votes by nationalities, although not fully accurate, showed that in Bohemia and Moravia, Communist strength was greater in predominantly Czech districts—districts with a Czech ethnic majority of about 90 per cent—(13.6 per cent in Bohemia and 11.5 per cent in Moravia-Silesia) as compared with predominantly German districts (9.6 per cent in Bohemia and 4.7 per cent in Moravia-Silesia). In Slovakia, however, the picture was reversed. Communists received 24.1 per cent of the vote in predominantly Hungarian districts and only 11 per cent in predominantly Slovak districts.[7]

In 1929, in the third general election, Communist support decreased, but it was not commensurate with the losses in Party membership. The Communists still polled 753,444 votes. Their losses were primarily in the Czech and Slovak districts, while in the national minority districts they showed a slight gain since 1925. In the next general election, in 1935, Communist electoral support was again somewhat greater than in 1929. The Party polled 849,515 votes and was third in strength in the state—behind the Agrarian and Social Democratic parties (not counting the Sudeten German Party). This time, in sharp contrast to 1929, its support increased in the Czech and Slovak districts (especially in Slovakia) by about 160,000 votes, while it lost 60,000 votes in the predominantly German districts. (Table 5.)

An interesting feature of Communist electoral strength was its equal distribution between the countryside (towns and villages with less than 5,000 inhabitants) and urban areas (towns with a population of more than 5,000). The Communist Party was in fact the only party in Czechoslovakia attracting equal support in town and country. The causes for its relatively good showing in the countryside—especially in Slovakia and in the nationality districts—might be sought in the existence of an agrarian proletariat numbering about 400,000. However, the social composition of rural communities also must be kept in mind. Many workers lived in towns with fewer than 5,000 inhabitants. In one district of great industrial concentration—Plzen (armaments and heavy industry)—the Communists made a consistently bad showing. This district remained a Social Democratic stronghold even in 1925, when that party suffered disastrous losses elsewhere. The Communist Party fared better in other industrial districts. In Kladno, it usually polled a larger number of votes than the Social Democratic Party. In Moravska Ostrava, it fell behind its Marxist rival, but amassed a percentage of votes considerably in excess of its national average.

The electoral support marshaled by the Communists did not necessarily reflect endorsement of their ideology. The Party had its best year in 1925, when it had not yet developed a Bolshevik line and was still associated, in the popular mind, with left-wing social democracy. Its worst year at the polls was 1929—when the ideological debate was at its height. The fact that its support in urban areas dropped more sharply at this time than in rural areas indicated perhaps that ideological considerations were of greater importance to industrial workers. But even in 1929, the Party retained a large core of supporters who showed little concern about ideological matters.

Just what the Communist vote represented was difficult to determine with any accuracy, for the nature of the Party and the policies it advocated permitted a large number of people to support it for a variety of reasons. Representing as it did a cross section of the country's nationalities, and advocating a policy of national self-determination, the Party attracted a fair amount of the ethnic protest vote. But this was unstable support, for when a more effective political force appeared on the horizon, promising the fulfillment of the aspirations of one or another ethnic group, the attractiveness of the Communist Party dwindled. In 1935, when the Sudeten-German Nazi movement surged forward with an impressive show of strength, Communist support in the German nationality districts dropped sharply. Conversely, in the same year, the Party's attraction for the Czechs increased—not for ideological reasons, but as a result of the patriotic overtones of its policies and the impending conclusion of a mutual-assistance agreement with the U.S.S.R., which met with public approbation.

Representing close to 10 per cent of the electorate in a country where no party received more than 14 per cent of the vote, the Communists were a potentially strong political force. Their potential, however, remained unfulfilled. Their main source of strength was the support they received at election time. It was based on twin pillars of social and national discontent and, as such, it represented divergent and not easily reconcilable interests. Mass electoral support on the part of the Czechs was not translatable into revolutionary action. The Czechs gave the Communists no mandate to overthrow the Republic. When they voted Communist, they did so because the Party appealed to their egalitarian predisposition, not because it held out the prospect of social revolution. To favor revolution would have meant to jeopardize national independence. In case of severe internal strife, Czechoslovakia surely would have been easy prey for its predatory neighbors. Few Czechs could have been induced to overthrow their government under these circumstances. Other nationalities, in turn, were motivated primarily by a desire to alter the form of state and secure self-rule for themselves. It is not difficult to see that the heterogeneous nature of Communist supporters had a deleterious effect on the striking power of the Party. As a revolutionary force, it amounted to nothing. As a parliamentary factor, its influence was also nil.

In order to assert itself, the Party would have needed to shed its multinational character and to opt in favor of the Slavic element in the Republic. It also would have had to abandon some of its basic ideological tenets—adopting a positive attitude toward a unified and centralized republic of Czechs and Slovaks, and agreeing to reform the existing social and political institutions rather than to overthrow these by revolutionary means. Such adjustments to the exigencies of the specific country requirement were ruled out within the framework of Comintern policy. This is not to say that the Communists did not make minor tactical concessions. The united front policy of the 1930's and the guardedly patriotic overtones of their propaganda at the same time represented steps in the right direction. The more patriotic the Party seemed to be and the more closely it could be identified as the left wing of social democracy rather than the negation of social democracy, the more its stock rose with the Czechs. Nevertheless, the Party could not—or at any rate did not—go far enough to meet the preconditions that would have enhanced its effectiveness.

Essentially, the Czechoslovak Communist Party, like many of its sister parties, was too weak to change forcibly the environment in which it operated, and not adaptable enough to take advantage of the limited opportunities that were available to it under the given conditions. In order to assert itself, the Party would have to wait until more powerful forces came to its aid by changing the external (international) and internal (domestic) environment in its favor.

PART TWO

Prelude to Power:
The War Years, 1939–45

5. COMMUNIST STRATEGY AT HOME AND ABROAD

THE END OF the First Republic also marked the termination of the legal existence of the Communist Party. The government of the so-called Second Republic, which displayed a marked totalitarian penchant, moved quickly to suppress Communist political activity. In October, 1938, all Communist publications were prohibited. In December, the Party was outlawed. A month later, three Communist deputies—Antonin Zapotocky, Vlado Clementis, and Ivan Sekanina (who was executed during the war)—made a final effort to test the validity of the ban. When the electoral court refused to validate their mandates as deputies in Parliament, the Party was definitely driven underground.[1] From then until May, 1945, when Czechoslovakia was liberated, the Communist Party functioned as an illegal organization and, like all other major political parties, it had representatives abroad.

Under the impact of international and domestic developments, the Communist apparatus in Czechoslovakia broke into two major components—one centered in the Czech lands, the other in Slovakia. Communication between the two centers was sporadic, and their activities during the war developed independently. In addition to the two domestic centers, headquarters were set up abroad, first in Paris (by Sverma, Kohler, and Siroky), then in London (by Nosek, Hodinova-Spurna, and Clementis).

The leaders of the Party—Gottwald, Slansky, and Kopecky, who managed to escape from Czechoslovakia—went directly to Moscow. Sverma, Kohler, and their Slovak colleague, Viliam Siroky, joined them there after completing their Paris assignment.[2] In addition, a surprisingly large number of Communists of lesser stature eluded the German authorities and made their way to the Soviet Union before 1941.[3]

The Communist Underground in the Czech Lands

The underground activities of the Communist Party in the Czech lands have been scantily documented. The reluctance of the Communists to glorify their exploits is probably due to the paucity of heroic deeds to recount, and to the insignificant influence of the "domestic resistance" in shaping Party policy after the war, as contrasted with the "Moscow emigration."[4] The silence of their detractors, in turn, must be taken as an indication of the unavailability of evidence in support of the charges of collaboration with the Germans, between 1939 and 1941, which from time to time have been leveled against the Communists.

The story of the underground is not particularly exciting. Banning the Party was regarded with considerable apprehension by democratic leaders who felt that, in the struggle against Nazism, the cooperation of all antifascist elements would be needed.[5] However, the attitude of the Communists toward the Czechoslovak cause varied greatly for some time. It did not crystallize until the Soviet Union entered the war.

The patriotism of the Communists, so blatantly displayed at the time of Munich, remained high during 1938 and the spring of 1939. The death of Karel Capek, the celebrated national writer, in the winter of 1938, was regarded by the Czech nation as a symbol of its tragedy. Capek was popularly believed to have died of a broken heart. The Communists eulogized Capek, describing him as a "representative of the left bourgeois democratic camp" who strove effectively to "advocate the democratic program of Masaryk and Benes." He was also seen as "most closely connected with the existence of the free and democratic Czechoslovak Republic . . . whose peaceful existence corresponded to his character."[6]

The German occupation of Bohemia-Moravia hurt the Communists badly, for a large number of their followers were quickly rounded up and imprisoned by the Gestapo. Nevertheless, they participated in the modest demonstrations of patriotic opposition that followed the German occupation. Their propaganda continued to glorify the heroic Hussite past of the Czech nation, though it mingled these praises with accusations of the contemporary Czech bourgeoisie and of social democracy for "the part they played in undermining the safety of the Republic."

The Russo-German Pact placed the Party under a heavy strain. Propagating the Moscow-imposed line denouncing the imperialist war waged by the West, and deprecating the Czechoslovak liberation movement in exile (headed by Benes) were not popular undertakings. The Party's behavior during the Nazi-Soviet honeymoon was ambiguous. It attempted to belittle the struggle of the Western powers against Hitler, while promising early liberation to the Czech people. Its criticism of Benes, though mild at first, rose to a thundering *fortissimo* at the end of 1940.[7] Although the Party did not at any time openly collaborate with the Germans, its stock with the Czech people fell, and it existed in relative isolation. This isolation and the relative freedom from molestation by German authorities facilitated the development of a widespread underground network with a stable central leadership and a corps of instructors. The organizational foundation laid during this period helped to carry the Party through the more difficult years that followed, when three successive Central Committees were destroyed by the Nazis. Continuity in leadership was fully interrupted only in 1944, when the last Central Committee composed of old stalwarts was liquidated. After a break of several months, however, a new leadership was formed, combining a group of intellectuals with a number of young Communists who had not been prominent in the Party apparatus before the war.[8]

With the German assault on the U.S.S.R., the Party's negative attitude toward the war changed abruptly. The attacks on Benes ceased.[9] But the nature of its activities did not change; it still devoted most of its attention to propaganda and to maintaining an organizational network. The absence of overt resistance to the Germans was as characteristic of the Communists as it was of the entire Czech nation.

Perfunctory as their overt acts of resistance were, their verbal militancy was far more pronounced than that of any other underground group. The advantages that accrued to the Party in this period stemmed from two sources. First, it was the only political party to maintain an organizational network. Every other party disintegrated completely. Second, toward the end of the war, the Communists heeded the demands of their exiled leaders to create "revolutionary national committees." The formation of these committees was intended to spur the struggle against the Germans and to provide organs of state power after the liberation. Although the committees failed to carry the battle to the Germans, they did come into the open at the time of liberation. Since they were the only organized nuclei of political power, they bolstered the position of the Communist Party.

With two exceptions, the Communists did not cooperate with other resistance groups, although overtures were made to them.[10] In the closing days of the war, they united with prominent democratic personalities to form a Czech National Council (Ceska Narodni Rada—CNR), which represented supreme political authority in the Czech lands, and negotiated the surrender of German forces in Prague. Josef Smrkovsky, the leading Communist representative, was a Vice-Chairman of the National Council, in which he exercised much influence. The only group the Communists cooperated with prior to this was headed by Alois Petr, a former trade-union deputy of the People's Party. Petr was not closely identified with the political leadership of his party. Moreover, like the Communists, he sought to break with the past and to encourage younger, politically uncompromised individuals to rebuild the Republic. The wartime comradeship with Petr paid its most rewarding dividend in February, 1948, when he, together with Josef Plojhar (a priest with concentration camp experience), defied the elected leadership of his party and led it into the Communist fold.

The initial aloofness of the Communists might have been due to a desire to avoid political entanglements with exponents of the old order. After 1943, the changes in the fortunes of war, the growing likelihood of liberation from the East, and knowledge of the increasing influence of the Communist leadership in exile probably obviated the necessity for cooperation with other political groups.

The influence of the Communist underground movement cannot be accurately determined. According to an anti-Communist resistance leader, the Communists were definitely in ascendance over non-Communist groups after the summer of 1942. Although it may be safely assumed that the attractiveness of Communism grew as liberation approached, the caution of the Czech people prevented all but a few hardy souls from associating themselves with the Party. In May, 1945, its membership in the Czech lands stood at 27,000. Considering prewar figures and the claimed loss of 25,000 Communists during the war, not many could have been new members.[11]

The Communist Underground in Slovakia

The situation in Slovakia was radically different. Looser political controls by the puppet government of Jozef Tiso, a more favorable terrain, and easier access to the Soviet Union encouraged more active resistance. In the spring of 1939, the Slovak Communists became an independent section of the Comintern (Komunisticka Strana Slovenska—KSS), although they continued to be subordinated to the guidance of the national Czechoslovak Communist leadership.[12] Attempts to direct developments in Slovakia from Moscow went awry, however, largely because of the alertness of the police. Emissaries from the Soviet Union were apprehended shortly after their arrival: Viliam Siroky in 1941[13] and Karol Bacilek in 1943.[14] Only Karol Smidke eluded the police, but he did not have great prestige, nor did he enjoy Gottwald's full confidence. The direction of the Communist underground passed into the hands of Gustav Husak and Laco Novomesky, domestic leaders who had little experience and no training in Moscow.

They worked with Smidke, but since they lacked firm guidance, particularly after the dissolution of the Comintern in May, 1943, they became prey to "national bourgeois" deviationist tendencies, as did most underground Communist parties in Eastern Europe. They underestimated the necessity of maintaining and developing a strong, separate organizational network and of persisting in the class struggle, differentiating their efforts from those of others, who also strove for emancipation from fascist rule. Instead, they assigned highest priority to a national Slovak struggle for liberation in a broad antifascist front. They joined democratic opposition leaders in the creation of a Slovak National Council (Slovenska Narodna Rada—SNR) in September, 1943, and worked out an agreement three months later. Communists and democrats were represented in equal numbers in the SNR.[15] Together they enlisted the aid of dissident officers of the Slovak Armed Forces (including the Minister of Defense, General Catlos) in the preparation of an uprising that would free Slovakia of its puppet government and remove the stigma of collaboration from the entire Slovak nation, thus strengthening its claim to self-government within the Czechoslovak Republic. The uprising was sprung prematurely, on August 29, 1944, because of a change in the plans of the German military to occupy Slovakia sooner than had been anticipated. Smidke, who had flown to Moscow to acquaint the Communists and the Soviet authorities with the plans of the underground, was still there when the revolt broke out.

The results of his negotiations have not been divulged, but the cryptic references by Zdenek Fierlinger and Vaclav Kopecky, who have chronicled these events several years apart,[16] indicate that Smidke's mission was regarded with suspicion in Moscow. Czechoslovak and Soviet Communists had misgivings about any indigenous movement with a chance of succeeding, for fear that the participants would derive great prestige and acquire vested power, which would make them dangerous competitors. Although the social and political composition of the Slovak insurgents was far less objectionable than that of the Warsaw rebels, who rose against the Germans almost at the same time, neither the character of the insurrection, nor the persons involved were to the liking of the Muscovite leadership.

Immediate action was taken to forestall untoward developments, and Jan Sverma and Rudolf Slansky were hastily dispatched to serve, respectively, as political and military advisers to the insurgents.[17] Slansky had received training at partisan headquarters in Kiev and was attached to the staff of General A. N. Asmolov, a Soviet military officer in charge of partisan operations. Sverma was sent directly from Moscow. Other Czechs and Slovaks in exile (e.g., the Social Democrat Bohumil Lausman) joined partisan units that were parachuted into Slovakia—as much to balance the armed might of the insurgents as to fight against the Germans.

According to eyewitnesses, Sverma had serious difficulties asserting his authority. On the one hand, he was confronted with a functioning "supreme organ of power," the SNR, which had emerged from illegality on September 1, and arrogated to itself the executive and legislative prerogatives of a government, issuing decrees and creating executive-administrative departments (poverenictva) for the conduct of daily business. On the other hand, he was faced by ultra-left Communists, who favored the creation of a Slovak Soviet Republic to be incorporated in the Soviet Union. They perpetuated an ideological deviation that had been widespread among Slovak Communists in 1941 and 1942.[18]

The defeat of the rebel forces and the capture of their capital, Banska Bystrica, by the Germans, late in October, reduced the efficacy of the insurrection. In the retreat through the mountains, large numbers of partisans, including Jan Sverma, were lost.*

The liberation of Slovakia was delayed and was ultimately carried out by the Soviet Army, which eliminated any serious threat of the establishment of an administration rivaling that proposed by the Communists in exile. However, both Benes in London, and Gottwald in Moscow, had to recognize the SNR as a legitimate governing body, having an executive as well as a legislative arm, and to accommodate the members of the SNR as spokesmen of their nation in the new Czechoslovak Administration.

The Communists were in a particularly delicate situation; they were loudly championing equal rights for Slovaks in the "reborn Republic," and for this reason could not easily suppress institutions that gave substance to these rights.

Although it was defeated, the uprising strengthened the Slovak bid for self-government and brought about political arrangements to that effect. Further, it ensured the Communists of one-half of the posts in all Slovak public institutions and led to the formal

*After the liberation of Czechoslovakia, Sverma's body was taken to Prague and given a hero's burial. Years later, Rudolf Slansky was accused of having willfully caused Sverma's death. Although Slansky was not rehabilitated in the course of de-Stalinization, he was absolved of the absurd charge of having contributed to Sverma's death. V. Kopecky gives an authoritative account of the partisans' retreat and leaves no doubt that Sverma was ill and could not be saved. See V. Kopecky, *CSR a KSC*, pp. 366–67.

unification in Slovakia of the Marxist left. At the height of revolutionary excitement, the Social Democratic Party, at that time
represented mainly by a younger generation of officials (the old
leadership was either dead or in prison), merged with the Communists under the latter's label. But the uprising and the preceding developments served as a cause of dissension and rivalry
within the Communist Party—between the leaders who had prepared the revolt and those who were in Moscow or in prison, and
thus barred from participating. As the liberation of Slovakia progressed, the leaders of the resistance were not given the recognition they might have expected; Muscovites and ex-prisoners took
over active direction of the Party's affairs, and while open clashes
were avoided, personality and ideological differences were evident. This friction lingered on, and, long after the coup, caused
Husak and Novomesky to be expelled from the Party and imprisoned.

The Communist Movement Abroad

At the onset of the war, the attitude of the Communist political refugees toward the Czechoslovak movement headed by Benes
was ambiguous.

In the summer of 1939, when Benes arrived in London to lay
the foundations of a political movement in exile, a group of Communists, including Vaclav Nosek, Anezka Hodinova, Josef Valo,
Gustav Beuer, and Karl Kreibich, offered to collaborate with
him. In October, in Paris, he was approached by Jan Sverma,
who tried to entice him to transfer headquarters to Moscow.[19]
According to Benes, Sverma envisaged the liberation of Czechoslovakia entirely as a result of a great revolutionary victory of the
Soviet Union, and wanted to win Benes to this viewpoint. It was
evident to Benes that Sverma and other Czechoslovak Communists were wholly under the influence of their Soviet comrades.
They considered the Soviet-German pact as an expedient, permitting the U.S.S.R. to stay out of the war until the very end,
when both warring camps would be near exhaustion and unable
to prevent a social revolution in their countries. Benes, who did
not share Sverma's views and expected the Soviet Union to be
drawn into the war much earlier, declined to leave the West at
that time. But he regarded cooperation with the Communists in

the future and under more propitious circumstances as a fore-gone conclusion.

Following the Sverma-Benes encounter, but not necessarily be-cause of it, the Communists adopted a reserved attitude toward Benes,[20] which turned to open hostility after December, 1939, when the Kremlin broke all ties with the Czechoslovak exile movement, shut down the Czechoslovak Embassy in Moscow, and ordered the withdrawal of Ambassador Zdenek Fierlinger, who until then had been permitted to remain at his post in an unoffi-cial capacity.[21] Attacks followed on Benes and his bourgeois-demo-cratic associates, who were condemned as the guilty men of Czechoslovakia. Despite such vituperation, Benes continued to urge his compatriots not to lose faith in the possibility of cooper-ating with the Communists, for he expected them to change their views radically as soon as the U.S.S.R. became involved in the war. Indeed, the strained relations did improve rapidly after the Soviet Union entered the war and renewed diplomatic rela-tions with Benes' exile government. In 1942, five Communists—Vaclav Nosek, Josef Valo, Anezka Hodinova, Karl Kreibich, and Ivan Petruscak—were appointed to the State Council, a sort of parliament in exile. A sixth, Bohuslav Vrbensky, served *in ab-sentia,* from Moscow. Although this was the extent of formal Communist participation in the government, informal contacts between Czechoslovak Communists and non-Communists were numerous and friendly. Many Communists were given employ-ment in the various administrative bodies maintained by the government. Others received some kind of assistance from the Czech authorities. Communists as individuals were part of the Czechoslovak exile movement in London.

The groundwork for the future participation of the Commu-nist Party in the Czechoslovak Government was laid in Moscow in December, 1943. Earlier that year, Benes had initiated nego-tiations for the conclusion of a mutual assistance treaty between the Soviet Union and Czechoslovakia. Preliminary discussions be-tween Benes and A. Y. Bogomolov, the Soviet Ambassador ac-credited to the Czechoslovak Government in exile, were held in March, and early April, 1943.[22] By June, substantial agreement had been reached on the underlying principles. The Soviet Gov-ernment had, among other things, approved Benes' proposal to expel the majority of the German-speaking population from Czechoslovakia.

The signing of the treaty was delayed for several months, allegedly because of objections interposed by Anthony Eden, who considered Benes' haste ill-advised and suggested waiting until an armistice with Germany had been signed.[23] Benes was not pleased at the prospect of postponing the formal conclusion of the alliance. For, he claimed, the signing of a treaty then "would show the whole world . . . what the Soviet Union wants and what policy it intends to pursue after the war," and would therefore enhance a rapprochement between the Soviet Union and the Western Allies.[24]

Late in the fall of 1943, following the Moscow conference of the Foreign Ministers of Great Britain, the U.S., and the U.S.S.R., Eden apparently relented, and Benes was free to embark on his historic journey to Moscow.

He regarded the treaty as the cornerstone of Czechoslovakia's future foreign policy, if not of the country's entire existence. It specified close cooperation and mutual assistance, especially in stopping another "Drang nach Osten." Benes' yearning for his country's security seemed to be fulfilled. The treaty also stipulated strict observance of "noninterference in each other's domestic affairs," and thus bolstered hopes for a tranquil reconstruction of Czechoslovakia.

Negotiations with Benes

Negotiations with the Communist leadership were a natural corollary of Benes' official discussions with Stalin and Molotov. The constructive participation of the Communists in rebuilding the Republic was not a matter of debate, but the terms and conditions for Communist adherence to the government needed to be clarified. The second week of his sojourn to Moscow was devoted largely to political discussions with Gottwald, Slansky, Sverma, and Kopecky, who acted as spokesmen for the Communist Party.[25]

Altogether, four meetings—lasting close to twenty hours—were held at Benes' residence. The discussions were of a preliminary nature. They covered a wide range of subjects from exile politics to the disposition of political forces in Czechoslovakia after the liberation, and were conducted in a friendly atmosphere.

Benes' opening gesture was to invite the Communists to send two representatives to the London cabinet, in order to give overt expression to the unity that actually existed between Communists and non-Communists in exile. His offer was rejected on the ground that the Communists could not associate themselves with several representatives of rightist groups who were then serving in the cabinet, and a drastic reshuffle of the cabinet to suit their demands probably would not be feasible in London. Benes had to agree with the latter argument. The Communists therefore remained outside the government, although they subsequently exercised considerable influence over its actions.

Now that the question of Communist participation in the exile government was settled, the talks turned to the future of Czechoslovakia. Gottwald, the chief Communist spokesman, expressed the view that a "revolution against the Germans and the guilty Czechs" would be necessary and "National Committees" representing the working people of town and country would have to be introduced, not only as revolutionary bodies, but also as permanent organs of state power, giving the civil administration an entirely new, popular character.[26] Benes concurred in the need for administrative reform and the introduction of popularly elected National Committees which, as he pointed out, were well rooted in the Western democratic tradition.[27]

Gottwald also expected a "revolutionary shift" to the left in the political orientation of the Czechoslovak people, entailing a socialist majority and a big defeat of the "rightist bloc."[28] He envisaged close cooperation among the three socialist parties—the Communist, Social Democratic, and National Socialist. But he turned down as premature Benes' suggestion of a formal merger.[29] His counterproposal was to create a "National Front" including the three socialist parties and such nonsocialist parties as would be permitted to operate. The Front would insure the unity of the broad strata of the population. It would also guarantee the implementation of a national political platform, for all parties would commit themselves to solidarity in it.[30] The influence of the socialist parties in the Front would be further assured by the creation of a socialist bloc, committed to the closest possible cooperation.

Turning to more concrete issues, the Communists did not object to Benes' suggestion that elections be held no later than six months after liberation. However, they proposed that the "left" be strengthened, even before the election, by appointing one of its representatives (not a Communist) as Prime Minister, and by giving important portfolios in the cabinet to leftist parties. The Communists held out for several of the key posts in the government, but did not specify which ones they had in mind. There was general agreement on the desirability of limiting the number of political parties in Czechoslovakia. Although no specific proposals were made, the Catholic People's Party was approved as an admissible nonsocialist force. There seemed to be a tacit understanding between Benes and the Communists on outlawing the former rightist parties, but closer scrutiny of the problem of a party representing peasant interest was shelved for the time being.

In addition to the very large area of general agreement, there were points of disagreement. These centered on four issues: Benes' capitulation at Munich, the conciliatory attitude of the London government toward the Czech Quisling (Hacha) regime, the reluctance of London to incite the Czechs to revolutionary activity against the Germans, and the centralist viewpoint of the London government concerning the future organization of the Republic. (It was here that the Communists introduced the concept of complete equality of the various Slavic elements in the country.)

Gottwald's concern with the moral consequences of Benes' capitulation at Munich could hardly be understood in other than ideological terms.[31] Similar considerations must have prompted him to take issue with Benes about active resistance to the Nazis. Gottwald probably feared that the Czechoslovak people might go through a second revolutionary period—the first having been their emancipation in 1918—without acquiring revolutionary experience. Leninism takes a dim view of peoples and classes lacking in revolutionary experience, for it holds that only in revolutionary battles can a nation or class acquire a taste for truly Bolshevik tactics. The penchant of the Czechoslovak Communists for constitutionalism and legalism before World War II was to a large measure ascribed to their lack of this experience, and Gottwald wanted at all costs to avoid a repetition of these conditions.

The issues on which Benes and Gottwald did not agree were

not of prime importance, and Benes left the meetings obviously satisfied. The unity of the nation—always of paramount concern to him—now appeared assured. The Communists would work with him rather than against him and, in this manner, the quick and peaceful reconstruction of Czechoslovakia appeared well within the realm of possibility. Although the Communists had raised a number of controversial issues, they had been less obstreperous than might have been expected. Their demands did not seem to Benes either excessive or specific enough to worry about greatly. Points of disagreement could be worked out if Gottwald were amenable to *quid pro quo* compromises, as Benes hoped he would be.

While in Moscow, the President became aware of what he might expect from the left wing of the Social Democratic Party. Zdenek Fierlinger, the Czechoslovak Ambassador who had been re-accredited to the Kremlin after the restoration of formal relations in 1941, was a Social Democrat of lifelong standing. He made it unmistakably clear to the President that he had agreed with the Communists on a common policy and a common approach to the political problems facing Czechoslovakia.[32] In answer to the President's query, Fierlinger asserted that he had been authorized to speak on behalf of the entire left wing of the party. He stressed the bankruptcy of the prewar Social Democratic policy and emphasized the need for solidarity on the left. He deplored the ideological split that plagued the Social Democrats even in time of war, and intimated that while neither one of the exile factions had a right to speak on behalf of the whole party, the "left" would make a strong bid for supremacy and would not tolerate the revival of "rightist" tendencies.[33] Benes then offered to invite one member of the Social Democratic "left" to join his cabinet—two "rightist" Social Democrats were already serving in it—but Fierlinger refused the offer as a sop that would not reconcile the fundamental differences between the two Social Democratic factions.

Fierlinger's emergence as the leader of the "left" socialists and the obvious use he made of his ambassadorial office for partisan political purposes was highly irregular. Under his management, the Czechoslovak Embassy was little more than a Communist and Soviet listening post. The impropriety of his behavior actually led several members of the London government to demand that he be recalled. But Benes would not hear of it.

In his dealings with the Communists, Benes once more acted as a self-appointed spokesman for the nation and for all non-Communist parties. Although no formal commitments were made at this time, the agreements in principle entailed strong moral obligations, which the democratic parties could not easily disregard. Moreover, Benes took it upon himself to convey the gist of the conversations to appropriate members of the London government and to deliver letters from the Communists and from Fierlinger to their comrades, setting forth their side of the talks and their terms of collaboration among political groups in exile.* Although the substance of Benes' negotiations with the Communists could not be heavily censured, his procedure seemed reprehensible. He did not consult the spokesmen of non-Communist parties before he went to Moscow, he gave the Communists an opportunity to express themselves first, and agreed to act as an intermediary between them and the democratic leaders, confronting the latter with a *fait accompli.*

As a result of the stance of the Communists and "left" socialists, the President found himself and his government in an anomalous position. A large and powerful bloc of the Czechoslovak political forces remained outside the government, refusing to take responsibility for its decisions. Yet little, if any, government business could be transacted without reference to the factions standing aside, for their eventual participation in running the affairs of state was taken for granted. The Communists and the "left" Social Democrats thus enjoyed a double privilege. They did not bear responsibility for the government's actions, yet at the same time, they exerted a strong if not a decisive influence on it.

The knowledge that the Communists would in effect censor all

---

*The letters were documents of first-rate importance foreshadowing the arrangements for the political future of the Republic. Although their content was well known to the President and a large number of persons abroad, it was concealed from politicians in Czechoslovakia, for fear that it would cause an adverse reaction among them and among the people. Many Czechs and Slovaks learned of these documents long after they fled their country following the Communist coup d'état in 1948. (Excerpts from the letters are printed in *Nase Cesta*, a journal edited by Social Democrats in exile, March 6, 1955, pp. 2–4. The Communist text is in Gottwald, *Spisy*, XI [1955], 259–72.)

decisions made prior to their entry into the government profoundly affected the activities of many Czech *émigré* politicians, who had an eye on their political futures, and who did not want to incur the displeasure of the Communist leadership.[34] Observing the behavior of Czechoslovak political factions, one could hardly fail to conclude that the center of power no longer resided in the London government. The decisions of the government were regularly cleared with the Moscow Communists and, while the government seemed to shift about uneasily, as if in doubt what to do next, the Communists went ahead boldly, enunciating an action program. Despite the subservient attitude of its individual members and the deference the government showed toward the Communists, friction between London and Moscow could not be avoided.

The Communist Action Program Takes Shape

The Communist action program was brought to the attention of the exile movement in the form of articles in *Ceskoslovenske Listy*, a Czech journal first published in Moscow in August, 1943. Appropriate excerpts were transmitted to Czechoslovakia in broadcasts from Moscow, or dropped in leaflet form over the country and distributed by the Communist underground.

The Communist action program as it was unfolded in *Ceskoslovenske Listy* could leave little doubt about the Party's intentions. The major articles, written by Gottwald, Sverma, Slansky, and Kopecky, made it clear that far from aiming to improve the political and economic structure of the pre-Munich Republic, the Communists wanted to place the country on entirely new foundations. Gottwald did not mince words in denouncing "the pre-Munich bourgeois democratic republic, in which power was in the hands of a relatively narrow group of big capitalists representing finance, industry, and large landholding interests. . . ."[35] He spoke boldly of the "re-examination of values" that occurred under the impact of "five years of subjugation . . . so that the entire political life of the pre-Munich republic and of its individual tenets would be transformed."[36] Articles by Gottwald and Sverma spelled out the Communist concept of National Committees as elected revolutionary bodies of popular government operating in towns and villages, districts, and on the land (province) level. They would perform executive, legislative, administrative, and even judicial functions.[37] Sverma's detailed description of the methods of creating National Committees, and the functions for which they should prepare, was broadcast to Czechoslovakia and distributed there in pamphlet form as a directive for the underground.[38]

These pronouncements were couched in unmistakable Marxist-Leninist terminology, leaving no doubt about the character of the National Committees as "soviets" adapted to the needs of Czechoslovakia.[39]

Sverma also projected the development and organization of trade unions as a "mighty association serving the working class as a whole." He reviewed the weaknesses and errors of the past, and asserted that "old party obstacles must be suppressed . . . the united union organization will be built on the basis of true workers' democracy . . . [the unions] will be independent organs of the working class and cannot be instruments of party politics."[40]

The Communists emphasized the unity of the working class and the decisive role it would play in the Republic "as the solid foundation of a new life in the nation."[41] The implications once more were clear. Under the old regime, the Social Democratic and National Socialist parties, who were members of the government, were responsible for splintering the working class into antagonistic political factions, thereby depriving it of its rightful power. Under the new regime, the working class would be united, and therefore powerful.

Kopecky presented a comprehensive analysis of the Communist concept of equal status for the various Slavic nationalities in the Republic and put the Party on record as a champion of the cause of Slovak autonomist aspirations.[42] Rudolf Slansky wrote on economic matters and Jiri Kotatko outlined the Party's agricultural policy.

In addition to emphasizing national unity, especially the unity of the working class, Communist writers paid heavy lip service to the reawakening of a new Slavic consciousness and brotherhood. Naturally, they pictured themselves as the standard-bearers of this new "Slavic policy which . . . cleaned of all Pan-Slavist elements, of Czarist imperialism, assumes a truly democratic character, such as it has always had in the hearts of the Czech people

. . . who lost their aristocracy after the battle of the White Mountain [in 1620] and struggled back to life as a nation of 'small people.' "[43]

Ceskoslovenske Listy also published the battle cry of left-wing Social Democrats for a change in their party's orientation. The new course was charted in the following terms:

> The Social Democratic workers recognized that the coalition policy of the Social Democrats was not the democratic way toward ever greater progress, which their leaders claimed it was. The handcuffs of coalition policy [with the bourgeoisie] prevented social democracy from implementing an independent workers' policy, and finally led it to a fatal dependence on the right wing of the coalition, which in the decisive moment chose the road of direct cooperation with the treacherous Henlein [Sudeten German] opposition. . . .
>
> Social Democratic workers desired the closest possible fighting unity [of the working class] and soon developed a positive attitude toward the Soviet Union. . . .
>
> The necessity of unity in the Czechoslovak workers' movement is today almost universally recognized among Social Democrats.
>
> The Social Democratic workers never abandoned the principles of socialism and democracy. . . . Ideological and programmatic rapprochement [among the workers' parties] aiming at the creation of a single party is necessary. . . . A clear program boldly aimed at the thorough rebuilding of the social order will be a guarantee that . . . the work of the national revolution will be completed in the social field.
>
> Let us not forget that the reaction, compromised as it is as a result of its treacherous policy before Munich and during the occupation, will remain politically strong so long as it will be strong economically. . . . This danger will be the smaller the closer the unity of all workers and especially of the workers' bloc will be. . . .[44]

Preparations for the Return Home

Meanwhile, preparations for a return to Czechoslovakia were taking concrete shape. Benes was urged by the Communists to issue a decree defining the competence of the National Committees. The decree was duly issued in December, 1944. A draft prepared in London was sent to Moscow for clearance.[45] The final version included every correction the Communists had suggested and resembled closely the formula Gottwald and Sverma had earlier enunciated. Vaclav Nosek hailed it as one of the basic measures taken by the government in exile, "permitting a transition free from upheavals to the new conditions."[46]

With the penetration of Soviet armed units into Czechoslovakia at the end of 1944, the transfer of the seat of government and the question of the time and place for reorganizing the cabinet became acute. This subject, briefly and inconclusively discussed by Benes and Gottwald in December, 1943, now became a burning issue. Nosek had indicated in July, 1944, that the proper time would come when a part of the country had been liberated.[47] Moreover, the Communists in Moscow intimated that during the closing stages of the war the government should transfer its seat from London to the Soviet Union.[48] Benes preferred to put off the formation of a new government until the liberation of Prague. He also wanted to return from London directly to the capital, either with the old government intact, or in a "state of resignation." He did not want to reshuffle the cabinet without the participation of Czech domestic resistance elements. The Communists, however, were adamant, and during the winter of 1944 applied increasing pressure on Benes to induce him to change his mind.[49] The Moscow leadership looked askance even at preliminary negotiations between Benes and Nosek in London, for fear that Nosek, the principal Communist spokesman in the West, might not be able to act with the desired firmness. In its view, binding decisions could be reached only in Moscow, in plenary discussions with Gottwald and the top echelon of the Communist Party.

The reasons for the Communists' insistence on their terms were obvious. Delaying the creation of a new government until the entire country was liberated might put them at a considerable tactical disadvantage. The London government, returning to Prague intact, probably would receive an expression of public confidence of such magnitude as to reduce the Communists' bargaining position for key cabinet posts. Moreover, the Communist Party would be deprived of directing and taking credit for the implementation of crucial revolutionary measures immediately after liberation. In order to gain its objectives under these circumstances, the Party either would have to resort to armed uprising or other forms of violence which it sought to avoid, or it would face a difficult uphill struggle in its effort to entrench itself in the government. Conversely, determining the composition of the new government in Moscow, before the liberation of Czechoslovakia was completed, would impart great political and psychological advantages to the Communists. Returning to Czechoslovakia as full-fledged members of the government, they would benefit in terms of power and prestige. Their participation would be interpreted as moral approval by Benes. They would also be able to issue authoritative instructions to comrades still in occupied territory. Seeing their representatives in this position would have a beneficial effect on the daring of Communists throughout the country.

After a series of frantic exchanges between Moscow and London, the Communist view prevailed. It has not yet been revealed why Benes conceded this crucial point. However, the trend of events in the Carpatho-Ukraine, the most Eastern province of Czechoslovakia, which had been liberated before any other part of the country, might have decisively influenced the President's decision. In the Carpatho-Ukraine, the attempts of an official government delegation headed by Frantisek Nemec—a rightist Social Democrat—to re-establish Czechoslovak sovereignty met strong resistance and ended in failure. It was of little consequence that the delegation had been dispatched there in accordance with the terms of an agreement with the Soviet Government and with its explicit approval and cooperation. Local Communists led by Ivan Turjanica, a Czechoslovak officer of Carpatho-Ukrainian descent, and operating under the protection of Soviet soldiers and political police, staged a plebiscite demanding the incorporation of this territory into the Soviet Ukraine.* The attitude of the authorities in Moscow toward the "spontaneous" popular movement was one of "reluctant but benevolent" approval, and the

---

*Turjanica became regional secretary of the Ukrainian Communist Party, in charge of the entire Carpatho-Ukraine. He served in this capacity until his death, in the early 1950's.

Benes government was confronted with an accomplished fact.[50]
The complicity of the Czechoslovak Communist leadership in this
affair has not been substantiated; in fact, it seemed at the time
that Gottwald and his colleagues had been taken by surprise.
Naturally, whatever their true feelings, they could not but heart-
ily support developments to which the Kremlin had given its
stamp of approval. The subtle threat of a repetition in Slovakia,
or at least in the eastern portion of that province, was additional
pressure on Benes.

The President and his entourage arrived at Moscow on March
17, 1945, and remained until March 31. In this period, the composition of a new government and its formal program were
worked out.

The Fate of the Republic Is Settled

The outcome of the Moscow discussions was disastrous for the
democratic parties. The Communists won every major point.
They demanded and obtained key government posts such as the
Ministries of the Interior, Agriculture, and Information. Their
claim was based on the unsubstantiated assertion that, during the
war, their party had become the strongest political force in Czechoslovakia.[51] All told, the Communists held eight of twenty-five
posts in the new government, which was called on to direct
Czechoslovakia's affairs during the crucial months of reconstruction. These included two posts in the Council of Vice-Premiers,
the Ministries of the Interior, Information, Education, Agriculture, and Labor–Social Welfare. One of their members was chosen
Under-Secretary of State for Foreign Affairs.* Ludvik Svoboda,
the commanding general of the First Czechoslovak Brigade in the
U.S.S.R. (who later joined the Party, but was then neutral), became
Minister of National Defense at the recommendation of the Com-

---

*The Foreign Minister was Jan Masaryk, a likable but ineffectual person
without political-party affiliation. The son of the founder of the Republic,
he had served as his country's ambassador to the Court of St. James's before
World War II, and had earned a reputation at home as an international
playboy. He joined Benes' exile government, lending it the luster of his
family name and his many useful contacts in London. His retention in the
postwar cabinet helped to mislead Western diplomatic circles, which tended
to attach undue significance to the presence of Masaryk in a responsible
post and to overestimate the prestige and influence he had among his people.

munists. Zdenek Fierlinger, also a Communist choice, received the premiership.[52]

The government included a disproportionate number of Slovaks, in recognition of their newly won importance in the state. By contrast, not a single Communist or non-Communist from the Czech lands was appointed. In a sense, this was understandable. Bohemia and Moravia were still under German occupation, many political leaders were in concentration camps, and those who were at liberty had not been able to join their colleagues for consultation. However, the failure to provide for the inclusion of Czech leaders, either by keeping certain posts open for them, or by making interim assignments of portfolios pending the liberation of the whole country, connoted a curious attitude. Although the government called itself provisional, it had no intention of reconstituting itself before the selection of a National Assembly.*

The Communists were well pleased. They preferred to keep control in the hands of a few trusted leaders, and looked apprehensively even on the domestic leadership of their own Party. The composition of the government assured them of the desired control, and gave them a lien on the political careers of the democratic cabinet ministers, of whom several were under obligation to the Communists. In direct competition with domestic leaders, they might not have obtained the endorsement of their respective parties for such high office.

This was not all. While the government was being formed, the composition of the National Front also was decided, and Klement Gottwald became its chairman.[53] The parties represented in the National Front and the cabinet were identical, and the Front served as a shadow cabinet, where issues could be thrashed out with greater informality and frankness. The existence of this dual

---

*No member of the Czech National Council was admitted to the government. On the contrary, after the liberation of Prague, the government moved with precipitous haste to divest the Council of any incipient authority, and to deny it any claim to political recognition. This was made possible by the immediate transfer of the seat of government to Prague. The liberation of the capital coincided with the arrival of Soviet troops, signaling, at the same time, the collapse of the last vestige of German resistance. The National Council had been active for a short time only, and its undoubted accomplishments were overshadowed by the triumphal entry of Soviet troops and Czechoslovak representatives from abroad.

system, embodying one formal and one informal cabinet, remained one of the peculiarities of Czechoslovak political life until the coup.

One of the crucial decisions reached at Moscow concerned the limitation of the number and type of political parties in Czechoslovakia. All rightist parties were outlawed. This removed from contention the Agrarian Party, the most influential prewar party. It had traditionally held the key positions, most of which were now taken over by the Communists. The Agrarian Party was not outlawed without good reason. It had, *de facto,* collaborated with the Germans. But perhaps more important was the consideration that it had not been popular with any of the parties that had participated in the Moscow negotiations. Its political philosophy had not run on tracks parallel to Masaryk's. The Agrarians had also "ruled" with a heavy hand. They were far more authoritarian than any of the other Czechoslovak democratic parties, and they gave unmistakable evidence of knowing how to convert a small electoral advantage to disproportionate influence. All this did not endear them to their rivals. The Agrarian leadership had consistently opposed Benes, having sought to undermine his prestige while he was Minister of Foreign Affairs, and even having nominated its own candidate for the presidency in 1935. For this reason and others as well, the Agrarian Party was on bad terms with the National Socialists. It often clashed with the Social Democrats, and even the People's Party rejoiced at the disbandment of the Agrarians. For the People's Party relied heavily on peasant support, especially in the wealthier agricultural areas in Moravia. With the Agrarians out of the way, it hoped to capture a large proportion of politically homeless peasants.

* The Communists encountered no great difficulty in extracting democratic consent for prohibiting the rebirth of the Agrarian Party in any way, shape, or form. According to the best available evidence, only one voice was raised in opposition. But the Communists went further. They made sure that the Agrarian Party would not be revived, and they also occupied its traditional strongholds in the cabinet. The other parties seemed to act in the belief that the peasants would not "go Communist" and that, once given a chance to extricate themselves from the stranglehold of the Agrarian leadership, would vote for "Masaryk's de-

mocracy." As usual, the democratic parties failed to show an appreciation of the importance of controlling tangible instruments of power and persuasion that can help to secure the allegiance of one or another stratum of the population.

The rightist parties were banned arbitrarily, in contravention of normally accepted notions of political freedom. Subsequent endorsement by public opinion did not erase the spurious validity of this decision. The parties that formed the government essentially represented a closed corporation. They conspired to direct the expression of political sentiments into pre-existing channels. Obviously, all hoped to benefit from this deal. What the democrats seemed to overlook was that they had willingly cooperated in destroying, or at least in curtailing, one of the cardinal principles of democracy, and by so doing had strengthened the hand of the Communist Party, unless they themselves were prepared to go further in the use of undemocratic methods.

The program of the newly constituted government incorporated the major features of the Communist action program. It committed the new regime to far-reaching political, military, economic, social, and cultural reforms. It embodied the principle of equality between Czechs and Slovaks, making for a dual administration in the state. It called for a reorientation of the Czechoslovak Army along the lines of the Red Army. It stipulated severe punishment for war criminals and prohibited the former rightist political parties.[54]

The triumph of the Communists was decisive, and they did not hesitate to remind the people of it. As Klement Gottwald put it, ". . . if we examine the program of the present Czechoslovak Government, the program formulated in Moscow in the spring of this [sic] year, and if we recall our first negotiations with President Benes in the fall of 1943, we see that every major, basic, and fundamental point contained in the government program already had been in these meetings with the President in . . . 1943."[55]

Rudolf Slansky, speaking at a regional conference of the Party in Moravska Ostrava on March 17, 1946, gave this account of the formation of the government:

When President Benes came to Moscow in December, 1943, we got together with him and had discussions . . . that lasted a full twenty hours. Comrade Gottwald told him then, "Mister President, if you wish to avoid civil war after the liberation, it is necessary that we carry out basic changes in our economic life . . . that we establish National Committees, expel the Germans, solve our relations with the Slovaks, and everything else that was in the Kosice* program." We, the Moscow Communists, are the authors of the Kosice program of the government.

When in April [sic] of last year the gentlemen came from London to Moscow, and we asked them what sort of program they have, they told us, none.

When the government was to be formed, we told them, first [we shall have] a program—and we submitted to them the Kosice program, which, with minor stylistic changes, was accepted. [Then] we took a gold fountain pen and everyone who wanted to be a member of the government had to commit himself by his signature that he would implement the program. Only then was the government formed.[56]

Slansky's assertion, exaggerated as it may seem, went unchallenged by the non-Communist participants in the negotiations.

In the light of subsequent developments, the wisdom of Benes' rapprochement with the Communists, and his capitulation at Moscow, can be—as indeed it has been—seriously questioned, for at this time the cards were not altogether stacked against him. Had he decided to force the hand of the Communists and of his Soviet allies, he either might have extracted some concessions from them, or compelled them to sack him, and thus, in effect, to dishonor their agreement with him. In the latter case, the whole world would have been dramatically alerted to the Communists' postwar designs. However, Benes was not much given to forcing an opponent's hand, and he was certainly not inclined to exchange the Presidency of the Republic for the dubious distinction of martyrdom on behalf of the West. His primary interest was in restoring Czechoslovakia's independence and integrity,

---

* Kosice was the town in Eastern Slovakia where the new Czechoslovak Government established headquarters before moving to Prague and where its program was announced.

and the surest way to accomplish this was to avoid quarrels rather than magnify them. It was natural, therefore, that he should go to extraordinary lengths to accommodate the Communists. In evaluating Benes' behavior, the element of personal vindication must also be taken into account. The West had let him down ignominiously in 1938. The Munich episode was distasteful to Benes not only because his allies had deserted him, but also because throughout the crisis they had acted as though moral right were not on his and on his country's side, and as though he, rather than Hitler, were the aggressor. It must have given him considerable satisfaction to return to Czechoslovakia as President with the help of his Eastern, rather than his Western, friends.

Aside from these overwhelming considerations, there were other reasons that permitted him to rationalize his capitulation. He was still convinced that Stalin would give tangible evidence of gratitude for the services he had rendered the Soviet leader by informing him of the Tukhachevsky plot.[57] (Benes believed quite firmly and sincerely that Tukhachevsky had plotted with the Germans against Stalin, and that he [Benes] was responsible for the detection of this plot, which saved the Soviet dictator from possible disaster.) Benes also believed that the Czech Communists—especially Gottwald—were democratically inclined, and would calm down as soon as the first wave of popular enthusiasm and radicalism had spent itself. He had faith in the good sense of the Czech people, and did not expect them thoroughly to endorse the Communists.[58] If, then, the Communists would abide by the people's expressed wishes, a more equitable division of forces would be restored.

While Benes was suffering one of his worst political defeats, the Communist Party, which before 1938 had been unable to assert itself effectively, scored the greatest victory in its history. It had set itself four objectives. It had insisted that a postwar government should be formed before Czechoslovakia's liberation, and that it should be formed in the East. It had claimed several key posts in the government. It had sought to stamp out right-wing political opposition before it had a chance to develop. It had urged the creation of a National Front. All these objectives were achieved. The Party emerged from the Moscow meetings as the strongest element in the government and as the author of its program. It had won commanding political heights at the green table rather than on the field of battle. Its ability to meet the challenge of a revolutionary situation remained untested. The problems confronting it consisted not in conquering power, but in utilizing its operational bases to expand the limits of the very considerable power it already held, and in fully exploiting the psychological advantages it enjoyed.

PART THREE

*The Technique of Power Seizure:
The National and Democratic
Revolution, 1945–48*

6. THE SETTING

THE GENERAL setting in which the reconstruction of Czechoslovakia got under way was one of change. Six years of occupation and war had effectively destroyed the country's institutional system. The international order also had been profoundly altered. A realignment in Czechoslovakia's foreign political orientation and a thorough revamping of its political, social, and economic structure were in order.

The specific features characterizing the liberation of Czechoslovakia were the presence of the Red Army as the agent of liberation—and thus, perforce, as the revolutionary agent—an upsurge of enthusiasm for the Soviet Union, and the intermingling of national and social strivings on the part of the people as the leading ideological motives of the "revolution." (The role of the American Army will have to be discounted, for United States troops occupied only a relatively small portion of Czechoslovakia, and the psychological climate around them was not comparable to that existing in Soviet-occupied territory.)

The Red Army

Although the influence of the Red Army on internal developments in Czechoslovakia was indirect and limited in time, it was of great benefit to the Communists.

The Red Army did not elicit a uniform response from the population. As a liberating force, it received a sincere and enthusiastic welcome. But enthusiasm soon gave way—at least in a significant portion of the population—to fear and hatred.[1] Both the enthusiasm and fear helped the Communists. A large number of people in their first rush of enthusiasm embraced the Communist Party, while fear prevented others from opposing it.

99

The presence of the Red Army had an incalculable effect on the mobility and daring of the Communists during the all-important initial phase of the "revolution," when the rate of change was greatest and the political and economic foundations of the new Republic were being laid. For example, teams of Communist organizers followed closely in the wake of the Red Army as it swept through Czechoslovakia from east to west, and helped everywhere to secure disproportionate influence for local Communists.[2] Measures taken at the instigation of these teams during the first few days after liberation were often irreversible.

Soviet troops remained in Czechoslovakia for six months. By the time they left, the Party was strongly entrenched in the administration, and major economic reforms, i.e., land reform and nationalization, had been enacted by law. This is not to suggest that the situation would have been significantly different had the Red Army withdrawn sooner. Its assistance to the Communists was most effective during the first few weeks of its stay. But the mere presence of Soviet troops probably retarded the crystallization of an opposition to the rapid expansion and consolidation of Communist control over the vital instruments of power, and inspired the Communists to act with greater boldness than they might have been inclined to show under different circumstances.

The Soviet Union

Although the Red Army's presence as an occupation force was not regarded as an unmixed blessing, the emergence of the Soviet Union as the strongest European power and the penetration of Russian armed forces deep into Central Europe were greeted with general approval. The German attack on the Soviet Union, and the "holy war" nature of the Nazi campaign in the East, rekindled a strong bond of friendship between Czechs and Slovaks on the one hand, and the Russians on the other. Pan-Slavism was restored to a high place in the sentiments and thinking of the Czechoslovak people, and Russia was now overwhelmingly regarded as a protective Slavic brother, rather than as the spawning ground of Soviet Communism.

The reorientation of Czechoslovakia's foreign policy toward the East needed no selling to the population. Czechoslovakia's ties with the West had received a severe jolt at Munich. The acquiescence of Great Britain and France in Hitler's plan to annex the so-called Sudetenland was regarded by the Czech nation as "treason." Despite the healing effect of time, of the Western war effort, and the hospitality extended by Great Britain to Benes' government in exile, the aftereffects of the traumatic experience suffered by the Czechs at Munich lingered on. Confidence in the integrity and reliability of the Western powers was badly shaken and could not be restored to its prewar level. So strong was the people's aversion toward the West that the results of the 1946 election in Czechoslovakia, which gave the Communists a strong plurality, were interpreted by many Czech political observers as a "vote against Munich."[3]

This was probably an exaggerated and inaccurate appraisal of the public mood. But a predisposition to cooperate very closely with the Soviet Union was strongly in evidence. The alliance with the Soviet Union, which Benes concluded in 1943, reflected a natural reaction to the disappointing experience with the West, and a realistic anticipation of a shift of the center of gravity of international politics to the East. The Soviet Union indeed emerged as the dominant power on the Continent, and the fate of Czechoslovakia was closely linked with its great Eastern neighbor. Benes' notion that the U.S.S.R. held the key to European stability was more valid than ever.[4]

All political parties accepted the alliance with the Soviet Union as a bona fide cornerstone of the country's new foreign policy. Although the non-Communist parties certainly hoped to maintain good relations with the West, they acquiesced in the limiting features of their relationship with the U.S.S.R. and were prepared to go far in trading independence in foreign affairs—with its largely illusory advantages—for security against German aggression, which the Soviet Union seemed quite able and willing to provide, and for national revenge on the Teutonic enemy, which the Russians also appeared to support.

Lingering misgivings about the threat of Soviet Communism to Czechoslovakia's internal stability and to the freedom of its institutions were almost completely dissipated. The groups that had most vigorously opposed Bolshevik practices, and had reason to fear them, were in disrepute. The majority of the people felt deeply committed to the implementation of extensive social and economic reforms, and they knew that Bolshevism menaced primarily reactionary nations, classes, and individuals. President Benes and his close associates maintained the view that the enormous suffering endured by the Soviet Union and the colossal triumph it scored in the war would have a purifying effect on the Communist regime, which would grow tamer, more liberal, and more tolerant—at least of democratic socialist practices. It would in no way endanger the humanist values cherished in Czechoslovakia.

Benes advocated friendship toward the U.S.S.R. not only for his people, but for all Central European nations, which would thus be assured of protection against external aggression and would be able to develop freely within their frontiers.[5] The prospect of coexistence with Russia along these lines was little short of idyllic. These optimistic appraisals were based mainly on a misjudgment of the evolutionary trend of the Soviet system and on a desire to get along with the Russians at all costs. Benes and his associates were convinced that their sincere friendship would be reciprocated, and that the Soviet Union would act in good faith toward Czechoslovakia. They looked for preferential treatment from Russia, and did not expect the application of inflexible standards that would lead to the transformation of Czechoslovakia into a mirror of the U.S.S.R. Despite accumulating contrary evidence, the Czechoslovak leaders clung to their mistaken notions, shaking off an occasional gnawing doubt, until the coup d'état, in February, 1948.

The nation readily accepted the views propounded by leaders whom it had learned to respect and to follow. The Czechoslovak Communists, of course, benefited from these attitudes. The great prestige in which the Soviet Union was held contributed to an uncritical acceptance of the Communist Party. If the motives of the U.S.S.R. were honorable, those of the Communist Party could not be less so, and if close cooperation with the Soviet Union was desirable, what party was better suited to lead the nation than the Communist?

Reassessment of Values

The Munich crisis and the German occupation of the Czech lands caused a resurgence of rabid nationalism and a radicalization of the political and social orientation of the population.

Munich represented an internal as well as an international crisis for Czechoslovakia. It marked the breakdown of Masaryk's democracy and accentuated awareness of the social, political, and national cleavages in the country. The shock of the collapse of the First Republic was magnified by the short-lived experience of the Czechs under the authoritarian government of the so-called Second Republic. During the long years of war, there was ample time to mull over the shortcomings of former Czechoslovak regimes and to plan for the future. Perhaps no other nation devoted as much attention to analyzing the failures, weaknesses, and imperfections of its political, social, and economic systems. The amount of self-criticism and mutual recrimination between political parties and individuals that came to light during the war was extraordinary, and from a diligent reassessment of the past was born a conscious determination to rectify mistakes and make a fresh start toward a better future.

Overhauling the Party System

The Czechoslovak party system was due for a thorough overhauling. The extreme atomization of parties, characteristic of the prewar era, and their self-centered, narrowly sectarian tendencies, as well as their propensity for avoiding responsibility, were severely criticized. In their hour of atonement, even politicians agreed that the country had been overpoliticalized and that irresponsible and extensive partisan agitation had been detrimental to the development of a constructive political life and to the best interests of Czechoslovakia.[6] Profuse self-criticism of the party system resulted in avowals to simplify it by decreasing the number of parties to three or four, to reduce the area of political strife, and to increase political responsibility and morality.

The revision of the party system was aided by spontaneous developments during the war. Immediately after the occupation of the Czech lands, the stock of the political parties whom the public held at least in part responsible for the catastrophe that had struck was very low.[7] During the occupation, party differences were secondary to the common struggle against the national enemy. This did not mean total obliteration of political rivalry, but it created an atmosphere in which appeals to national unity and solidarity far outweighed sectarian considerations.

In the course of time, as liberation drew nearer, several prewar parties, particularly those left of center, seemed to regain some of their lost prestige. The political orientation of the nation had unquestionably shifted toward the left, and dislike for the rightist parties—especially the Agrarian, because of their collaborationist tinge—remained strong. The decision, reached at Moscow, to outlaw the rightist parties gained much approval. The most conservative of the four parties permitted to operate in the Czech lands—the People's Party—had been popularly regarded as a slightly left-of-center party. Revaluation of the party system left the Communists in a favored position, for they, having borne no governmental responsibility before 1938, were not encumbered with the sins of the past. Moreover, the simplification of the party system caused a relative shift in the traditional positions of the moderate left-of-center parties, who were now by definition representatives of the right.

Social and Economic Reforms

In addition to the overhaul of the party system, articulate Czechoslovak spokesmen favored fundamental changes in the social and economic structure of the country. They felt that stunted progress along these lines had been the bane of the First Republic.

"Our house must be rebuilt both politically and socially, with a new content, new people, and often with new institutions," said President Benes, in February, 1945, and one of his close collaborators asserted that "the necessity of fundamental changes in our economic and social life . . . was understood by all of us."[8] As far as the Czechs were concerned, liberalism, with its economic laissez faire, was dead. The era of "socializing democracy" had dawned. The passing of liberal democratic capitalism and the advent of socializing democracy were eloquently and forcefully hailed by Benes, who said that liberalism had produced a "sick and uncertain society," characterized by political and cultural chaos and class war:

> Prewar democracy proved to have many deficiencies and in many countries it helped to a great extent to bring about the advent of totalitarian dictatorships. It will have to be reformed and fully regenerated. After [World War II] political

democracy will have to develop systematically and consistently into a so-called economic and social democracy.

According to Benes, the "new postwar democracy" would be the product of both a struggle against the aggressor (Nazism) and an "internal revolution."[9] In this context, he recalled that the aspirations of the Czech people tended to be "permeated with longing for social and economic justice" going straight to the conception of "the socialization of modern society."[10] He also reminded his listeners that "the national struggle [of the Czechs] . . . especially from the middle of the nineteenth century [had been] above all a social struggle."[11]

> We lost the aristocracy and our higher classes at the time of our political decline, and when we created our new bourgeoisie, we were already entering a period in which modern capitalism was doomed. Our economic and social emancipation coincided with our national emancipation, with the fight for our national freedom. Let us not forget that to a great extent it also made possible our present great revolution.

Benes himself declared that he rejected the "purely political conception of democracy in a liberalistic sense" and understood it "as a system in the economic and social sense also."[12]

Fundamentally similar views were expressed by the National Socialist Party in one of its more serious political statements, drafted in the fall of 1947, in which its conception of the philosophical underpinnings of the new constitution was outlined. It denounced both "natural law and liberalism," proclaiming liberalism to be "superannuated," and asserting that "between liberalism and democracy there is not only a quantitative difference, but a direct qualitative difference, which stems from the most consistent forms of both—anarchism, as the extreme form of liberalism, and socialism, as consistent democracy, that is, democracy spanning both the area of politics and economics."[13] The National Socialist Party spoke in this manner, notwithstanding its rejection of dialectical materialism and its claim of "unswerving faith in the dignity of the individual as an end in himself."

Nor was Benes' socializing concept predicated on Marxism. He did not feel that Marxian philosophy provided a valid, let alone the sole possible, basis for "socialization," and he most emphatically denied that the evolution of societies from a lower to a higher stage could take place only through class war, by abrupt jumps, as envisaged by the dialectical method, entailing not only violence but also the denial of all the values of the "lower" phase as soon as the "higher" is achieved. On the contrary, he asserted that in a mature state such as Czechoslovakia, the transition to socialism could be achieved gradually and peacefully by blending diverse views and approaches into a mold best suited to ensure "reasonable evolution in accordance with the natural economic, social, geographical, ethical, and juridical conditions of the national society concerned."[14] Although he expected developments in his country to be influenced by the example of the U.S.S.R., he maintained that "even the Soviet Union and Russian Communists acknowledge the possibility for gradually transforming a liberal democracy into its higher state—into a socializing democracy."[15]

Socialism was of overriding concern to the Czech people, so much so that any party seriously opposing it, or obstructing progress toward it, stood little chance of surviving. The Communists, advocates par excellence of radical social and economic changes, were now in the comfortable position of having nearly everybody agree with them. They could point to the prewar record of the other parties and, by innuendo or direct reference, cast doubt on the ability (or sincerity) of these groups to guide the nation. The serious substantive difference between Benes' and the Communist Party's concepts of socialization was not brought to light for some time. For tactical reasons, the Communists did not correct Benes' misinterpretation. Ultimately, of course, a parting of the ways was inevitable.

New Nationality Policy: Germans and Hungarians

Experience with the German and Hungarian minorities living in the Republic convinced the Czechs and Slovaks of the desirability of ridding themselves of the menace represented by them, and of reconstituting Czechoslovakia as a national state of Slavic peoples. As it turned out, the Czechs were able to expel almost all Germans from Bohemia and Moravia. The Slovaks had less luck with the Hungarians. But the crusade against the Germans was of greater significance—because of the large number of people involved, its emotional content, and its far-reaching social and economic consequences.

The expulsion of the Germans was accompanied by the confiscation of all their agricultural, commercial, industrial, and personal property. As a result of a vast increase, during the war, in German-owned and controlled property in Czechoslovakia, about 60 to 70 per cent of the country's economic wealth was involved.[16] Nationalization of German-owned industrial plants could not be opposed.[17]

As President Benes put it:

> German interference in Central Europe, and above all the establishment of the Protectorate of Bohemia and Moravia, assumed in a great measure the form of economic subjugation. The Germans expropriated and administered all key industries and banks, and in this way automatically prepared the nationalization of Czechoslovak industry from the economic point of view. The Czechoslovak state after its liberation could not satisfy numerous individuals by restoring to them the properties they formerly had owned; often they had sold them voluntarily to the Germans. There also were instances in which great properties had been stolen from Jews, who afterwards were killed or who perished without leaving heirs. And there were many other similar cases. It was impossible to return this sort of property or distribute it to individuals. It seemed more advantageous then to leave it in the ownership of the state, even though the decision was to administer it in accordance with the principles of private enterprise.[18]

The physical transfer of 2.1 million Germans—among whom were nearly 150,000 farmers, over 500,000 industrial workers and day laborers, 40,000 shopkeepers, and more than 100,000 clerical employees—caused a serious labor shortage and brought about a permanent dislocation in the economic structure.[19]

Hardest hit were the glass, paper, textile, and mining industries, in which the Germans had represented, respectively, 60, 58, 56, and 45 per cent of the total labor force. Before 1938, textiles and glass had been among the chief items of export. The atrophy of these industries tended to shift the country's industrial structure from predominantly consumer-goods to capital-goods production. The loss of the miners was irreparable. (Although after 1948 the number of miners in Czechoslovakia actually increased over the prewar total, due to the greater demands of the vast industrial expansion undertaken within the framework of the five-year plan, per capita output dropped, and the entire industry was in chronic crisis, because of the lack of enthusiasm and skill of the new miners, most of whom had been arbitrarily assigned to their jobs.)

The depletion of the border areas of their normal population induced considerable social mobility among the Czechs and Slovaks. Many administrative posts had to be filled, and thousands of confiscated plants, workshops, and stores required temporary "national managers," (narodni spravce) until a final disposition of these properties could be made. Over 100,000 farms lay fallow, and the demand for skilled labor was great. Good housing, the chance of acquiring household goods, real estate, and perhaps a small shop, spurred a mass migration to the areas abandoned by the Germans. Opportunities for enrichment were so great that, by the end of 1946, over 2 million Czechs and Slovaks had moved there from the interior of the country.[20]

The hatred vented on the Germans, the chaotic conditions in the border areas, and the tremendous amount of economic wealth suddenly available for distribution or for state retention exuded possibilities for political exploitation. Here, in one package, were the major ingredients required for a thorough uprooting of the old social order. The Communists did not fail to seize this opportunity.

New Nationality Policy: Czechs and Slovaks

Another major issue demanding urgent solution was the settlement of the relations—both constitutional and actual—between Czechs and Slovaks. In 1939, with Hitler's help, the Slovak "autonomists" attained their most exalted goal: secession from the Czechoslovak Republic. From March 14, 1939, until August, 1944, Slovakia enjoyed a sort of pseudo independence under German tutelage. The pinch of war and the heavy boot of German occupation were not felt until the fall of 1944, when the front drew near and a mass uprising against the puppet regime took place. Although their sovereignty was more apparent than real, the Slovaks valued it for two reasons. First, there were plenty of jobs, and within limits, Slovak officials had real responsibility for running their country. Second, Hitler's decision to turn Slovakia into a "model satellite," as well as special war circumstances, substantially increased the economic well-being of this province until the very end of hostilities. Before the war, only one-third of the electorate openly supported autonomist strivings; now such sentiment was universal, and it was bolstered by the existence of a Slovak legislature, the SNR, and an executive, the Board of Commissioners (Sbor Poverenikov—SP).

The principles of Slovakia's new status were enunciated by Klement Gottwald, on April 5, 1945. Speaking for the national government and the Communist Party, he pledged that the relations between Slovaks and Czechs would be based on full equality (*rovny s rovnym*), that the SNR would be acknowledged as the sole source of governmental power in Slovakia, that all common problems would be solved in closest cooperation between the government and the SNR, and that the interests of the Slovaks in the central administration (including the apparatus of foreign affairs) would be protected by proportionate representation in numbers as well as in the importance of the posts assigned to them. For the army, he promised the formation of separate Slovak units, headed by Slovak officers.

This proclamation, frequently referred to by the Communists as the "Magna Carta of Slovak rights," formed a part of the government's official program. The specific terms of agreement on the executive and legislative competence of the SNR and the SP, and their relation to the central authorities, were to be worked out within the framework of a new Constitution.

This departure in the settlement of the affairs of the two Slavic components of the Republic was as necessary as it was promising. In practice, the adjustment of relations between them left something to be desired. Many Czechs felt that the Slovaks possessed undeserved advantages. Consequently, efforts were made to curtail them. The Slovaks, in turn, resented any encroachment and sought to enlarge the area of their freedom, preferring to administer their province with as little reference to the Czech lands as possible.[21]

The Communists had excellent practical reasons for posing as champions of Slovak rights. Failure to do so would have been tan-tamount to political suicide in that province. By catering to pub-lic opinion, they hoped to capture the electorate. Perhaps they re-membered the upsurge of socialist sentiment after World War I and expected to win a majority of the votes, which would place them in a favorable position to exert pressure on the central gov-ernment. If this was their hope, they were disappointed, for they fared much worse in Slovakia than in Bohemia and Moravia. But the reversal did not cause them serious damage. The incapacity of Czech and Slovak democrats to unite in a common anti-Commu-nist front, and the unsettled conditions in Slovakia, gave the Communists an opportunity to intervene and to achieve by manipulation what they could not attain by open competition.

Deterioration of Moral Standards

Six years of foreign occupation had deleterious effects on both political and personal ethics. A quantitative measurement of mo-rality is difficult at any time and under any circumstances, as is a qualitative appraisal of the influence of a high or low degree of morality on the fortunes of competing political parties. Never-theless, it seems reasonably safe to assert that morality had de-clined and that the Communists were the primary beneficiaries.[22]

One astute observer summed up the case as follows:

The revulsion caused by the helpless loss of national integrity in October, 1938, and of independence in March, 1939, after only twenty years of restored independence, induced in the country a malaise that easily might become either cynical re-nunciation of national ideals that had been fostered for a hundred years, or else a readiness to seek salvation in a philosophy that offered light and salvation from the East. Six years of unwilling service to the triumphant invader also was in itself demoralizing. For six years, it had been a patriotic duty to go slow and to sabotage, to destroy and not to build; and six years of such habits, of subservience, humiliation, and starvation, both physical and intellectual, leave their mark on a people and leave them ready either to seek new reme-dies or to believe that there is no remedy at all.[23]

The circumstances under which the entire nation had lived, fighting for survival, and the conditions to which many people had been exposed because of their religious or political beliefs and their national origin, were not conducive to the advancement of morality. The difference between life or death, freedom or imprisonment, well-being or suffering, often hinged on the degree of resourcefulness or ruthlessness with which individuals were able to take care of their own interests. Material interests took precedence over ethical considerations, and the predatory nature of man was perhaps nowhere as apparent as in prisons and concentration camps. In terms of postwar development, this meant a generally hardened attitude toward life, marked by an interest in material rewards or power, or both, as compensation for the years of suffering. The Communist Party offered the greatest promise of fulfilling such desires.

Positional Advantage of the Communists

The Communist Party, in addition to its tactical advantage, enjoyed a positional one.

Among the political parties charged with the reconstruction of Czechoslovakia, the Communist Party stood out as the best organized and most ably led. Its superiority was largely the result of training and foresighted preparation, which enabled it to maintain some sort of organization under the most adverse political conditions, and caused it to save as many of its leaders as possible while grooming new ones, even as part of the old leadership was being liquidated by the Nazis. At the end of the war, it had a well-trained, young, capable, determined, and disciplined elite. No other party possessed an equal "capital." All of them had been crippled organizationally, and their losses during the war had almost wiped out their traditional leadership, for which there was no systematic replacement. Only the Communist Party had anything approximating a well-defined program or platform.

The partners—or opponents, as the case might be—of the Communist Party were the National Socialist, Social Democratic, and Catholic People's parties, in the Czech lands and the Democratic Party in Slovakia. (In 1946, the number of parties in Slovakia was raised to four by the addition of the liberal, predominantly Catholic, Freedom Party, and the Labor Party, an ill-disguised refuge of the right-wing Social Democrats, who had been left homeless by the merger of their party with the Communists.)

THE NATIONAL SOCIALIST PARTY. The National Socialist Party was the Communists' most formidable opponent. An old party, dating back to 1897, it attempted to combine moderate socialist aims with nationalism in a home-grown political philosophy greatly favored by the Czech people. It claimed to be the spiritual trustee of the Masaryk-Benes tradition and appealed to the electorate as the standard-bearer of national heritage. Nationalism was the strong element of its ideology. The National Socialists were ardent exponents of a policy best identified as "Czechoslovakism." They favored centralization of power in Prague, opposed Slovak autonomist efforts, and sought to develop a distinct national individuality by welding the Czech and Slovak peoples together in an indivisible national and political unit. The socialist tenets of the party's repertoire were mild. It had rejected both the Second and Third Internationals and opposed state socialism. After World War II, it supported a program of nationalization limited to a few key industries, but wanted nationalized enterprises set up as corporations administered on the principles of private enterprise.

Before the war, the National Socialists' popularity had been greatest in Bohemia, among the middle- and lower-middle-class elements (civil servants and skilled workers). It had had a strong following among the legionnaires (veterans of the Siberian campaign of World War I), and had controlled a powerful mass (gymnastic) organization, the Sokol.

The leadership was decimated during the war. Only one member of the prewar executive committee, Jaroslav Stransky, escaped abroad. The new executive included a large number of persons who had made good in London (e.g., Hubert Ripka, Prokop Drtina, Frantisek Uhlir, and Julius Firth). The new party Chairman was Petr Zenkl, former Lord Mayor of Prague, who had spent six years in German concentration camps. The Secretary-General was Vladimir Krajina, a professor of botany. He had distinguished himself by his underground activities, primarily as President Benes' most reliable source of information. But he was new at the game of politics.

Although Zenkl was a popular choice, he could not easily command full allegiance. He did not have the prestige needed to control various prima donnas who thought themselves equally well suited to lead the party. Zenkl had not attained political heights before the war. Neither was he a politician in the true sense of the word, and he was so stubborn and forthright in his dislike of the Communists, that he embarrassed many colleagues who inclined toward a more appeasing attitude.

THE PEOPLE'S PARTY. The People's Party—the only nonsocialist party in the Czech lands—had been a minor political force before the war. Its appeal was limited by its Catholicism, which, in a country officially nonsectarian but actually anticlerical, was not a recommendation for great popularity. This party originated after World War I, as a result of the merger of two Christian Social factions previously operating in Bohemia and Moravia. Despite the merger, the Bohemian and Moravian wings were never close to one another. The Moravian wing held the upper hand, since the party achieved its greatest success in that province, drawing heavily on the support of well-to-do farmers. Fundamentally, the political ideology was based on the papal encyclical, *Rerum Novarum*, but the clerical element in it was always weak.

Except for the Communists, the People's Party was the only one that did not lose its leader during the war. Monsignor Jan Sramek, who had been at the helm for many years, escaped to London in 1939, and returned to Prague in 1945, to continue as chairman. His advanced age (he was in his seventies), however, did not promise vigorous leadership. For example, a long illness prevented him from attending cabinet meetings throughout 1947. But this was not the only source of the party's weakness. In the postwar period, its status as the only nonsocialist group in Czechoslovakia automatically made it a refuge for some of the more conservative elements, who tried, albeit unsuccessfully, to wrest the power from Sramek. The existence of widely divergent factions within it reduced its operating efficiency. The factions ranged, left to right, from the orientation of Alois Petr (who later worked with the Communists), to the liberal Father Frantisek Hala, to Sramek, who stood at center, to Adolf Prochazka on the right, and to Mrs. Helena Kozeluhova, Pavel Tigrid, and Bohdan Chudoba on the far right of the party.

THE SOCIAL DEMOCRATIC PARTY. Of all the political parties, the Social Democrats were in the worst shape in the immediate postwar period. Their wartime losses seemed heaviest, and the surviving members of the executive committee were either too old and tired to assume responsibility, or they suffered from acute moral remorse about the mistakes of the past—a disease afflicting Social Democrats more frequently than adherents of other political faiths. The leadership thus fell into the hands of Zdenek Fierlinger and a group of younger, left-wing socialists, returning from exile, whose views were akin to the Communists', and who had committed themselves to close collaboration with the Communist Party.

The economic radicalism of the Social Democrats was both inevitable and necessary under the prevailing circumstances. But it did not enhance their popularity with the workers. The Social Democrats were unable to challenge the Communist Party's hegemony in the Marxist left; nor was their radical leadership inclined to do so. Maintaining a separate Social Democratic Party was chiefly a device to increase the power and influence of the Communists. In the initial stages of reconstruction, when party representation in various government and professional organizations was determined on the basis of a parity formula alloting each Czech party 25 per cent of the seats, the Communists and Social Democrats together could never be outvoted. Had there been only three instead of four parties in the Czech lands (as a result of a Communist–Social Democratic merger), the Communists would have found it difficult to claim more than one-third representation. In Slovakia the situation was different, because the Social Democrats did merge with the Communists, temporarily leaving only two parties to share power.

Retaining the identity of the Social Democratic Party was also useful, since it helped to harness to the combined Communist–Social Democratic engine the support of moderate socialists, who continued to vote for the party label, although the policies of the leadership did not reflect their views. This support might have been lost to the National Socialists, had a merger been effected. Of course, as long as the energies of moderate Social Democrats were misused by the leadership to aggrandize Communist power, there was always a latent danger of a revolt within the party. This did happen, in the fall of 1947, when the moderates, in a last display of courage, threw off the shackles of their leftist, pro-Communist leadership. But the damage had been done. By 1947, the trend toward totalitarianism was too strong to be stopped or delayed by the resurgence of a moderate Marxist party.

THE SLOVAK DEMOCRATIC PARTY. The Slovak Democratic Party
was a newcomer, a synthetic product of the war years. Originally,
it embodied former center and rightist groups that had opposed
the Tiso regime. Its leadership consisted exclusively of former
Agrarians. Soon—in the spring of 1946—the Democrats concluded a
formal agreement with exponents of Catholic interests, who until
then had been *de facto* deprived of political representation, because their party, the Slovak People's Party, had been banned for
its fascist record.[24] By virtue of this agreement, Catholics were
assured of two-thirds of the seats in the party's governing body,
and of the same ratio of the positions the Democrats would secure
in the cabinet, the National Assembly, and the local administration.[25] This agreement left the Democrats open to attack for permitting the re-entry into politics of morally reprehensible elements. At the same time, they definitely stole the march on the
Communists, who also sought to cater to the vast mass of politically homeless adherents of Slovak conservative separatism, but
who could not actually enter into open agreement with clerical
representatives. Catholic support assured the Democratic Party
of an overwhelming victory in the 1946 elections.

The victory was significant, for if nothing else, it forced a
revision of Communist policies regarding Slovakia. But the contribution of the Democrats to the over-all strength of the anti-
Communist forces was of dubious value. Their outspoken conservatism, the obvious influence in the party of reactionary
elements, the self-centered and often irresponsible policies that
placed a higher value on privileges obtainable locally than on
contributions to the general welfare of the Republic, and the repeated—albeit weak—attempts to revive the Agrarian organization
in the Czech lands, were not endearing to Czechs of any political
orientation. Many Czechs intensely disliked the Democratic Party,
which they regarded as a metamorphosed version of the Hlinka
Party.[26] Finally, its equilibrium was never stable, for the Catholic
and Protestant components (almost all former Agrarians were
Protestants) had a long tradition of hostility to each other. The
Democratic Party was a maverick political force, tending to create
a larger number of problems than it could solve.

The positional advantage of the Communists was enhanced by
two more factors, national representation and the inability of

their opponents to join forces. The other parties were confined either to the Czech lands or to Slovakia, and they quarreled among themselves. The National Socialists were antagonistic toward the Slovak Democrats, because of their separatist tendencies. Obversely, the Slovak Democrats considered the National Socialists the foremost exponents of the hated policy of "Czechization." There was friction between the National Socialists and the People's Party, because of the former's outspoken anticlerical attitude, and because these parties vied for the favors of the same constituency. The National Socialists and Social Democrats were continually at loggerheads. Their traditional rivalry was exacerbated by postwar conditions. To some extent, they too were contending for the favors of the same constituency, and the National Socialists exerted great pressure to wean away the moderate wing of the Social Democratic Party. Nationwide representation gave the Communist Party greater maneuverability. The conflicts between its opponents, which for a long time prevented the formation of anything approaching a coherent anti-Communist front, gave the Communists an opportunity to exploit these "indirect reserves of the revolution."

7. THE COMMUNIST PARTY: POLICY, COMPOSITION, AND LEADERSHIP

THE SETTING in which the reconstruction of Czechoslovakia began was unquestionably favorable to the Communist Party. But environmental factors—the Communists might call them objective conditions—could not by themselves automatically assure the Party of success in its quest for power. Of decisive importance was the Communists' recognition and astute appraisal of the intrinsic potential of these factors and situations, and the skill with which they turned them to good advantage.

The question is frequently asked whether the Communists in Czechoslovakia and elsewhere in Eastern Europe proceeded according to a plan conceived and elaborated in advance. The answer in the Czech case is certainly affirmative. But the nature and scope of advance planning must be defined. In a sense, the entire training of the Communist parties focused on the techniques of seizing power. Concretely, advance planning was limited to identifying major institutional targets and devising an over-all strategy that took into account the salient features of the domestic and international scene. It did not concern itself with tactical details —although it is safe to assume that the Communists had a fair idea of just how they would try to execute certain maneuvers—nor did it set a rigid timetable for the accomplishment of the terminal goal, complete seizure of power, or, for that matter, of any specific intermediary goal.

The extent of planning done before Czechoslovakia's liberation has already been indicated in the discussion of Communist policies and activities during the closing stages of the war. On the country's liberation, an assessment of the situation, in terms of the actual conditions was necessary. An authoritative analysis of the internal situation and a blueprint for action were provided by Klement Gottwald in a policy speech of major significance, on July 9, 1945. The speech was meant for the assembled Communist functionaries only, for it was one of the few political addresses delivered by Gottwald not to be published immediately in the press, or in the form of a pamphlet. It was brought to light for the first time in 1947, in a volume of Gottwald's selected writings.[1] It was then too late to serve as a warning to the democratic opponents of the Communist Party, but early enough—the coup had not yet taken place—to qualify as authentic evidence of a priori planning which was unlike the famous "salami" speech given by the Hungarian Communist leader, Matyas Rakosi, in 1952, and was therefore suspect as a retrospective systematization of strategy and tactics.[2]

The Grand Design Unfolds

As Gottwald saw it, Czechoslovakia was passing through a truly "revolutionary period," and the main problem in every revolution, as Lenin had said, is "the question of power; which class or nation has power, or rather into the hands of which nation or class power is passing."[3]

What was the situation in Czechoslovakia in this regard? "Power is passing from the German occupation authorities . . . into the hands of the Czech and Slovak nation," said Gottwald.[4] At the same time, the "struggle is aimed against the Czech and Slovak reaction" as well.[5] In this manner, the "revolution" had both a "national . . . and democratic" character.[6] Defining the revolution in these terms carried with it the connotation of a broad coalition of "the working class, united and led by the Communist Party," with "the masses of the peasantry, the middle strata of the urban population, the working intelligentsia, and a portion of the Czech and Slovak bourgeoisie."[7] It also implied a gradual rather than abrupt seizure of power. Gottwald cautioned against rushing headlong into socialism, because the possibilities for exploitation offered by "the national and democratic revolution" had by no means been exhausted.[8] "We must continually remind ourselves," he said, "that in the present phase we are following the line of the national and democratic . . . and not the line of the socialist revolution."[9] He held that, with the proper skill, the Communists could "gain the majority of the nation, the majority of the people," which is the "most important thing for all revolutions and all progress."[10]

To be sure, the road to victory would not be easy. Although the "bourgeoisie as the leading class, especially the 'haute bourgeoisie,' has discredited itself in the eyes of the nation," the struggle for "the soul of the nation" was only beginning. It would be an "ideological, political, administrative, economic, and power struggle, briefly, a struggle on all fronts."[11] However, in their struggle, the working class and the Communist Party possessed great advantages. For "as everyone could see, this was not the pre-Munich regime," it was not a formal parliamentary democracy, but a "people's democratic regime, which is characterized by the fact that the people's elected deputies not only vote for laws but . . . the execution of laws is also in [their] hands. The political line of the government is determined . . . by the workers, and the working people, with the Communist Party at their head."[12] In addition, the working class and the Communist Party had the backing of the "powerful Soviet Union" and "were confronted with a favorable situation, seldom likely to be repeated in history," in that they were "carrying out the revolution from above and below simultaneously."[13]

Finally, Gottwald pinpointed the institutional targets whose conquest and utilization would be most instrumental in securing a dominant position for the Communist Party:

Our first task is to secure and anchor the system of national committees . . . Our Party and all its organizations must realize that precisely the national committees are the tools with which it is possible to change the entire state structure from top to bottom.

[Second] . . . the Party must pay particular attention to the building of a really popular national security apparatus that could never be used against the working class, against the people. The third important task is to create a really popular democratic army that is united with the people. *You know that next to the civilian security apparatus, the army is the instrument of political power.* [Our italics.]

The fourth task is . . . to occupy the salient positions in the national economy, by confiscating German and Hungarian property, and by introducing a system of national administrations in positions formerly occupied by traitors and collaborators. . . .

Further, comrades, we must build and consolidate the united organizations of the working people of town and country, primarily the trade unions, cooperatives, youth organizations, and the United Farmers' Association. . . .

The decisive role played by the working class . . . is due largely to the unity of these organizations. But for their unity, the reaction would have already raised its head. Therefore we must realize that the reaction will aim its attacks . . . on these organizations.[14]

The program outlined by Gottwald was a warning to the democratic parties that the Communists regarded the coalition in which they participated as a temporary expedient.* At the same time, it served to caution overzealous and anxious Communists to make haste slowly.

Fundamentally, the policies of the Czechoslovak Communist Party in the immediate postwar period were predicated on two major assumptions: the possibility of winning a majority of the population—thus coming to power by democratic means—and the necessity of controlling, under any circumstances, the decisive instruments of power.

In its essentials, Gottwald's analysis followed Lenin's appraisal of the alignment of class forces in the "democratic revolution" and suggested an attempt to maintain the "revolution in permanence"—that is, to proceed by stages, from a broad class alliance

---

*The Communist concept of the coalition was much more explicitly stated by Antonin Zapotocky, in December, 1947: "In order that we be understood, we emphasize clearly that the significance of the agreement [for cooperation between Communist and non-Communist parties] rested in its aim to avoid further struggles, not in avoiding socialism. Today we do not yet have a Socialist republic. We want to [have it], however, and all of us have promised to work toward this goal." (L. Frejka, *26 Unor v Ceskoslovenskem Hospodarstvi* [*The Meaning of February 26 for the Czechoslovak Economy*] [Prague: Orbis, 1948], p. 12.)

A full text of the parliamentary speech from which this quotation is taken, is printed in Antonin Zapotocky, *Jednota Odboru Oporou Boju za Socialisaci* (*The Unity of the Trade Unions Supports the Struggle for Socialization*) (Prague: Prace, 1951), pp. 111–37. The quoted passage is on p. 135.

directed against the national enemy and a numerically limited stratum of the population identified as "the reaction" or the "haute bourgeoisie," to successively narrower class alliances aimed against ever more inclusive strata of the bourgeoisie.

The over-all strategy indicated by Gottwald was not peculiar to the Czechoslovak Communist Party. Caution and moderation in varying degrees characterized the actions of all East European Communist parties in this period.[15] Certainly the common ideological heritage of these parties and the practical preparation of their leaders in Moscow had something to do with the broadly uniform design of their policies. However, in no other East European country was the gradualist approach adhered to so consistently, extensively, thoroughly, and for such a long time as in Czechoslovakia. Ultimately, force had to be used to effect the transition from a formal parliamentary system of government to a Communist dictatorship. But so thoroughly had the Communists softened up Czechoslovakia, that violence could be kept at a minimum, and Soviet interference could be limited to psychological pressure instead of active intervention, if by no other means than the presence of troops.

The causes of this difference must be sought in the strength of the Czechoslovak Communist Party as well as in other favorable conditions in Czechoslovakia. By strength, the availability of a relatively large trained elite, a sizable number of members of long standing, and a reserve army of sympathizers running into the hundreds of thousands, should be understood. None of the other Communist parties in Eastern Europe—Yugoslavia excepted—had similar capital to work with.* But what were the other conditions? They transcended the bounds of objective con-

---

*The leadership of the Czechoslovak Communist Party was more numerous and more homogenous than were the other East European Communist elites. Its members had worked together for many years, and they knew each other well. The other parties were beset with ideological, personal, and generational conflicts that derived primarily from the long period of illegality in which they had existed, and from the enforced separation of members at home from leaders abroad. Although these conflicts were held in abeyance in all parties during the period of power seizure, they constituted a potential source of dissension and only thinly veiled incipient personal rivalries. The Czechoslovak Communists enjoyed a greater degree of spontaneous harmony in their midst, and this undoubtedly aided them in the smooth application of their strategic designs.

ditions listed in the preceding chapter, and engendered other less tangible factors.

Successful planning requires a high degree of predictability of future conditions or, what amounts to the same thing, control of as many of the variable factors that are likely to arise as possible. The Czechoslovak Communists did well in this regard. They managed to control, in advance, some of the crucial potential variables (e.g., the elimination of rightist opposition) and made an accurate estimate of future conditions. In this respect, too, they seemed to have an advantage over their East European comrades, who had been away from their homelands for a considerably longer time, and were therefore out of touch with the people and unfamiliar with the institutions of their country and their political opponents. The Czechs knew their country and, most important of all, they had an excellent line on their opponents. The manner in which they handled Benes, in particular, indicated beyond doubt that they knew their man. All this reduced the hazards of advance planning and facilitated the implementation of a comprehensive strategic plan. At no time were the Czechoslovak Communists confronted with a serious challenge. The behavior of their opponents seldom departed from the expected pattern. This is not meant to imply that everything went like clockwork for them. They suffered minor setbacks, fumbled on occasion, and had their anxious moments. By and large, however, they won their goals without ever having their political acumen severely tested.

Chronologically, the national and democratic revolution can be conveniently divided into four distinct phases. Such a breakdown does not imply a detailed timetable, nor is it meant to endow the Communist leaders with infallible foresight. But the terminal dates of several of the phases are so well defined as to give a clear perspective of the flow and ebb of the revolution.

May–October, 1945. This was a period of intense revolutionary excitement, during which the Communists made rapid strides toward conquering the political and economic heights of power. The outstanding features of this phase were: utilization of the key posts in the government as operational bases to expand the area of their influence; creation of a network of National Committees as organs of state power on the local, district, and land (province) level; absence of a duly elected legislature; enactment of fundamental legislation by simple presidential decree.

October, 1945–May, 1946. This was a period of decreasing revolutionary excitement. Its distinguishing feature was the re-establishment of a semblance of parliamentary government, in the form of a Provisional National Assembly indirectly elected by the political parties. This phase culminated in a general election, from which the Communists emerged with a large plurality.

May, 1946–July, 1947. This phase was marked by a relative lull in political activity, though it was not devoid of skirmishes. No significant changes in the internal power balance took place, though the duly elected National Assembly gradually gained in prestige and served as a stabilizing factor in internal politics. The terminal date of this period coincides with the Czechoslovak Government's decision to attend the Marshall Plan Conference, and with the stern rebuke it received from Moscow, causing it to reverse its decision.

July, 1947–February, 1948. This was a period of increasing political agitation, terminating in a coup d'état. It was characterized by intense Communist efforts to atomize the political opposition, to infiltrate and compromise opposition parties—especially through the use of *agents provocateurs*—and to introduce new social and economic demands designed to put the opposition parties on the defensive. It culminated in a coup d'état, which marked the abrupt termination of the national and democratic revolution and the onset of the dictatorship of the proletariat.

Membership and Organization

In keeping with the gradualist strategy of the Party, which entailed open competition for public support, Communist recruitment strove for mass enlistment, opening the ranks to all comers, and offering many inducements to join. New members did not have to pass strict ideological tests, and their privileges far outweighed their duties.

The membership body was not encumbered by a multitude of functions on behalf of the Party; it was not asked to attend innumerable meetings, to study the philosophical tenets of Marxism-

Leninism, or even to acquaint itself with the more practical aspects of Communist history. There was little encroachment on private lives.

The benefits were many. Gratification could be attained in a variety of ways, material and spiritual, tangible and intangible, in the form of authority and power, greater access to material goods, preferential treatment, rapid upward mobility in the social scale, or a feeling of riding the wave of the future and participating in the creation of a better world, a world which every Communist was free to picture for himself in the image of his own desires. There was nothing rigid or narrowly circumscribed about the Communist program. It was so broad, its platform so inclusive, and the practical goals so pleasing, that identification with one or another facet of the program was greatly facilitated.

The results of the Communist membership policy were spectacular. In May, 1945, the Party had 27,000 members. A year later, just before the general election, there were 1,159,164 registered Communists; of these, 1,007,834 were in the Czech lands, and 151,330 in Slovakia.[16] This was more than twice the number of Communists in Russia four years after the Party's seizure of power. Recruiting tapered off after the election, and a check of Party cards carried out under the guise of "re-registration," in the fall of 1946, showed a membership of 1,043,754 in the Czech lands, and 191,882 in Slovakia.[17] A new drive began in January, 1947. It moved slowly until the fall, when Gottwald set a goal of 1.5 million members by the time of the next scheduled general election in May, 1948.[18] The response in the Czech lands surpassed expectations. The Party reported an average of 40,000 to 50,000 new applications per month from November, 1947, to February, 1948. In Slovakia, meanwhile, only 18,340 new members were enrolled during the entire year of 1947. At last count before the coup, on January 15, 1948, membership in the Czech lands stood at 1,329,450, and at 210,222 in Slovakia.[19]

The Communists claimed—probably correctly—that their membership exceeded the combined total of the other three parties in the Czech lands, and asserted that while the other parties were organized in 60 to 70 per cent of the communities, Communist cells blanketed 96 per cent of all localities. Only in hamlets with but a few dozen families was there no Party organization.[20]

Regional distribution of membership was uneven. The disparity between the Czech lands and Slovakia was striking in absolute figures as well as in proportion to total population: approximately 14 per cent in the Czech lands, and less than 7 per cent in Slovakia. This was due to a lower degree of political awareness and interest in Slovakia, and a measurable lag in the subjective skills of the Slovak Communist Party in recruiting and organizing members. It was in part a reflection of the dissimilar wartime experiences of the Czechs and Slovaks that gave rise to a strong orientation to the left among the former, while in Slovakia, conservative, proclerical tendencies became more strongly entrenched than ever. Finally, barring Hungarians from active participation in politics had more far-reaching consequences for the Communists in Slovakia than a similar move against the Germans had in the Czech lands, since the proportion of Hungarians in the Communist Party in Slovakia had been very high.

The concentration of members was not uniform throughout the Czech lands. It was greater in Bohemia than in Moravia, and was pronounced in large urban-industrial centers such as Prague, where there were 190,000 Communists (as compared with 6,000 before the war),[21] and Brno, where there were 122,000.[22]

The social composition of the Party reflected a departure from tradition. At the Eighth Congress, in March, 1946, 57 per cent were industrial workers; 8 per cent were white-collar employees. Artisans accounted for an additional 5 per cent, and the remaining 30 per cent, for which no breakdown was given, were composed of peasants, representatives of the free professions, and other bourgeois elements.[23] One-third of the members were women, and a bare majority—51 per cent—were under forty-five years of age. Only 18 per cent were less than twenty-five years old.

Under circumstances and conditions in which the standards of competition were still operative, the presence of more Communists in more places than members of other parties was of inestimable value to the Party. Yet, rapid growth and large membership held obvious disadvantages too. Quality was sacrificed for quantity. Instead of being a fighting vanguard of the proletariat, composed of disciplined and devoted professional revolutionaries, the Party was, more or less, an aggregate of card-carrying individuals, with all the weaknesses that that entailed. The problems of organization and control were considerable. Moreover, at any given time, the loyalty and reliability of the rank and file, who had to offer little, if any, proof of their motives for joining, were questionable.

The Communist organizational network, as it existed at the end of the war, was not geared to a smooth absorption of the avalanche of new members. This problem was solved, however, by subdividing the basic units of the Party into groups of eight to twelve members, each under the leadership of a trustee (desitkar), who, in fact, became the most important connecting link in the hierarchy.[24] Aside from this innovation, the Party structure conformed to the customary geographic pyramid. Its basic units were of either the local or factory variety, with the former predominating in a ratio of three to one. In ascending order from the basic unit there were district and regional organizations and, finally, the central organs of the Party.

The geographic pyramid was complemented by strongly centralized functional channels of command, especially in the economic field. Officials entrusted with work in the economic field were organized in sections, commissions, and subcommissions—each covering a well-defined area of the country's economic institutions.[25] In this manner the Party could watch developments "in every sphere of activity."[26] Functional centralization led to the concentration of authority and responsibility for Party policy in the hands of a small number of reliable cadres with considerable training, experience, and devotion to the Communist cause.

Leadership

The central leadership was composed of old wheel horses who had risen to prominence with Gottwald in 1929, and who had formed the hard core of the Party since then. Although the losses sustained by the Communists were heavy—they claimed that sixteen of the fifty members of the last elected Central Committee had perished during the war[27]—a surprising number of leaders survived and returned to Czechoslovakia to play significant roles in the postwar period.

Within the leadership, a certain amount of stratification appeared to take place, based primarily on considerations of the residence of any given Communist during the war. In this respect, there were roughly four distinct groups: the Muscovites, the London contingent, leaders of the domestic resistance, and those who spent several years in prison or in concentration camps. Some overlapping occurred, but with a few insignificant exceptions, identification with one or another group was possible.

In the Communist Party, as in the government and in other political parties, the *émigrés* dominated the scene. Among them, in turn, the supremacy of the Muscovites was incontestable. They occupied the policy-making positions: the chairmanship and secretary-generalship, posts that were held by Klement Gottwald and Rudolf Slansky, respectively. Gottwald was also the Party's chief representative in the government, first as Deputy Premier, and later as Premier. Slansky did not hold office in the government. In addition to these two men, Marie Svermova (the widow of Jan Sverma) held a key position in the administrative apparatus of the Party, as head of its organization department. All three had been in the Soviet Union from 1938 until 1945. Gottwald's leading position could be taken for granted. He had been top man since 1929, and had given no cause for demotion. The emergence of Slansky as second in command—some believed that his position was stronger than Gottwald's (a belief not founded in fact)—and Svermova's elevation to a high post were not equally foreseeable.

Slansky had been a member of the Communist inner circle before the war, but did not seem to be in the immediate line of succession. There were a number of other leaders with prior claim to such honors, by virtue of seniority or status. Slansky's star, however, rose in Moscow, although until the end of 1944 he was still outranked by Jan Sverma—if the roles played by the two men in laying the foundation of the Party's postwar policy and their relative positions in the Slovak uprising are taken as criteria of measurement. The coincidence of Sverma's death with Slansky's advancement suggests the possibility of rivalry between them. Even Sverma's death did not sufficiently explain the choice of Slansky over Vaclav Kopecky, an old Comintern hand, or over Antonin Zapotocky, one of the founding members and one-time Secretary-General of the Party. Slansky's youth—he was born in 1901, and was one of the younger members of the Gottwald leadership—and his intellectual qualities might have tipped the balance in his favor.

The selection of Marie Svermova for a position of such responsibility, while not necessarily surprising, nevertheless deserves comment. If rivalry had indeed existed between her husband and Slansky, she would have been a logical choice to counteract Slansky's great influence in the Party—a task which, in view of the prestige of her own position, was well within her means. Before her husband's death, she had been overshadowed by him, but she was a ranking Communist in her own right. She joined the Party in 1921 at the age of nineteen, soon became Secretary of the Komsomol in Prague, and then regional Party Secretary in Prerov. In 1926, she went to Moscow for two years. She was elected to the Central Committee of the Party at its Fifth Congress, in 1929, and edited the Communist theoretical journal *Bolshevik*. In 1931, she returned to the Soviet Union for another two years.[28] Her fortunes seemed to be declining in the middle and late 1930's, when she represented the Party at a number of international conferences, but did not figure prominently in a policy-making position in Prague. On December 31, 1938, she escaped to the Soviet Union, where she lived in relative seclusion until her husband died.

Other prominent Muscovites were: Gustav Bares, chief of the culture and propaganda department and first postwar editor of *Rude Pravo,* the Communist daily; Vaclav Kopecky, Minister of Information; Jaroslav Prochazka, head of the education and enlightenment department of the armed forces; Bedrich Reicin, chief of intelligence and counterintelligence in the army; Josef Kolsky, head of the organization department of the trade unions; Jiri Kotatko, in charge of the land reform section of the Ministry of Agriculture. Arnost Kolman, the Party's leading theoretician, was the most "Sovietized" of the Czechoslovak Communists, having resided in Russia since 1915. He was a renowned mathematician and philosopher who at one time headed the section on dialectical materialism of the Soviet Academy of Sciences.[29] His return to Czechoslovakia after 1945 was probably prompted by the scarcity of outstanding Czech theorists on Marxism-Leninism.

Still other Muscovites held more innocuous, but only slightly less significant, posts: Josef Krosnar was chairman of the regional National Committee in Prague; Josef Juran held the same post in Brno; Jan Harus (who had emigrated to the Soviet Union in the early 1930's and spoke Czech with a Russian accent) shared control of the Liberec region with Rudolf Vetiska; Vlastimil Borek was an influential official of the Ministry of Foreign Affairs; Bozena Machacova-Dostalova was in charge of the women's section of the Party's secretariat.

The prominence of the Moscow group was not surprising. An attempt had been made at the outbreak of the war to concentrate in Moscow as many members of the leadership as was possible. Moreover, those who had been under the close scrutiny of Soviet Communists and were up-to-date on the Party's strategic and tactical plans had an obvious advantage. The reliability of Communists who had not been in the Soviet Union was not necessarily in doubt, but it was only proper to test them at first, and even if they were above reproach, they were handicapped—especially those who had spent a long period behind bars—by having been out of touch. The number of responsible positions to be filled was so great, however, that the services of no Communist of some standing were spurned. Even those who had been expelled from the Party before the war were reinstated. For example, a group of alleged Trotskyites, including Milan Reiman, Dufek, and Kalandra, who had been ousted in the late 1930's, and during the war formed the Great Council (Velka Rada), had no difficulty in reentering and securing important positions.

The Western contingent, larger than the Moscow group, also fared well. In the economic sphere in particular, top posts were occupied by individuals with considerable Western exposure, and little or no Moscow training or experience. Ludvik Frejka, who became Gottwald's economic advisor and headed the Party's economic commission, had been in London during the war, as had Josef Goldmann, an outstanding economic theorist, as well as Eugene Lobl, Edward Outrata (a postwar convert to Communism), and many others. Western representation was not confined to the economic sphere. Vaclav Nosek was Minister of the Interior, Anezka Hodinova was prominent in the National Assembly, and Vladimir Clementis was Under-Secretary of Foreign Affairs. Finally, a special contingent of Westerners—veterans of the Spanish Civil War, who had been interned in France, were subsequently freed, and spent the war years in England—became strongly ensconced in the police apparatus.

The "graduates" of concentration camps and prisons did well, though, with some exceptions, their rise was less spectacular. Four leading Communists—Antonin Zapotocky, Gustav Kliment, Jaromir Dolansky, and Ladislav Kopriva—who had made an unsuccessful attempt to escape together to the Soviet Union and instead had spent six years in German concentration camps, found their way back to high positions quite easily, although some took longer than others. Zapotocky was immediately entrusted with one of the crucial jobs, as the head of the trade unions. Kliment became prominent in the presidium of the unions. Kopriva became chairman of the National Committee for Bohemia, not a post of first-rate significance, and Dolansky had to wait until 1946 before he was advanced to cabinet rank. Other concentration camp "graduates," such as Jindrich Vesely and Emil Hrsel, were placed in the security apparatus, and still others of lesser stature were given assignments in the central secretariat (e.g., Jiri Hendrych) or in the regional committees of the Party (e.g., Antonin Novotny, Kvetoslav Inneman). The weakest representation was accorded to the leaders of the domestic resistance movement. Only Josef Smrkovsky attained national stature soon after the liberation. Others, such as Lumir Civrny, Viktor Knapp, Vaclav David, and Vladimir Koucky—all members of the last illegal Central Committee in the Czech lands—had to spend some years in apprenticeship before they were promoted to high rank.

There were several reasons for their poor showing. Those who had been left in charge of the Party were killed by the Germans. The last illegal Central Committee consisted entirely of younger, previously untried members. Although their services to the Communist cause were appreciable, in that they safeguarded the Party's organizational continuity, they made no outstanding contribution to the liberation of the country, nor did they distinguish themselves as fighting heroes. Thus, their claim to recognition was slight. The death of prewar leaders like Eduard Urx, Julius Fucik, the brothers Synek (Otto and Viktor), and Frantisek Tausig reduced potential power conflicts within the Czech Party. Had some of them survived, a situation similar to the one that ultimately arose in Hungary and Poland, where strong men of the domestic resistance (Rajk and Gomulka) came into conflict with their Muscovite comrades, probably could not have been avoided. Such a conflict was limited to Slovakia, where the supremacy of the Moscow leaders was reaffirmed with even greater decisiveness than it was on the national level in Prague.

The chairmanship of the Slovak Communist Party went to Viliam Siroky (one of Gottwald's closer collaborators who had been in Moscow at the beginning of the war, before his return to and imprisonment in Slovakia), while Stefan Bastovansky (another old Moscow hand and Siroky's prisonmate) became Secretary-General there. Julius Duris, a member of Siroky's entourage, at least by institutional affiliation, received the most prominent cabinet post held by a Slovak. Novomesky, Husak, and Smidke obtained posts in the provincial administration.

The Party had a large manpower pool to draw on. Few recent recruits were able to achieve important positions without seasoning. Exceptions could be found among economic technicians, and one person, Alexei Cepicka, appeared headed for a meteoric rise through his marriage to Gottwald's daughter. In two years, he rose from obscurity to become Minister of Internal Trade and was on his way to even greater glory.

The disposition to be made of the Sudeten German members was a thorny problem. Official government and Party policy concerning the Germans distinguished between Nazis and "antifascists," and in many ways sought to ease the hardship of the latter. In practice, these distinctions faded. So great was the hatred of the people, and so powerful the momentum of the national purge, that few individual Germans could hope to re-enter public life. The Party had to bow to overwhelming popular sentiment. It could not reinstate its Sudeten German members to good standing and make room for them in the higher councils. To be sure, the Party made use of Germans who were willing to serve in the border areas, where there was a shortage of personnel. But it did so surreptitiously, and where detection was impossible to avoid, as often happened, it hastened to deny these practices or to blame them on irresponsible local organizations.

The better-known Sudeten German Communist, such as Bruno Kohler, Paul Reimann, Karl Kreibich, and Gustav Beuer, were not given positions of public trust and responsibility before the coup d'état. Whether they fulfilled important tasks behind the scenes was a matter of speculation. Beuer, for example, was utilized for publicity functions abroad. His book on postwar developments in Czechoslovakia, published in Great Britain, was intended to spread the myth of peaceful coexistence between Communists and non-Communists in the shadow of the Kremlin.[30] Kohler acted as liaison officer with the East German Communists until 1947, when he reportedly turned up in Prague in an undisclosed capacity. His wife served as Gottwald's personal secretary. The earliest reference to Reimann's activities occurred in 1947, when he was lecturing at the Party's central school. No publicity accompanied his quiet return to active duty.*

Other, lesser-known, but not necessarily less important, Communists of German or German-Jewish background appeared on the scene during 1946 and 1947. Zikmund Stein had been prominent in the Party during the 1920's,[31] but had then vanished without a trace. His return to Czechoslovakia sometime after the war was totally unheralded and might have remained concealed but for a chance identification by an old casual acquaintance in the street. The nature of Stein's functions stayed undisclosed, but non-Communist intelligence reported, on good authority, that he headed the Party's legal department.[32]

The Party's *eminence grise,* shrouded in mystery, was Bedrich (Fritz) Geminder, alias Bedrich Vltavsky. He had spent much time in the Soviet Union in the 1930's, returning to Czechoslovakia only occasionally, and holding no official position in the Party.[33] Some people claim that he was a close personal aide of the Bulgarian, Georgi Dimitrov, whom Stalin made Secretary-General of the Comintern in 1935. Geminder's first publicly noted performance in Czechoslovakia was innocuous. A special issue of *Rude Pravo,* celebrating Gottwald's fiftieth birthday in 1946, carried, among other testimonials by distinguished Communist and non-Communist personalities, an article by Bedrich Vltavsky, praising the journalistic talents Gottwald had displayed early in his career.[34] Geminder's next public appearance was in the col-

---

*After the completion of the Communist power seizure, these veterans were reinstated in influential Party and public posts, and the part they played in the Communist administration was openly acknowledged.

umns of the Cominform journal, "For a Lasting Peace, for a People's Democracy." He was one of the journal's chief contributors from Czechoslovakia, writing at first under the name of Vltavsky-Geminder, and he was identified as a member of the editorial board. Actually, he had returned to Prague from Moscow in the spring of 1946 to participate, in some way, in the Party's Eighth Congress. Later that year, he was given charge of the international department of the Party's secretariat. In this capacity he kept a close watch over the country's foreign affairs.[35] But perhaps more important than the specific nature of his responsibilities was the fact that he constituted a foreign element in the Party, could in no way be identified with the traditional leadership, and, as such, unmistakably represented a form of supervision by Moscow.[36] The secrecy surrounding his activities bore witness to the mental climate in which the Party operated. One wonders to what extent his presence, which could not be concealed from the top echelon of Party officials, was a cause of discontent and resentment.

The supremacy of the Moscow leaders appeared to be accepted without noticeable grumbling, but the soft, gradualist approach of the Party did not meet with unanimous approval. In 1945, immediately after the liberation, the opportunity for an outright seizure of power was so excellent that to pass it up seemed like folly to those Communists who had not been appraised of the latest shifts in grand strategy.

In some ways the path chosen by the Party was more complicated and more difficult than a direct revolutionary assault might have been. By occupying posts in the government that were considered indispensable for an ultimate seizure of power, the Party also assumed the lion's share of responsibility for the reconstruction of Czechoslovakia. Working simultaneously toward both ends —a monopoly of power and a speedy restoration of normal conditions, especially in regard to the economy—unquestionably taxed the capabilities of the Party, since one effort was destructive and the other constructive.

There was danger that the Party would take its constructive responsibilities too seriously. As time passed, revolutionary ardor would wane and the onset of normalcy would militate against the seizure of power. Apprehensions increased in the second and particularly in the third year of the national and democratic revolution, when the Communists appeared to make no appreciable headway toward the achievement of their ultimate objectives. As Gottwald summed it up some months after the coup, "it was not surprising that . . . especially in the last period before February [1948], when the reaction raised its head with increasing impertinence . . . impatience and even doubt concerning the correctness of [the Party's] policy arose . . . in our own ranks."[37]

Whatever the undercurrents of conflict within the leadership, they did not visibly impair the Party's operating efficiency. No significant changes in the composition of the top command were made between 1945 and 1948. From this, one may infer that the individual members of the hierarchy were pulling their weight, even if some possibly performed their tasks with reservations.

The cohesive forces at work were powerful and by far overshadowed the divisive influences. The leaders who found a gradualist approach to their liking probably outnumbered the impatient radicals. Never in the past had the Czechoslovak Party shown outstanding revolutionary propensities, and there was no reason why it should now abruptly step out of character. The knowledge that the international and internal power configurations favored them, that they did not have to fear police interference, and that they could rely on rescue by the Soviet Union if they encountered serious trouble, provided the Communists with a margin of safety they never before possessed. It gave them a feeling of security and caused them to act boldly, and with unprecedented self-confidence.

8. *THE CONQUEST OF POLITICAL INSTITUTIONS*

UNDER NORMAL circumstances, the key to power—and this is what interested the Communists—lies in the control of the traditional and accepted loci or agencies of authority. Marxism-Leninism teaches that the proletariat, in seizing power, cannot simply "lay hold of the ready-made state machinery and wield it for its own purposes."[1] Whatever the validity of this maxim is in a typical revolutionary situation, it was not fully applicable in Czechoslovakia, under conditions of a gradual seizure of power, rather than a concentrated frontal assault on the bourgeois state. Gradualism necessarily entailed retaining many of the traditional institutions and using them as weapons, instruments, and operational bases in the struggle for power.

Actually, the Communists combined three different approaches to enhance their position in the machinery of the state. First, the executive and—with minor modifications—the legislative branch of the government retained their customary structure and functions. The Communists sought to entrench themselves as strongly as possible in these agencies and to use especially the executive —which admirably lent itself for that purpose—to carry out "the revolution from above." Second, a part of the bourgeois state machine, the entire structure of local administrative bodies, was completely eliminated and replaced by a new, simplified system of popularly elected National Committees. These Committees served to displace a strongly entrenched bureaucracy and to implement the revolution from below. Third, a reserve locus of authority was created in the form of the National Front, to which actual state power could be, and indeed was, transferred at the crucial time.

The Executive

Properly speaking, two separate agencies have to be considered under this heading: the presidency and the cabinet. Of the two, the cabinet had always wielded greater power. It was the most powerful agency of the government. The President had little authority over the cabinet, and the legislature never exercised effective control over it.

As a chronicler of Czechoslovak democracy put it, before 1938 the "Cabinet treated its Parliament as a willing and obedient steed. . . . Parliament dutifully discussed the proposals laid before it by the Cabinet, respected the latter's wishes, and carried out its directions . . . (but) nothing of importance was ever changed in the Government's Bills."[2] Legislation for the most part originated in the cabinet, and the constitutional powers of individual ministers were so great as to make them dictators in their sphere of jurisdiction.[3] There was no reason why these relations should be altered after the war.

THE PRESIDENCY. The Constitution left the President bereft of real power. Great authority nevertheless resided in this office before 1938. This was due to the prestige and moral influence of T. G. Masaryk, who had held the office without interruption from 1918 to 1935. Benes, his successor, could not match Masaryk's prestige, but he did wield considerable influence. After the war, he was unanimously re-elected President and, since his popularity seemed to be far greater than at any time before 1938, he theoretically was in a good position to exercise vigorous leadership. But he did not take advantage of this opportunity. He pulled few wires behind the scenes and rarely injected himself into controversial issues. He had a great stabilizing influence on the population, but he was not the rallying point of democratic political activity. His aloofness toward the parties, including his own (the National Socialist), from which he completely dissociated himself, and his studied impartiality, made him useless as an anti-Communist leader. On the contrary, his attitude played directly into the hands of the Communists, who capitalized on it in their propaganda.

THE CABINET. The power relations between Communists and non-Communists in the cabinet remained unchanged between

1945 and the coup d'état in 1948. The cabinet, which assumed office at Kosice in April, 1945, was formally reorganized in the fall of 1945, and again after the general election, in the spring of 1946. Its composition was not significantly affected. The Communists retained their hold on the important Ministries of the Interior, Agriculture, and Information. In the spring of 1946, they acquired the premiership as well, for it was traditional that a member of the strongest coalition party should be prime minister. This meant only that Gottwald, who had been one of the vice-premiers, moved up a notch to continue exercising—more formally, perhaps—a dominating influence. At the same time, the Communists traded the Ministry of Education for two other cabinet posts—Internal Trade and Finance. This was not due so much to depreciation of the Ministry of Education as to recognition that, under existing conditions, it was impossible to introduce radical organizational and ideological changes in the Czechoslovak educational system. Thus, after the spring of 1946, three important Ministries—Foreign Trade, Justice, and Education—remained outside the scope of direct Communist influence.

Of the various cabinet posts, the Ministry of the Interior, headed by Vaclav Nosek, was unparalleled in securing a privileged position for the Communists. Nosek's selection for this key post was probably motivated by the good reputation he enjoyed among many non-Communists. He spent the war in London, where he acted as the chief Communist spokesman. In his negotiations with Benes and his activities in the State Council, of which he was a Vice-President, he always displayed a high degree of reasonableness. He was a person with whom one could do business. As a result, he was described by his non-Communist associates as a decent, or honorable, man. His appointment, and not that of another individual with a more dreaded reputation, made the seizure by the Communists of this cabinet post more palatable to a large number of people. His selection was interpreted as an indication of the moderation of the Communist Party, and it instilled confidence that the Ministry would not be misused for partisan purposes.

The personality of the Minister, however, had little bearing on the uses to which the Ministry was put. To be sure, during the national and democratic revolution, the Ministry of the Interior was not primarily an instrument of terror. But this was due to deliberate political choice, not to the personal preference of the Minister. The strategic importance of the Ministry was inherent in its traditional responsibilities and in new, exceptional duties that were bestowed on it after the war.

In Czechoslovakia, as in many Continental countries, the Ministry of the Interior controlled the police and exerted preponderant influence over all aspects of the civil administration. The Agrarian Party, which had a monopoly on this portfolio before 1938, derived much of its continuing influence and power from it. There was no reason why the Ministry should not serve the Communists equally well. The people had learned to acquiesce in the wide privileges enjoyed by this Ministry.

In addition to its time-honored functions, the Ministry was entrusted with several special tasks of a temporary nature, but of very great significance. It was put in charge of national purification, and it directed the expulsion of Germans from the country, as well as the resettlement of Czechs and Slovaks in former German-inhabited territory.

Since it was the directing center as well as the last instance of appeal in matters concerning loyalty to the state, the Ministry of the Interior was in an excellent position to make friends for the Communist Party and to break its enemies. National purification received highest priority in the immediate postwar period, and the stamp of loyalty to the Republic was a prerequisite for each man's enjoyment of basic civic rights, let alone for self-betterment. Every individual's loyalty had to be attested by the local security authorities, which were under the Ministry's jurisdiction. What prevented the Communists from fully exploiting national purification was the scrupulousness of the special courts that were set up to try collaborators. These were under the jurisdiction of the Ministry of Justice, which was controlled by the National Socialist Party. But the courts were able to act only in cases that were brought to them by the police. Their ability to redress obvious wrongs was therefore greatly limited.

Inasmuch as the transfer of Germans was directed by the Ministry of the Interior, this truly national undertaking took on the appearance of an exclusive achievement of the Communists, who capitalized on the thirst for revenge and for acquisition of other people's property exhibited by a surprising number of Czechs and Slovaks.[4] By virtue of its control of the machinery of resettlement, the Ministry of the Interior was in a position to check the identity of would-be settlers at the source as well as at the point of destination, and to induce the "proper" people to move. The importance of control over the movement of millions of people hardly needs explaining. It is difficult to see why this responsibility was not entrusted to an interdepartmental agency which, even if not truly nonpartisan, could have at least partially blocked the unilateral exploitation of these opportunities by the Communists.

Next to the Ministry of the Interior, the Ministry of Agriculture served as perhaps the most important base of Communist operations in the cabinet.* Between 1918 and 1938, this Ministry, too, had been an exclusive domain of the Agrarian Party. The Ministry's role in the distribution of farm machinery, price fixing, purchasing of grain, and its influence on the Peasant Bank, to which the vast majority of peasants had had to turn for loans at one time or another, had greatly enhanced the Agrarians' electoral appeal. Now it was the Communists' turn to reap similar benefits. Through the good offices of the Ministry of Agriculture, which was, among other things, in charge of implementing the land reform decrees of 1945, the Communists once again were in a position to turn to partisan ends measures that had the wholehearted approval of the entire nation and of all political parties. The land reform decrees limited themselves to the confiscation of agricultural property owned by Germans, Hungarians, and collaborators. They were motivated by nationalistic rather than purely social and economic considerations.

The land reform section of the Ministry was headed by Jiri Kotatko, a Communist of long standing who had been in Moscow during the war. The National Land Fund section was in the charge of Josef Smrkovsky, a young, able Communist who rose to prominence during the closing stages of the war as one of the underground leaders of the Party in Bohemia. In individual localities, the confiscation of landed property and its redistribution to

---

*As one Czechoslovak political refugee remarked ruefully after 1948, "a hold on the Ministry of Agriculture served the Communists nearly as well as their control of the Ministry of the Interior." (Duchacek, *The Strategy of Communist Infiltration*, p. 23.)

claimants were in the charge of Communist-dominated Farmers' Commissions. The agricultural departments of the National Committees were also dominated by the Communists, who were clever enough to take full credit for the speedy distribution of the loot, but who made certain that no permanent titles to property were issued for some time. In this manner, they made doubly sure of the allegiance of their newly won peasant supporters. The efficacy of this approach was at least in part reflected in the 1946 elections, in which the Communists scored heavily in a large number of rural districts.

Another cabinet post of great importance was the Ministry of Information. Vaclav Kopecky, the Minister, was an old Party stalwart, a close associate of Gottwald's, with considerable experience, acquired in the Information Section of the Comintern in the 1930's and early 1940's. He was known for his uncritical Sovietophilism. Several top posts in the Ministry were occupied by Communist literati such as Ivan Olbracht, who was in charge of the broadcasting division, Frantisek Halas, who headed the publishing division, and Vitezslav Nezval, who supervised motion-picture production.

The contribution of this Ministry to the Communist cause was of an auxiliary nature until the coup. At that time, however, its full potential was deployed and its first-rate significance was demonstrated beyond any doubt. The Ministry tried, of course, to slant its output in favor of the Communist Party and, to the extent that it controlled the sources of propaganda and information, it did so unabashedly. A case in point was the Czechoslovak Broadcasting Service. Broadcasting had been a state monopoly in Czechoslovakia and after the war the broadcasting service, also headed by a Communist (Bohumil Lastovicka), operated under the Ministry's supervision. The programming and presentation of news and political topics revealed an obvious pro-Communist and pro-Soviet bias (the head of the political section of the broadcasting service was the Communist Jiri Hronek). Much time was set aside for news and editorial comments, and Communist commentators and speakers had a priority on radio time.

The Czechoslovak News Service (Ceskoslovenska Tiskova Kancelar—CTK), another centrally controlled organization operating under the Ministry, was also enlisted in the service of the Communist Party. But the CTK was not the only distributor of printed news, and it was not compulsory to publish its stories. In the broader cultural sphere, the Ministry's efforts to infuse Czech motion pictures, the theatre, and drama with socialist content were subjected to a twofold limitation. First, the Communist Party's official line at the time was one of moderation. Second, the Ministry had at its disposal only limited means to silence its critics and the opponents of "progressive" art and culture. Some Czech artists with conservative leanings could be effectively muzzled by invoking war-guilt charges against them. The majority, however, could not be so disposed of and the cultural field soon became a scene of lively and animated debate between Marxists and non-Marxists.

The Ministry's influence over the daily press was also limited. Licensing, a prerogative of the Ministry, was handled as a matter of routine. No political party or major organization was deprived of its privilege to print as much as it wished. Only once did the Ministry attempt—unsuccessfully—to resort to its prerogative to revoke a license.

The Ministry also controlled the allocation of newsprint, which was in very short supply, and thereby possessed a potentially powerful lever against its enemies. While it may have engaged in discriminatory practices, no evidence came to light indicating that non-Communist parties or organizations were deprived of newsprint in large enough quantities to hamper their propaganda and information activities.

The Communists had claimed the Ministry of Education in the first postwar government. They gave the post to Zdenek Nejedly, a long-time secret member of the Party and an ardent admirer of the Soviet Union. He, too, had spent the war in Moscow, and had been elected to the Soviet Academy of Sciences—an honor rarely bestowed on foreigners. Immediately upon returning to Czechoslovakia, Nejedly made threatening gestures presaging the Sovietization of the country's school system. But the sweeping changes he planned were not implemented. The failure to do so might have been due to a number of reasons, among them the order of priority the Communists themselves assigned to the accomplishment of certain tasks. For, in the spring of 1946, when the cabinet was reorganized following the general elections, the Communists gave up the Ministry of Education in return for two other cabinet posts—Finance and Internal Trade—whose possession they obviously deemed more important. Had they been vitally interested in retaining their hold on the educational apparatus, they unquestionably could have done so. As a result of the swap, the Ministry of Education passed into the hands of the National Socialist Party, under whose management the Czechoslovak educational system retained the features that characterized it in the prewar period.

In considering Communist influence in the cabinet, one inevitably questions to what extent the Communists were able to exclude outside forces from the Ministries they held, and how thoroughly they succeeded in penetrating Ministries under the control of other parties. There are only partial answers, suggesting that, in Ministries held by the Communists, outside influence was kept to a minimum, while in other Ministries, Communists asserted themselves in varying degrees. Figures released by the Communists show that among chiefs and deputy chiefs of departments and chiefs of sections, the proportion of Party members fluctuated from 5 to 20 per cent.* Their numerical strength, of course, does not reveal the extent of their influence on policy and administration.

The quantitative and qualitative aspects of Communist infiltration of the entire government apparatus were aptly summarized by one highly placed non-Communist "participant-observer":

> Justification for the many promotions of Communists to high positions in the police, the army, and the civil service was of two kinds. First, a "moral" qualification for office was to replace the old bourgeois demands for schooling or training. A fighting or resistance record, as vouched for by the Communist-sponsored Union of Partisans, was considered higher qualification than a university degree, or military academy training. And fighting experience with the Red Army was the highest qualification of all. Second, the Communists

---

*In the Ministry of Foreign Affairs 6 "leading posts" (as defined above) out of a total of 68 were held by Communists. In the Ministry of Education, the corresponding figures were 19 out of 105; in the Ministry of Justice, 3 out of 40; and in the Ministry of Foreign Trade, 4 out of 82. (Milos Klimes and Marcel Zachoval, *Prispevek k Problematice Unorovych Udalosti*, pp. 215–16.)

claimed that twenty years of bourgeois and Agrarian government had excluded them completely from government positions and that they were therefore entitled to a generous
share of the postwar administration. Since the National
Front government professed a willingness to mend all past
wrongs, this injury to the Communists while they were in
opposition should be redressed too. This unheard of claim
was only feebly resisted by the non-Communists. The above
arguments were usually stressed for penetration of government departments headed by non-Communists. In those directed by Communist ministers, very little trouble was taken
to justify the "blitz promotions" of Communist officials.[5]

In November, 1945, a purge commission for public officials was
set up under the Ministry of the Interior.[6] It did not operate in
an impartial manner, although the picture was not entirely one-
sided. There were non-Communist employees in Communist Ministries too, and even the police was not at any time before the
coup staffed exclusively with members of the Communist Party.

In the Ministries held by non-Communist parties, the success of
Communist infiltration seemed to be partly dependent on the personality of the Minister. Two contrasting examples are the Ministries of Justice and Foreign Trade, both held by National Socialists. In the first, the Communists could not make headway.
They were unable to influence the policy of the Minister, or to
penetrate effectively into high positions. From 1945 until 1948,
they were forced to fight from outside through the police, who
had an opportunity to block certain types of judicial procedure;
through the trade unions, via demonstrations and propaganda;
and in the National Assembly, by means of verbal diatribe. The
Ministry, however, remained impervious to these attacks.

The Ministry of Foreign Trade presented a different picture.
Some Communists and left-wing Social Democrats occupied influential positions. Jan Fierlinger (Zdenek Fierlinger's brother)
was in charge of the Russian desk. Evzen Lobl, a Communist, occupied an even higher position as division chief. The policy of
the Ministry was affected not so much by Communist personnel
on the inside as by over-all cabinet supervision. The foreign relations of the country, whether political or economic, were more
the concern of the government than of a single Ministry. The

chief effort of Communist personnel in the Ministry of Foreign Trade and in other government departments controlled by weak non-Communists centered on keeping a close check on day-to-day activities of the staff, becoming acquainted with the personnel, classifying it according to its reliability (from the Communist viewpoint), and, finally, preparing for the neutralization and seizure of these Ministries in a crisis. Thus, when the crisis actually came, the Communists knew exactly whom to dismiss or send on temporary leave, what offices to occupy, and how to run the Ministry.

The crucial difference between the Communist Party and the other parties was in the use to which they put the Ministries they respectively controlled. The non-Communist parties, who were not steeped in any kind of revolutionary strategy and tactic, to whom the crass or subtle manipulation of power was largely alien, and who for a long time were unaware of the fact that they were engaged in a life and death struggle, had nothing in their repertoire to enable them effectively to counter the deliberate policy of the Communists, who were undermining the substance of coalition government even while retaining it in form.

The Legislature

Fearing that the convocation of a legislative body would slow down, or possibly even thwart, the enactment of legislative measures designed to institute far-reaching political, social, and economic reforms, the Communists insisted on passing all major reform legislation by presidential decree before they consented to calling an Assembly. On the issue of government by presidential decree, considerable friction developed between the Communists and all the other parties, for the others (even the Social Democrats) wanted to elect an Assembly at the earliest possible time. The Communist view prevailed, and no Assembly was allowed to meet until the last of the major decrees—four decrees of nationalization—were signed by the President.

The Provisional National Assembly convoked on October 28, 1945, was unorthodox in its composition and in the method by which it was selected. It was a unicameral Assembly. The abolition of the Senate did not cause controversy, however, since the apportionment of party strength in the two chambers had always been identical. The Assembly was unique in that it included members not only of the parties, but also of the major nonparty mass organizations. Candidates were nominated by the respective groups, and approved by electors who were chosen at meetings of district National Committees.

In the Provisional Assembly, each one of the parties had an equal number of delegates (40), and 60 seats were reserved for representatives of interest groups. In view of the fact that the Communist Party submitted two sets of candidates, one for Slovakia and one for the Czech lands, it had 80 deputies (out of a total of 300). An additional 18 representatives of interest groups identified themselves as Communists, so that the Party had 98 representatives, or 2 short of a full 33 per cent. Social Democrats and Communists together had 149 representatives, or 1 short of 50 per cent.[7]

The functions of the Provisional Assembly were largely decorative. It approved wholesale many of the government measures taken between May and October of 1945, and prepared for the election of a Constituent National Assembly in May, 1946, for a two-year term. The chief function of the Constituent Assembly was to give the country a new organic law. In the election, which was genuinely democratic, the Communists gained 38 per cent of the total vote, thereby strengthening their claims on a leading position in the government. They had 114 deputies and, together with 37 Social Democrats, held a slim 1 per cent majority. The electoral victory of the Communists gave them control of important parliamentary committees such as the Interior, Security, and Labor–Social Welfare. They could have claimed the speakership in the National Assembly too, but instead used it in the bargaining for cabinet posts. This was possible because, by custom, the tenure of the Speaker, chosen immediately after the election, ran for only thirty days, after which time he was either re-elected or a new permanent Speaker was chosen.

The Communist Zapotocky was elected for the thirty-day term and could have been re-elected easily. However, the Communists agreed to the selection of Josef David, a National Socialist, in order to strengthen their claim on additional cabinet posts. Once the trading was done, the Communists moved to adopt new parliamentary rules divesting the Speaker of his traditional authority in favor of the presidium of the National Assembly, on which every party had one representative, for a total of six. This gave the Communists two representatives, and together with the Social Democratic representative (Frantisek Tymes and later Jaroslav Hladky), they could not be outvoted. By an "odd coincidence," the other three council members were not the staunchest of anti-Communists. The speaker, Josef David, belonged to the left-wing of the National Socialist Party and often sided with the Communists. The People's Party was represented by Alois Petr, and the Slovak Democrats by Jan Sevcik, who was later identified as an agent of the Soviet secret police. (He led the regenerated Slovak Democratic Party after the coup, until the summer of 1952, when he fell victim to an extensive purge.)

Despite their advantageous position in the Assembly, the Communists were unable to railroad legislation through it. As was to be expected, parliamentary procedure was hospitable to dilatory tactics, filibustering, and other maneuvers that delayed the enactment of Communist-sponsored legislation. Once, in the face of really stubborn opposition, the Communists tried to apply pressure from the outside. They called on peasant delegations to invade the Assembly to demand passage of several Communist-sponsored agricultural decrees. The maneuver failed.

The Assembly proved the most effective medium for checking Communist advances by legislative methods. Some of the debates in parliamentary committees produced the most outspoken criticism of the Communist Party, and in a few instances, the Communists were actually forced to retreat under fire in parliamentary committees. But the practical result of these efforts was negligible. Parliamentary oratory was not translated into effective political action. Even the publicity accorded to the anti-Communist successes was meager. The Assembly's strength was also its weakness; it was not suited to serve as an instrument for impairing Communist power positions.

Local Government

As Gottwald put it, the National Committees were ideally suited to change the entire state apparatus. The creation of a network of National Committees in localities (villages, towns), districts, and on the province (land) level received high priority from the Communists. The very circumstances in which these Committees came into being favored the Communists.

According to eyewitnesses and participants, National Committees were, for the most part, elected by acclamation at public meetings, hastily convened immediately after the liberation of a given locality. Sometimes the majority of the citizenry turned out for the election, which as a rule consisted of a show of hands approving a slate of candidates prepared and presented by the National Front. Sometimes attendance at these meetings was sparse. Whichever was the case, the list of candidates in the Czech lands included a great many more Communists than the 25 per cent to which that Party was entitled, according to a general agreement of the National Front calling for parity representation.[8]

Another method of selection was simply to appoint to office the National Committee, which had been formed as an underground unit during the Nazi occupation. In such cases, too, more often than not, Communists predominated.[9] In localities and districts inhabited preponderantly by Germans, National Committees were appointed by the Ministry of the Interior.[10]

During the initial period of their existence, when the channels of centralized authority had not been well established, local and district National Committees possessed *de facto* unlimited power over the citizenry. The Committees, specifically their security departments, were entrusted with ferreting out collaborators, and every citizen's loyalty to the Republic had to be confirmed by the Committee.[11] The Committee's refusal was tantamount to social ostracism at best; at worst, it entailed prosecution under war-crimes statutes. The Committees were also empowered to secure industrial and commercial property against sabotage, to confiscate the worldly goods of enemy nationals and Czech collaborators, and to appoint temporary trustees, officially designated as "national administrators" (narodni spravce), to manage confiscated plants and shops until such time as the government could decide what to do with them, i.e., to nationalize or assign them to private owners.

By the end of August, 1945, local National Committees had appointed 4,855 administrators, and district National Committees had designated an additional 2,740 as custodians of larger enterprises, giving preference to former political prisoners and "underground fighters."

The initial supremacy of the Communist Party in the National Committees gave it a political advantage that could not be overcome. In the autumn of 1945, nearly all chairmanships of National Committees were in Communist or pro-Communist (left-wing Social Democratic) hands. So was the leadership of most security and agriculture departments in local and district National Committees.[12] As political conditions became stabilized, the composition of National Committees was revised to conform more closely to the principle of equal representation for all parties. However, the Communists could not be dislodged from key spots, and the effects of measures taken immediately after the liberation could not be undone easily, if at all. The early unchecked reign of Communist-dominated National Committees left an indelible imprint on the country.

The general election of May, 1946, was followed by a reapportionment of seats in local, district, and land National Committees as well. Inasmuch as the Communist Party scored heavily in these elections—it carried a number of districts in the Czech lands by a clear majority, and had a plurality in many others—it was entitled to retain control of vital departments in the Committees. Of 154,000 members elected to local Committees, 69,786 (45.2 per cent) were Communists. Of 4,436 members of district and central (land) Committees, 1,947 (43.9 per cent) were Communists. In 37.5 per cent of all local Committees, the Communists had an absolute majority; they held the chairmanships in 55.1 per cent of the local Committees, and in 78 per cent of the district Committees.[13]

The Party, fully realizing the enormous power vested in National Committees, devoted minute attention to their activities. A commission for public administration attached to the Communist Central Committee supervised the selection and indoctrination of Communists serving on National Committees. It directed their day-to-day actions and checked their records. The Party published a fortnightly journal, *Lidova Sprava* (*People's Administration*), dealing exclusively with problems germane to National Committees.[14] Finally, in 1947, the Communists issued a comprehensive 659-page guidebook for officials of the National Committees.[15] No other party showed as much interest in guiding the Committees.

The National Front

In its conception as well as in its manner of functioning, the National Front was a potent instrument of political control serving the Communist Party.

The Front was a living symbol of national unity and solidarity as it existed in the heat of struggle against the enemy in the hour of revolution. Accordingly, it had a peculiar mystique of its own, and later, when unity and solidarity tended to break down, it was often enough to recall the idealized image of the Front in order to restore its influence in practice. Although the non-Communist parties—especially after 1946—tried to fend off Communist influence in the Front, they could never extricate themselves from the magic that kept them spellbound. To be accused of violating the principles of the Front, or of breaking it up, was the worst thing that could happen to them. This frame of mind was vividly illustrated in February, 1948, when the three democratic parties that resigned from the government loudly protested against Communist accusations that they had also withdrawn from the National Front.

The Front's existence thus stifled the development of free political parties and political activity. It ruled out the possibility of opposition in the full parliamentary sense, and perverted the customarily accepted interpretation of coalition.

The limitations implied by the Front, however, did not affect the Communist Party, which dictated its program and policies. Since this was the case, the other parties were in the uncomfortable position of having the ground cut from under their feet if they subscribed to the program, or of exposing themselves to charges of breach of faith or of antidemocratic and antinational attitudes if they opposed it. The Front therefore became a convenient instrument for keeping the non-Communist parties off balance, especially the three non-Marxist groups that were being pulled toward the left by their adherence to the Front, while the realignment of political forces tended to make them the repository of rightist sentiment.[16]

The manner in which the Communists dominated the Front reveals one of the basic techniques utilized in transforming a minority position within an organization into a majority position through a series of intermediary blocs and alliances.

The alliance between Communists and Social Democrats—in which the Communists were the stronger partner—served as a point of departure for the creation of majority opinion in the Front. This alliance was supplemented by a "socialist bloc of workers of town and country," into which the National Socialists were drawn against the better judgment of some of their leaders. Created in June, 1945, when revolutionary excitement still ran high and national unity was a meaningful reality for the people (if not for all politicians), the bloc "clearly represented the majority of the people."[17] The Communists secured the adoption of their views by prevailing upon the Social Democrats. The two Marxist parties then confronted the National Socialists and usually succeeded in inducing the latter to make the decision of the bloc unanimous. Once a unanimous decision was reached, it was presented to the National Front, where its acceptance was forced on the other, nonsocialist parties, with the argument that they could not oppose the "will of the bloc," that is, of a clear majority of the nation's working people.[18]

This technique was most useful during the early stages of the national and democratic revolution. By the summer of 1946, the socialist bloc was moribund as a result of objections by the National Socialist Party to the treatment to which it was exposed. The Communists did not press matters greatly, because their major objectives had been reached and a period of quiescence was setting in. This did not mean the complete abandonment of efforts to tie down the non-Communist parties through the use of coordinating committees of one sort or another. For example, in the fall of 1946, the Communists urged the establishment of such committees for the implementation of the two-year economic plan then being readied. Ultimately, they settled for coordinating committees publicizing the plan.

In the fall of 1947, when a temporary change of heart of the Social Democratic Party threatened for the first time to isolate the Communists in the National Front, they attempted to change the rules and urged the admission of Communist-dominated nonpolitical mass organizations, to give the Front a "truly popular character." This brazen attempt at packing the Front was successfully resisted by the non-Communist parties. Still, the Front did not become an anti-Communist instrument until the very eve of the coup. The non-Communist parties bowed to Communist wishes in the Front even on issues on which they took an antagonistic stand first in public, and finally in the government.

Several factors might be responsible for such Communist domination. Discussions were informal and behind closed doors. Little, if anything, about them was reported in the press. This made it possible—especially in the immediate postliberation period—to reach reasonable agreements. Perhaps the democratic parties found it easier to capitulate in private, as it were, rather than in the more formal atmosphere of the cabinet, which seemed to call for a stiffer attitude. The same informality gave the Communists a better opportunity to cajole and threaten without adverse publicity. According to Czech refugees who had sat in at meetings, they were quite outspoken in their references and allusions to open threats of Soviet interference should their wishes be thwarted. But, as with other matters, the outside world and the Czechoslovak nation itself learned of these things only after the coup.

The Instruments of Power

Although neither the police nor the armed forces were independent agencies, being under the ultimate jurisdiction of the Ministries of the Interior and National Defense respectively, they require separate treatment because of the importance given to them as instruments of power. Their evolution was very dissimilar, and the police were more prominent as a Communist tool.

THE POLICE. The role of the police was determined by the Party's over-all strategy. Between 1945 and January, 1948, the police were a potential rather than actual weapon in the struggle for power. There was little, if any, evidence of police power on behalf of the Party. Aside from arrests of several thousand people in Slovakia immediately after the liberation, reportedly by Soviet security agents, and a similar though lesser wave of arrests in the Czech lands, visitations by the secret police were infrequent.

One of the reasons for the inconspicuous part of the police was the Party's desire to avoid a terroristic label. In actual fact, the Communists yielded to pressure by the opposition on several occasions and modified some of the policies they sought to implement in the organization, disposition, and functioning of the police. These concessions were, however, mainly of a token nature. Never did the Communists permit serious encroachments on their hold over the police apparatus, and if it was not openly enlisted in their service, it was certainly denied to all opponents and did not meet the standard of an impartial force serving the interests of society. When the chips were down, as in January, 1948, no meddling by the democrats was allowed.

The organization of the police reveals the manner in which it was primed for use as a partisan instrument.

The need for purifying the police force, as it existed at the close of the war, was generally accepted, for its personnel throughout the nation had been strongly compromised. Seizing this opportunity and enlarging it well beyond the reasonable limits of necessary reform, the Communist Minister of the Interior wasted no time in transforming the police into a Communist tool. His first official order after returning to liberated territory called for the formation of a Commission of Internal Security to be composed of representatives of partisan units and the trade unions. The Commission was to act, temporarily, as the highest security agency in the country, and was entrusted both with matters of physical security and the apprehension of war criminals and collaborationists. Soon thereafter, the formation of a new national security corps (Sbor Narodni Bezpecnosti—SNB) was decreed. The SNB superseded all former police formations and absorbed the members of the regular police whose loyalty was approved by special screening boards. For the rest, its ranks were filled out with partisans and other armed members of the resistance movement. In practice, this meant infusing the corps with large numbers of people who had no formal police training. Thus diluted, the SNB was not necessarily exclusively staffed by Communists. Not all old-line policemen were, or could be, dismissed, and the Communist affiliation of many new recruits was of dubious nature. Under the circumstances, however, no more could be accomplished, and the most important thing was that the former identity of the police force was smashed. Although the SNB was not a wholly reliable Communist tool, it had the makings of one.

To cope with problems, the Minister of the Interior quickly ordered the formation of a readiness battalion (pohotovostni pluk), a flying squad of trouble shooters. It was commanded by Oldrich Krystof, a veteran of the Spanish Civil War, and was staffed exclusively by Communists. Its existence caused much uneasiness in the democratic ranks, and attacks on it finally became so vocal that it had to be abolished, in the fall of 1946. The victory proved hollow, for the original battalion of 1,720 men was replaced by special border battalions, 6,000 strong, heavily armed and motorized. Their creation was authorized by a law on the SNB, passed by the National Assembly after much wrangling and delay, in July, 1947.[19] Their alleged function was to protect the Republic against the heightened danger of sabotage and infiltration by German agents. In vain did the democrats protest that the German danger had decreased with the completion of the vast program of expulsion. The battalions were retained. Often units were stationed at strategic places in the interior of the country, as around Prague just before the outbreak of the coup. During the coup, these units played an important role—patrolling the streets of the capital.

In addition to the uniformed police, two other arms of the security apparatus—both plain-clothes outfits—existed. One was the criminal investigating service, whose jurisdiction extended over ordinary criminal matters; the other was the so-called state security service (Statni Bezpecnost—StB), better known as the secret political police. Both services were centrally controlled from the Ministry of the Interior. The man in charge of the StB was said to be Jindrich Vesely, a tough, Moscow-trained agent who had spent several years in Nazi concentration camps.

Along with the StB, the Communist Party enlisted the services of still another agency, the land security division, (Zemske Oddeleni Bezpecnostni—ZOB), which had come into being without legal sanction after the war. The ZOB was attached to the land National Committees in Prague and Brno. Why the separate territorial security divisions were needed was not clear. However, the fact that they were new creations without pre-existing tables of organization, thus lending themselves admirably to staffing by reliable Communists, seems like a plausible answer. The chief of ZOB in Bohemia was Emil Hrsel, a former Communist youth leader who spent the war in German concentration camps; the functions of the organizations under his command centered on spying on non-Communist political parties. The existence of ZOB infuriated the democrats, whose clamor brought about its abolition, though both its personnel and its functions were absorbed by the Ministry of the Interior.

The three separate arms of the police were not integrated into one organization until July, 1947, when a law defining the general scope of competence of the SNB was passed. Among other things, the law stipulated that in addition to Czechs and Slovaks, other Slavic nationals with at least five years' residence in Czechoslovakia could be enrolled in the SNB. It also set an unusually low upper age limit (thirty years) for the admission of new recruits, thus eliminating personnel more strongly' rooted in the political tradition of the prewar Republic.

THE ARMY. Although the army occupied a prominent place on the target list of instruments of power and Zdenek Fierlinger hopefully announced that the reorganization of the Czechoslovak armed forces along the lines of the "glorious" Red Army would be high on the agenda of his regime, the military neither developed into a reliable Communist striking arm, nor was it streamlined in accordance with the Soviet model prior to 1948. There were several reasons for this.[20]

The division of forces in the armed services was highly unfavorable to the Communists. The political orientation of old-line officers was preponderantly conservative. Although some officers compromised themselves during the war, a far greater number served their country's interests and, in view of their merits, had to be reinstated.[21] Only a few applications were turned down, for collaboration with the enemy and for political reasons (as in the case of General Sergei Ingr, the Minister of War of the exile government).

Despite a concentrated effort to build the new army around a core of units formed in the Soviet Union, important branches of the service were very much under Western influence. The air force consisted exclusively of British-trained personnel, and motorized units contained large contingents that had received instruction in the West.

The National Defense Minister himself, Ludvik Svoboda, might well have had Communist sympathies, although he was not formally a Party member. He had been chosen to lead the First

Czechoslovak Army Company in the Soviet Union, created in February, 1942, and he remained at the head of the First Czechoslovak Army Corps on the Eastern Front until his elevation to the cabinet.* He owed his position to the good will of the Communists, and could be relied on not to act vigorously against them. The chief of staff, General Bohumil Bocek, was reported to have become involved in some personal matter so that he, too, was at the mercy of the Communists. But several important posts were held by officers of Western sympathies. General Janousek, the head of the air force, was an assistant chief of the general staff, General Liska directed the military academy, General Bosy-Sklenovsky served as chief of the President's military chancery until 1946, when he was assigned to a regional command in Plzen. His place was taken by General Hasal-Nizborsky, another person of strong Western sympathies.[22]

Nothing less than a thorough purge of permanent cadres would have ensured the fealty of the army to the Communists. The political and technical obstacles to such a transformation were so numerous as to overtax the Communists' ability to cope with them.

For one thing, President Benes, as Commander-in-Chief, retained the prerogative of approving all promotions to general rank and while some promotions reportedly took place without his knowledge, large-scale rapid advancement of Communists to higher ranks could not be carried out without his knowledge and without alerting him to the inherent dangers of such moves.[23] Moreover, the training of reliable cadres takes time and requires extensive political indoctrination. The Communists had neither the time nor the inclination to arouse public hostility by introducing Marxist-Leninist political indoctrination into the army wholesale.

They managed to bypass and shunt off to innocuous regional command posts some of the officers who might have developed power. A case in point was General Kutlvasr, a popular man who

---

*Svoboda was an officer in the Czechoslovak Army before World War II. In 1939, he fled to Poland, where he helped to organize a fighting unit of Czechoslovak refugees. Retreating from the Nazis, he led his troops into territory occupied by the Soviet Union on September 18, 1939. His wife, who remained in Czechoslovakia, was executed by the Nazis in 1941, and his son died in the Mauthausen concentration camp.

had distinguished himself during the brief period of street fighting and military resistance in Prague at the close of the war. He was transferred to Hradec Kralove, where his influence was much impaired.

The Communists were also able to infiltrate the army's education and enlightenment department, and the intelligence and counterintelligence agencies. One of their members, General Jaroslav Prochazka, a graduate of Soviet military-political institutions, headed the education and enlightenment department (Hlavni Sprava Vychovy a Osvety—HSVO), which was actually the precursor of the political administration of the army, formally introduced only after the coup. Bedrich Reicin, a former Komsomol leader who, having served a brief prison term imposed by the Gestapo, escaped to Russia in 1940, was elevated to the rank of colonel with alarming speed, and headed the army's intelligence network (OBZ).

Enlightenment officers were assigned as deputy commanders to all army units of company size, or larger. However, there was a shortage of suitable personnel for this type of duty. In April, 1945, there were only 605 Party members of all ranks in Svoboda's Army Corps,[24] the vast majority being recent converts. Three years earlier, the number had been only thirty-five. Frequently, one person had to fill several posts. Alternatively, these posts remained vacant. There was considerable resistance among old-line officers to the appointment of cadres that did not measure up to the traditional educational and technical standards of competence required of commanders. Unwilling or unable to force the issue, the Communists had to satisfy themselves with an incomplete network of political controls.

In order to conceal their membership, Communists in the armed forces were not organized in separate Primary Party Units; instead, they enrolled in the particular locality where they were stationed. This led to a loose affiliation with the Party, and denied them the advantages of a hierarchy of Party cells within a closed organizational system.

Thus, the Communists did not dominate the army securely enough to use it in their own behalf. But they did succeed in neutralizing the only force even potentially capable of challenging the Party. During the coup, the army was dutifully confined to barracks, where it passively witnessed the seizure of power.

9. SOCIAL ORGANIZATIONS, THE ECONOMY, AND MASS COMMUNICATIONS

MASS ORGANIZATIONS are considered by the Communists as extremely important reserves of revolution, for they are eminently suitable for propagandizing and—under the proper circumstances —for mobilizing the masses. The infiltration and subversion of these organizations is a primary aim of all Communist parties, wherever they operate.

One of the prerequisites for effective exploitation of a mass organization is that it be as broadly representative of a particular interest (or professional) group as possible. The Communists have therefore been consistent advocates of united, nationwide trade unions, peasants' organizations, and other groups. The reason behind this is simple. If interest groups are split a number of ways, the task of penetrating them becomes excessively complicated. Moreover, winning over one or another organization under these conditions can hardly be termed winning control over a particular interest group. The case is different when a particular interest group is united. It is then politically less homogeneous, and the inevitable cleavages among various political factions in the organization are grist for the Communist mill. But even more important is the Communists' belief that their superior organizational skills will aid them in dominating a group in which they do not necessarily have overwhelming support.

The unification of professional and interest groups in nationwide, nonpolitical organizations was high on the agenda of the postwar Czechoslovak Government. All parties were agreed on this issue, just as they were on the simplification of the party system.

The excessive fractionization of trade unions, and of farmers', youth, and gymnastic organizations along party lines had been one of the less attractive features of political life before 1938. The activities of these organizations were filled with exaggerated political content. As a result, the more important ones, particularly the trade unions, were prevented from exerting the full measure of their influence. The assumption underlying the unification of professional organizations was that their removal from political contention would also reduce party strife. This was a wishful hope, because political strife could not be wiped out with the stroke of a pen. It was merely transferred from an intergroup to an intragroup basis. But it provided the Communists with the awaited opportunity.

The creation of united, nationwide mass organizations brought a new dimension into political life. For the first time since 1918, it caused a division and possible conflict between the political allegiance of a person and his other group associations, especially if one particular party could gain predominant influence in a mass organization and subject the adherents of other parties to propaganda and pressure. This is precisely what the Communists sought to achieve, and in at least two crucial cases—the trade unions and the host of partisan and freedom fighters' associations —actually accomplished. In the trade unions, workers who belonged to one or another non-Communist party were subjected to irresistible social pressure. In a crisis, the non-Communist parties could not count on the support of their worker-members. An equally striking example was offered by a series of organizations —of "partisans," "freedom fighters," "fighters of the barricades," and "former political prisoners and inmates of concentration camps"—which came into being immediately after the war.*

Partisans and Freedom Fighters

These were vocal groups—radical in their political views— which, by the nature of their membership, commanded much respect and a certain amount of fear. The Communists' leading

---

*The partisans were headed by Rudolf Slansky, Secretary-General of the Communist Party. The "freedom fighters' association" (Svaz Bojovniku za Svobodu—SBS), which eventually became a roof organization for sundry partisan associations, was headed by Ladislav Kopriva. Its Secretary-General was Jan Vodicka. Both men were old-time Communists who had been in concentration camps.

position in them was not undeserved. What made these organizations powerful beyond the limits of their own intrinsic importance was their representation of a meeting ground of Communists and non-Communists in a fraternity dedicated to radical solutions of political, social, and economic problems. No party could disdain its heroic members, who had suffered in prisons and concentration camps, or had risked their lives in the defense of their fatherland. On the contrary, they were entitled to, and received, special consideration. Yet, the presence of freedom fighters in the non-Communist parties often did not serve the best interests of these parties in their struggle against the Communists. For in a significant number of cases it was difficult to say whether the allegiance to their chosen party was greater, or smaller, than the solidarity they felt toward their Communist ex-comrades-in-arms. The divided loyalty of this radical element deprived the non-Communist parties of the wholehearted backing of exactly that part of their membership which might have poured a certain amount of fighting spirit into their activities.

Precise statistical analysis eludes us, but a few examples may be sufficient to show how the Communists benefited from the fighting camaraderie with individuals of other political faiths. Frantisek Tymes, a mild-mannered Social Democrat known as a moderate, in the hour of greatest need sided with the pro-Communist left wing of his party. When asked why he had done so, he gave as his reason the solemn promise of Social Democrats and Communists in German concentration camps (where Tymes had spent the war) "never again to betray each other." Alois Petr and Josef Plojhar, two prominent members of the People's Party who betrayed it during the coup, had prison and concentration camp experience behind them. Emanuel Slechta, a National Socialist who deserted his party in its hour of need, also had been a political prisoner. The same held true for Otokar Wunsch, a National Socialist newspaperman. Although he died before the coup, he had aided the Communists, for as his party's only representative on the presidium of the Central Council of the Trade Unions, he had consistently voted with them.

Trade Unions

Of all mass organizations, the trade unions (Revolucni Odborove Hnuti—ROH) were most solidly under Communist control and most influential in aiding the Party. They were the largest (in 1947, they had well over 2 million members), and the most militant. Their size and the social element they represented made them truly formidable.

Before the war, the Czechoslovak trade-union movement had been badly split. Every party had its own unions, and in addition there were a number of independent ones.

The picture after the war, however, was wholly different. The creation of a united trade-union movement after the war consisted solely of seizing union headquarters in Prague and giving the unions a revolutionary label. This was done sometime between May 5 and May 9, 1945, while the population of Prague engaged the German garrison in a final struggle.

The German occupation authorities had abolished the multitude of unions in Bohemia and Moravia and substituted two central unions, one for industrial and one for white-collar workers. They had also set up a regional network of trade-union centers, whose primary functions were to implement a recreation program patterned after the German *Kraft durch Freude* ("Strength through Joy") scheme. These unions were a collaborationist organization and were on the proscribed list of the government after the war—although in their case, as in the cases of a large number of Czech Quisling organizations, the concept of collaboration required close scrutiny. On the one hand, the Germans did not trust any Czech organization sufficiently to endow it with serious proselytizing or police functions. On the other hand, the Czechs joined Quisling groups in order to avoid possible persecution and hardship and, if given the opportunity, to use these organizations as centers of passive resistance. The unions were perhaps in a somewhat better position to afford protection, for the Czech working class had been treated gingerly by the Germans, who were primarily interested in high productivity and obtained it by refraining from terror against the workers. In the spring of 1945, over 500,000 workers paid dues to the German-sponsored unions.

The existence of a centralized organization made it unnecessary to build a unified organization from below. It facilitated instantaneous control from above, and those who would have desired to oppose the centralization of unions were at a disadvantage, both from a psychological and a power point of view. As it happened, at the time of Czechoslovakia's liberation, there were no vocal opponents to the unification of the unions.

The war had helped to break down the political and ideological barriers among the rank and file of the labor movement, to whom working-class unity had never lost its practical appeal. Now, when official differences between socialist parties tended to dwindle, and circumstances demanded solidarity, there was no reason why the workers' movement should once again split into quarreling factions. The workers were fully conscious of the fact —or if not, their leaders forcefully reminded them of it—that the lack of unity had cost them dearly in the past. They were determined not to repeat their mistakes, especially since the prospects of rising to a ruling position in the country were excellent, provided they remained closely knit.

The mere mood for unification does not explain why the Communists should benefit from it instead of the Social Democrats, who—after all—had been the stronger of the two Marxist parties before the war. The upsurge of pro-Communist sentiment is not easy to explain in rational terms. As one able Czech political observer put it, the workers may not have known much about Communist ideology; there could be no question, however, that emotionally they were in favor of the Communists. To them, as to many others in the country, Communism looked like the wave of the future. It held out the promise of fulfilling long-sought social and economic gains. The Party was buoyant, young, and dynamic, whereas the Social Democrats could not shake off the stigma of lassitude and old age. There was also the question of available leaders.

The losses in trade-union leadership suffered during the war affected the Social Democrats more seriously than the Communists. A particularly severe blow was the death of Antonin Hampl, long-time chairman of the party and head of the metalworkers' union. Along with him, the entire leadership of the union, the largest and most militant one, was decimated by the Nazis. By contrast, Antonin Zapotocky, the senior Communist trade-union leader, survived a six-year stretch in concentration camps; and, from the depths of the U.S.S.R., reappeared Josef Kolsky (he was flown to Prague from Moscow immediately after the liberation), who had once been a leader of the Communist metalworkers in Czechoslovakia, and who had long experience at the headquarters of the Red International of Trade Unions in Moscow. Kolsky became organizational secretary of the trade unions. The absence of outstanding Social Democratic leaders simplified the Communists' task, for they could easily steal the limelight from lesser union officials, the more so as the latter looked for guidance to the ardently pro-Communist leadership of their party, which did not encourage them to assert themselves against the Communists.

The Communists moved quickly and efficiently to seize control of trade-union headquarters and, from this vantage, shaped the structure of the unions and delineated their fundamental policies.

Structurally, the unions were tightly centralized, so as to permit the greatest possible concentration of power in a small group of leaders. The Central Council of the Unions (Ustredni Rada Odboru—URO), consisting of 120 members, was the general staff of the workers' movement. (The Council included 94 Communists, 18 Social Democrats, 6 National Socialists and 2 representatives of the People's Party.) This large and unwieldy body met only once every three months. Day-to-day business was carried on by a smaller body of 40 members, URO's presidium, which was headed by a chairman, Antonin Zapotocky, and a secretary-general, Evzen Erban.* Their authority was unlimited.

Assisting them in policy formulation were seven functional commissions—for organizational, social-political, economic, financial, cultural, public-relations, and factory-militia matters. These commissions were executive and administrative. They implemented URO policy.

Under this impressive superstructure, the unions were geographically organized. They had regional centers (Krajska Od-

---

*Erban was a Social Democrat who had not been outstanding in his party before the war. He had been an official of the German-sponsored unions during the war and then an ardent "left winger." His choice for the secretary-generalship, instead of any number of lesser Social Democratic union organizers of long standing in the party and the workers' movement, revealed what sort of Social Democrat the Communists regarded most suitable for elevation to high office.

borova Rada—KOR), district centers (Okresni Odborova Rada—OOR), and local and enterprise groups. Local groups functioned in communities where no industrial installation was large enough to have an independent trade union, i.e., none had more than twenty employees. A pyramidal structure—rapidly built up and staffed—based on a geographic rather than an industrial principle was the most efficient way to assure the unions of a single voice, since union organizations from top to bottom represented all the workers. In addition to contributing to the unity of the trade-union movement, the geographic principle of organization also tended to strengthen the over-all influence in the workers' movement of the more radical trades (metalworkers and miners), as against white-collar employees and others who might have inclined toward a moderate orientation.

The geographic pyramid was supplemented by a functional structure, patterned on the traditional industrial type of organization. There were twenty-one industrial unions representing the major trades and professions (metal, mining, transportation, teachers, etc.). These (industrial) unions, however, were being developed very slowly.[1] The sphere of their autonomous functions was not clearly defined and they were in every respect subsidiary to the over-all operations of geographic units. Industrial unions were in fact integral parts of the all-union organization. URO had the prerogative to create and abolish industrial unions at will. It appointed their leading officials and controlled their finances.

The relations of the revolutionary trade-union movement with the government were very close, and in principle, as well as in practice, the unions were staunch supporters of the National Front and its program. At the same time, not being directly represented in the government or the National Front, URO reserved for itself the right to criticize policy. In practice, it availed itself of this right sparingly, and then only to lambaste reactionary opposition to measures which the unions and the Communist Party, either separately or jointly, sponsored and supported. It was apparent to all that URO's attitude toward the government was far from subservient. On the contrary, the legal prerogatives of URO to participate in policy formulation were so extensive, and the pressure it could bring to bear on policy-making and administrative organs so great that, in some respects, it was superior in power to the government.

The unions were legally entitled to make their wishes known to the legislative and executive authorities[2] and to "send . . . workers' representatives to all larger bodies performing a public function."[3] The authorities, in turn, were under legal obligation to assist the trade unions in the realization of their tasks and to grant them, without charge or fee, such information as they needed to perform their duly constituted functions.

URO exerted decisive influence on the two Ministries primarily concerned with labor and industrial matters (the Ministries of Industry and of Labor–Social Welfare), and it also made its weight felt in the Ministries of Finance, Internal Trade, and Transportation. URO was instrumental in drafting the decrees of nationalization. It was represented in all economic planning bodies and was consulted on the appointment of managers in nationalized enterprises.

The far-reaching prerogatives of URO "at the top" were duplicated by the legal rights of works councils (zavodni rada) "at the bottom."

Immediately after the liberation, when centralized state authority was lacking and even centralized channels of control in the unions had not been established, hastily formed revolutionary works councils ruled supreme in industrial and commercial installations throughout the country. They purged traitors, assumed managerial functions, and took over responsibility for safeguarding property against sabotage and destruction by enemy agents or traitors.[4] Since their members in many cases served in local National Committees, the concentration of power in their hands was considerable. The works councils were quickly confirmed by decree, in which their extensive rights were also defined.[5] Accordingly, works councils exercised far-reaching supervisory functions over the management, although they were specifically prohibited from exercising managerial functions. Works councils had to be supplied by the management with detailed reports about the day-to-day operations of the plant, its financial status, its business transactions, and its future plans. The council had a right to be consulted on any contemplated change in administration or production, and it could offer suggestions on its own initiative, which the management could not dismiss without sufficient and good reason. The councils had access to company books and files at all times. They could examine them and, if they so desired, could request an expert audit by a competent public organ at the company's expense. Naturally, the councils had extensive rights, so far as the protection of workers' interests, the hiring, firing, and allocation of labor within the plant were concerned. Among other things, the works councils passed on the moral qualifications and national reliability of prospective employees. Extensive as these paper rights were, they were surpassed in practice.

The works councils were not actually trade-union bodies. They were the representatives of all workers—organized and unorganized—by virtue of their spontaneous origin and the functions assigned to them. Thus the problem of dovetailing their actions with those of the trade unions arose. It was obvious that they had to be brought in line with the union structure, and subjected to the control of URO. The existence in individual plants of two bodies representing the workers contained seeds of danger.

As quickly as was practicable, the unions reached out to dominate the works councils and to transform them into obedient tools. The trade unions had jurisdiction over the finances of the councils, and representatives of the regional trade-union councils were entitled to sit in on works-council meetings. Most important of all, however, was the method of selection of works-council candidates. The enterprise unit of ROH appointed an election committee, which drew up one slate of candidates.[6] The slate was then presented to the workers for approval. A four-fifths majority was necessary to elect the slate as presented. Failing that, the election committee was asked to draw up a new list. The power to select works-council representatives assured the trade unions of commanding influence in the councils. As a rule, several members of the executive committee of the enterprise unit of ROH also held office in the works council. Only the chairman of the trade-union unit was prohibited from holding office in both groups. In this manner, the possibility of developing the councils into competing organs with the unions was forestalled. In fact, the councils became effective go-betweens for the unions and the management, and served as instruments of control over the unorganized workers.

Turning the works councils into trade-union appendages was not accomplished without political struggle. Although the non-Marxist parties conceded the supremacy of the Communists in the unions, they sought to salvage a measure of influence among the workers. Therefore, they proposed schemes for equal representation in works councils based on political party affiliation. (a principle that was theoretically applied in National Committees), or proportionate representation based on such affiliation. Under the second alternative, the Communists would not have been deprived of a dominating position in the councils, but the other parties would have secured at least respectable representation, which was denied them under the Communist-sponsored election procedure.

The Communist view prevailed. The only concession to the democratic parties was the high percentage of votes required to carry the officially sponsored slate. This gave the workers an opportunity to express disapproval. Actually, the official slate was carried in 70 per cent of the plants on the first ballot, and in 20 per cent of the enterprises on the second ballot. Only in 10 per cent of the cases was there enough resistance to dictation to force a selection of works-council representatives by more democratic procedure.

In addition to its far-reaching legal prerogatives, ROH possessed a first-rate striking arm in the factory militia. Armed "factory guards" were formed at the time of Czechoslovakia's liberation. Their existence was justified especially in the border areas inhabited by Germans, where the need for physical protection of industrial installations was real. However, these armed units were not disbanded after conditions became stabilized and the threat of enemy sabotage receded. On the contrary, the trade-union leadership viewed them as nuclei of a future people's army and defended them as essential to the development of the new people's democratic system.[7] Because of pressure by the democratic parties, the militia was never accorded legal status and performed no public functions after its initial tour of duty—guarding industrial installations—was completed. But its units remained in active reserve, its supply of arms was not taken away, and it continued to be centrally directed. Its usefulness was fully demonstrated in the only instance in which it was really needed, and for which it was being held in readiness, the time of Communist seizure of power.

The vast powers with which ROH and its leading organ, URO, were endowed enhanced the attractiveness of the unions. They were in an excellent position to safeguard workers' interests, and to invoke sanctions and discriminate against those who did not go along with the spirit of the times. As a result, union membership was virtually mandatory, especially for industrial workers. Any thought of setting up a rival organization was futile. ROH was recognized by law as the sole trade-union organization in the country.

In May, 1945, there were 565,000 union members; by the end of the year, there were 1,442,000 unionists. In December, 1946, membership stood at 1,878,000, and at the end of the following year, the rolls stood at 2,249,976.[8] By contrast—according to official figures—only 5,500 members withdrew from ROH during this period.

Trade-union policy concerning the workers was based on a carrot-and-stick approach, with the carrot prevailing over the stick. Occasionally, pressure and even terror were invoked in order to ensure solidarity and to prevent defection. By and large, however, the union leadership relied for appeal on the tangible benefits it could offer. In addition to catering to the material interests of the working people, the unions were instrumental in providing legal protection for them, against prosecution for acts of violence committed in quest of Czechoslovakia's liberation. Loose interpretation of motives prompting acts of violence in fact served to legalize many transgressions of the law and of normally accepted standards of decency, particularly in the immediate post-liberation period.[9]

The knowledge that the unions had ample means to protect them, and that they were in fact a privileged caste, made the workers bolder in their actions and more radical in their demands.

ROH was a powerful organization, second only to the Communist Party. Indeed, at times it seemed that ROH overshadowed even the Party. Actually, this was not so. Despite the assiduously maintained fiction of ROH's independence, there was no evidence that the Communist leadership of ROH ever seriously challenged the Party, although identification with institutional interest appeared to take hold of Communist trade unionists, and divergent viewpoints were aired in closed meeting. Outwardly, however, no breach showed in the relations between Communists active in the Party and in the trade unions.

The firm hold on trade-union leadership contributed to the Party's strength and gave it unusual freedom to maneuver. URO representatives in government bodies and public corporations were nothing more or less than active supporters of Communist policies. But URO's official exemption from government responsibilities made it a pressure group of unsurpassed value. It permitted the unions to display greater radicalism and to mobilize the masses on behalf of the Communist Party on occasions when the Party, because of its policy of moderation, found it inconvenient or possibly embarrassing to resort to harsh tactics. For example, the unions staged a number of street demonstrations in support of national and local issues in which the Party had an interest. The unions also kept alive the question of additional nationalization—after the basic decrees had been enacted—while the Party professed disinterest in extending the public sector of the economy. Finally, the trade unions were prominently employed by the Party during the coup d'état.

Other Mass Organizations

Other mass organizations did not lend themselves as readily to Communist domination as did the unions, nor were they as important. The difficulties faced in the quest for control of these organizations varied. In none of them was the social base of the membership as favorable as in the unions. In none of them was there as advantageous a situation from an organizational point of view. The Germans had not been obliging enough to prepare the ground for unification in every field. Moreover, the non-Marxist parties were more firmly entrenched in other organizations, so that they could offer more effective resistance to techniques of conquest from within.

The United Farmers' Association (Jednotny Svaz Ceskoslovenskych Zemedelcu—JSCZ), for example, eluded outright Communist control, although Josef Nepomucky—a Communist—occupied the post of Secretary-General, and the Party itself attracted sizable peasant support. Nevertheless, a large number of independent farmers continued to adhere to the National Socialist and the People's parties, and in Slovakia to the Democratic Party. The greater ability of the non-Marxist parties to resist was apparent from the protracted parliamentary debate that delayed enactment of a law defining the status of the JSCZ. The Communists, hampered in the deployment of the full measure of their influence in the JSCZ, moved to circumvent it and established their own operational bases among the peasants. Under the auspices of the Ministry of Agriculture, farmers' commissions were established in every locality where land was to be distributed under the new reform bill. These commissions were auxiliary organs of the Ministry, helping with the implementation of the reform. Membership in them was limited to landless peasants and small farmers seeking land. The social composition of the commissions and the material interests of their members made for subservience to the Communist Party.

The unification of sport and gymnastic organizations made no progress beyond the establishment of a central council, in which various party-affiliated athletic organizations were represented. In practice, unification was effectively sabotaged, because the largest and most influential athletic organization, the Sokol, which obviously had to form the organizational base of the projected unified structure, was securely in the hands of the National Socialist Party. The Orel, another influential athletic organization, was, in turn, firmly controlled by the People's Party, which showed little enthusiasm for unification.

Youth groups presented still another type of problem. They were unified in 1945, when the Czech Youth Federation (Svaz Ceske Mladeze—SCM) was established. Initially, Communist influence in the SCM was considerable. But the principle of nonpartisanship—not honored in practice in any organization—was violated so brazenly in the SCM that the non-Marxist parties felt compelled to withdraw their membership in the spring of

1946. The National Socialists took the lead, restoring the independence of their party's youth movement in May of that year.[10]

From then on, the SCM, although parading under a national label, was in fact the youth organization of the Communist Party only with marginal Social Democratic support. Following the withdrawal of the non-Marxist parties, its popularity declined rapidly. The membership fell from 600,000 early in 1946, to 289,000 in January, 1948, and it was of limited usefulness as a proselytizing agent for the Party.

Concomitantly with the decline of the SCM, the Communists lost support among the university students, who had corporate membership in the SCM through the Association of University Students (Svaz Vysokoskolskeho Studentsva—SVS). Anti-Communist sentiment was especially marked in the second half of 1947. Its causes could not be accurately determined. It is likely that ideological considerations were not of primary significance. Rather, the students were inclined to react to intemperate attacks by Communists on the Ministry of Education and to the deprecatory views on culture and education expressed by Vaclav Kopecky, the Communist Minister of Information.

The trend of developments among university students heartened the democratic parties, who sought to interpret it as a harbinger of change in popular sentiment. For this reason, the student elections held at each university and in each faculty of learning in November and December of 1947 were publicized as if they were a major test of political strength. The psychological effects of the defeat of the Communists in these elections, and of the close cooperation between National Socialist and People's Party student groups, were not to be dismissed lightly. Nevertheless, it was probably clutching at straws to attribute much importance to the outcome of elections to student bodies. In such a struggle for power as was going on in Czechoslovakia, the role of university students was necessarily a modest one.

The failure of the Communists to secure a firmer hold on mass organizations other than the trade unions was in part a measure of their inability to make headway under circumstances that were not prevailingly favorable to them. It also reflected the possibilities that existed in Czechoslovakia for resisting Communist infiltration. So long as the trappings of democratic governmental processes were maintained—as was the case until February, 1948 —the Communists lacked the means to force their will against determined opposition. This does not imply that successful resistance was possible to an equal extent in all fields. It is likely that vigorous resistance would have precipitated a seizure of power sooner than it actually took place and without altering the final outcome. The inability of the Communists to line up every mass organization on their side hardly interfered with the implementation of their design. Only the Sokol possessed the means to challenge the Communists "in the street." But the Sokol was not geared to such a performance. It was neither armed, nor was its membership alerted to the possibility of acting as a political striking force.

The Economic Levers of Power

In Czechoslovakia, as in all other countries in Eastern Europe, land reform and nationalization served as economic levers that the Communists exploited to further their own political ends. Essentially, the Communist Party adopted sharply different attitudes toward these levers of change. It went easy on land reform, pressing for no more than a "national purge of Czech land," which met with popular approval. With regard to the nationalization of industry, it maintained a much tougher position.

AGRICULTURE. Communist agricultural policy before the coup reflected one of the major objectives of the Party, to maintain the closest possible class alliance between the proletariat and the peasantry or, in other words, to win as much peasant support for the Communist cause as possible.

To achieve this objective, twin approaches were chosen. On the one hand, the Party laid claim to the administrative instruments of control (Ministry of Agriculture), which in the past had proved to be a powerful means of extracting peasant support. On the other hand, it catered to peasant interests by pursuing a policy of moderation, which soft-pedaled "collectivization" both as an immediate and a long-term prospect.

The contribution of the Ministry of Agriculture to Communist successes among the peasantry has already been discussed. A considerable part of the credit for successes in rural districts must be assigned to the Party's moderation. The Party astutely took into account the economic and social realities of Czechoslovakia, which made land reform a far less urgent social question than it was in neighboring countries. As a result of land reform carried out after World War I, large estates had been partitioned, and only a small number of so-called "residual estates" remained. The crucial issue, therefore, was not to break the back of Czech and Slovak large landholders, who were few in number and who— deprived of their traditional political instrument (the Agrarian Party)—had no means of rallying. The important thing was to deprive Germans, Hungarians, and traitors of their holdings and to return such land to the Czech nation. Correspondingly, the land reform decrees issued on June 21, 1945, limited themselves to "confiscation without compensation" of land owned by these groups.

In this manner, some 2.4 million hectares of land in the Czech lands and 550,000 hectares in Slovakia became available for distribution.[11] Roughly half of this was farm land, the rest woodland, which was not divided among private owners. Farm land was quickly assigned in small lots to landless peasants and other claimants.* Such land hunger as existed was to a large extent satisfied. The fact that the land taken away from the Germans was not collectivized was interpreted as proof of the honest intentions of the Communists. It was difficult to realize, under the circumstances, that the Communists were merely biding their time until the next round, when they would start making inroads on the land holdings of Czech and Slovak kulaks as well.

Meanwhile, the Communists succeeded in strengthening their alliance with the lower peasantry, whose interests they purported to represent, and the kulaks as well. The latter were thankful that their holdings had not been affected. To be sure, the Communists' moderation was of limited duration. Late in 1946, they began agitating for a revision of the first (prewar) land reform,

---

*Three-fourths of the land distributed was in the border areas of Bohemia and Moravia, where 157,595 claimants received 937,745 hectares, an average of 6 hectares each. In the interior of the Czech lands, 65,909 claimants obtained 99,535 hectares. Many of these were garden plots and building sites allocated to workers who lived in rural communities. In Slovakia, 79,976 claimants were given 183,463 hectares, an average of a little over 2 hectares each.

seeking a reduction in size of farms that exceeded the legal limit (150 hectares) set by the prewar reform. This move was subsequently followed by a demand for a 50-hectare (about 130 acres) limit on land holdings. These demands were incorporated in the so-called Hradec program, formulated in April, 1947, which became one of the centers of controversy between the Communist Party and the democratic parties in the stormy period preceding the coup.

INDUSTRY. Nationalization, surprisingly, proved to be a more controversial issue than land reform, because the Communists, together with the Social Democrats, confronted the other parties with a far more comprehensive scheme than had been implicit in the agreement reached at Moscow. The tactic here was to take advantage of the workers' tremendous revolutionary excitement to nationalize a wide sector of the economy by executive decree before a Provisional Assembly was convoked. The Communists were afraid that delay would be prejudicial to their plans.[12] They were well aware of the possibilities for procrastination offered by the cumbersome machinery of parliamentary government, and did not cherish the idea of protracted debate over nationalization of small and medium plants, banks, and insurance companies.

Official responsibility for drafting the nationalization decrees rested with the Ministry of Industry, headed by Bohumil Lausman. Although he was a Social Democrat, his views on nationalization did not differ from those of his Communist colleagues.[13] Nevertheless, the Communists took no chances and secured powerful representation on the central working commission, which drew up the decrees. One of their members, Engineer Rada, was Vice-Chairman. But in addition to direct representation, which each party had, Communists participated in the guise of trade-union representatives and emissaries of the Central Association of Industry (Ustredni Svaz Prumyslu—USP). The trade unions had eight representatives in the commission, among whom were such influential Communists as Gustav Kliment and Ludvik Frejka. Frejka did not represent the unions at all. He headed the economic commission of the Communist Party and was Klement Gottwald's personal economic adviser. The National Socialist and People's parties also had one representative each in the trade-union delegation. But they were "left-wingers" who did not truly reflect the sentiment of the party leadership.[14] The Central Association of Industry was a "socialist" variant of the National Association of Manufacturers. Instead of being the spokesman of private manufacturers, it was an auxiliary organ of the government, entrusted with important controlling and directing functions over private industrial enterprises. Its chairman and the presidium were appointed by the Ministry of Industry and included two trade-union representatives (Jaroslav Hlavacek and Otakar Mrazek). The USP had two delegates on the working commission, Otakar Mrazek and Milan Reiman, a Communist close to Antonin Zapotocky. Reiman was the Secretary-General of the USP.[15]

The commission, which began working on July 18, 1945, presented a finished draft of the decrees six weeks later. At this point there was a delay. The non-Marxist parties attempted to bottle up the decrees in the government long enough to permit the convocation of a Provisional National Assembly. President Benes, in turn, was reported to favor less extensive and more gradual nationalization. At the same time, he was showing signs of displeasure with continuing government by decree, and rumor had it that he seriously thought of refusing to sign any more decrees until parliamentary government was restored.[16]

The decrees were held up for almost two months while the Communists and the trade unions showed increasing restiveness. Finally, the "Marxist bloc" prevailed, and the decrees were signed by the President, on October 25, 1945. They marked the end of government by decree and also the culmination of the first stage of the national and democratic revolution. The Communists were not able to ram all of their demands through the government. They had to compromise on the principles that were to govern the organization and administration of nationalized enterprises. What they accomplished was to force the adoption of a package deal including banks and insurance companies. Moreover, the scope of nationalization was so wide as to give the public sector of the economy decisive preponderance over private enterprise.

Altogether, 3,119 industrial installations were nationalized (16.4 per cent of the total), comprising 61.2 per cent of the country's industrial labor force.[17] The number of employees served as a basic criterion for nationalization. The limit above which all plants were nationalized varied from one industry to another, the lowest figure being 150, and the highest 500.

Having achieved their basic objectives in the economic field, the Communists espoused a moderate attitude toward nationalization. They professed satisfaction with the results and claimed to have no further intentions of making inroads on private enterprise. To affirm their honorable intentions, they included a pledge of "no additional nationalization" in the official program of the government created by Klement Gottwald after the general election in 1946.[18]

Nationalization was merely the beginning of systematic guidance of the economy. On January 1, 1947, a Two-Year Economic Plan was inaugurated to speed industrial recovery and to set the stage for more comprehensive long-range planning. The Plan had been worked out by a government commission under the chairmanship of Klement Gottwald.[19]

Meanwhile, the Communists entrenched themselves in the administration of nationalized industrial enterprises. Members of the Party held the post of director in 35 per cent of the individual enterprises. They served as deputy directors in the remaining ones, and had almost monopolistic control over sections and departments responsible for wages and personnel. In the central administration of nationalized industries, divided into eleven general directorates under the jurisdiction of the Ministry of Industry, the Communists had two directors-general (in charge, respectively, of mining, and the combined iron, steel, and machine industries—key branches of the national economy), and seven deputy directors-general. Four directors-general were Social Democrats, two were National Socialists, and three had no party affiliations.[20]

The substantial control they had achieved in nationalized industrial branches and the preponderance of the nationalized sector of the economy over the capitalist sector did not prevent the Communists from raising new demands for the curtailment of private enterprise as a part of their final bid for power.

Propaganda

Propaganda is an extremely important weapon in the arsenal of a totalitarian party. Given the gradualist nature of the Communist Party's seizure of power, propaganda acquired unusually great significance. Before touching on the substantive aspects of Communist propaganda, it might be well first to appraise the general status of freedom of expression and the related issue of the relative access of political parties to the mass media. The picture that unfolds is a curious one.

In some ways, there was greater freedom of expression between 1945 and 1948 than at any other time in the history of Czechoslovakia. For example, there was no formal censorship of any kind of the contents of either the periodical or nonperiodical press. In other ways, there were obvious restrictions, such as the ban on the publication of newspapers by private individuals. It must be noted, however, that all political parties concurred in this type of restriction. Book publishing and distribution were free of any restriction, and private enterprise in this realm flourished as never before. Literary tastes, always strongly West-oriented, had undergone no change, and Communist nonperiodical literature enjoyed a low degree of popularity.

In the more important realm of mass communications, the Communists held a decisive edge over their opponents. They controlled the Ministry of Information. In addition, the literary and propaganda output of the major mass organizations for the most part faithfully toed the Party line. Such formal advantages were supplemented and accentuated by informal arrangements of equal, if not greater, importance, which substantially restricted the area of free discussion and divested freedom of expression of much of its meaning. Certain topics—principally, the Soviet Union, Soviet political leaders, Czechoslovakia's relations with the U.S.S.R., and Czechoslovak foreign policy—could not be treated critically. These restrictions grew out of the political situation. Their observance was in part due to self-imposed discipline by the democratic parties, whose leaders, ever motivated by caution and a desire to avoid clashes with the Communists, kept the editors of their respective papers on tight reins. (The restraint on democratic editors and journalists, imposed by their own party bosses, revealed a grievous deficiency of an exclusively political press.) On the rare occasions when a discordant voice was heard in the chorus, the Communists, or the Soviet press itself, quickly moved to intimidate the critic, accusing him of inciting unrest and serving the reaction.

The situation before the coup was vividly illustrated by the case history of *Obzory (Horizons)*, a People's Party weekly that was unusually forthright and violated the tacitly accepted code of conduct by criticizing the Soviet Union. As a result, Vaclav Kopecky, the Communist Minister of Information, attempted to revoke *Obzory's* license, but he was voted down in the cabinet, and the periodical continued to appear.[21] Soon after this victory, however, the People's Party removed the editors of *Obzory* and directed the entire staff to tame its attacks. The periodical remained more outspokenly anti-Communist than other journals, but the chastisement caused the loss of a considerable number of readers and diminished its effectiveness.

Still, *Obzory* irritated the Kremlin sufficiently to elicit a strong rebuke in the fall of 1947, when it was accused in *Slavjane* (the publication of the all-Slav Committee in Moscow) of printing tendentious stories inimical to the U.S.S.R. *Slavjane* charged that through a special selection of articles from the Anglo-American reactionary press, *Obzory* attempted to show the Czechoslovak public that Soviet foreign policy was imperialistic. "This," said *Slavjane*, "proves that *Obzory* and its editor-in-chief, Ivo Duchacek, are working against the Soviet Union, and against friendly relations between Czechoslovakia and the Soviet Union." In elaboration, *Slavjane* went on to say:

> The Soviet people are convinced that the groups of ill-disposed reactionaries do not represent the Czechoslovak nation and that they will not succeed in destroying the solid friendship between the Soviet Union and Czechoslovakia. But the Soviet people cannot help noticing the fact that obstinate slanderers and enemies of Soviet-Czechoslovak friendship . . . unfortunately continue their work . . . in other newspapers as well. One cannot continue to harm the interests of the Czechoslovak Government . . . without punishment.

The implications of the criticism were clear, and the Communist press did not fail to exploit the issue.[22]

The substance of Communist propaganda was determined by the Party's avowed aims to build majority public opinion around itself. Foisting conceptual changes on the nation, or alienating by adverse propaganda any large stratum of the population, would have been inconsistent. On the contrary, expediency demanded that the mood and disposition of the greatest possible number of people be taken into account and that propaganda be designed to facilitate identification with one or another facet of the Party's platform. To achieve this goal, Communist propaganda displayed amazing versatility. It played on emotions, fears, beliefs, hopes, and aspirations. It exploited the persistent fear of a revival of German strength and aggression and turned to its own advantage the existing apprehension about Soviet intentions, as well as the strong residue of friendship toward Russia.

Revolutionary slogans were played down, and the Party piously professed to believe in peaceful evolution toward socialism. Insinuations—no matter how timidly uttered—that the Communists really stood for revolution, class war, and proletarian dictatorship were met with rebuttals reflecting hurt indignation.[23] The Communists repeatedly emphasized that, in Czechoslovakia, "all the prerequisites for a peaceful transition to socialism" existed, and asserted that "experience has shown and the classics of Marxism-Leninism have taught us, that there is more than one way to socialism."[24] By the same token, they did not advocate slavish emulation of the first socialist state, the U.S.S.R., although they naturally held it up as a model worth following. But far greater stress was placed on the specific "Czechoslovak way to socialism."[25]

The Communists did not deny their adherence to and belief in Marxist-Leninist theory.[26] They affirmed its superiority over other philosophical systems. But they invoked Marxism-Leninism primarily in its most innocent form—as an infallible guide to the proper analysis of the course of history and not as a revolutionary theory. For exegesis, the Party turned to Benes, rather than to Lenin and Stalin.

The Party strove to erase any lingering remembrance of its negative stand toward the First Republic and to establish itself firmly as the standard-bearer of Czech national tradition. It professed always to have been "a national party in the true sense of the word, because we [sic] have forever been linked with the popular roots of the nation. Only the traitors of our time declared us antinational."[27] To lend substance to its claim, the Party drew attention to the stand it took in 1938, just before, and at the time of, Munich, and pointed to its war record, omitting any mention of its behavior from 1939 to 1941. It eulogized its dead heroes as no other party did, and sought to transform them into true national martyrs. At the same time, by inference, it took credit for all of Czechoslovakia's fallen patriots.

The Communists associated themselves with the outstanding political, cultural, and national symbols—both ancient and more recent—that were cherished by the Czech people. Identification with the Hussite warriors and reformers was an old device. But now they went much further. The Eighth Congress of the Party, held in March, 1946, was described as "the most beautiful realization of traditional Czech humanist politics."[28] Concomitantly, they played down the bitter controversies they once had with T. G. Masaryk, and described themselves as his spiritual heirs in "a historical epoch that transcended the scope of his ideas," implying that Masaryk, were he alive, would "go with" the Communists.[29] They used Benes even more brazenly, turning to him for exegesis time and again, and invoking the moral sanction of his words. They did not stop far short of monopolizing Benes as a patron saint. Among other things, his picture adorned the wall next to Gottwald's at the Party Congress in 1946.[30]

This indirect but open exploitation of Benes' authority was one of the anomalies of Czech political life after the war. In deference to the President's desire, the political parties agreed not to involve him in partisan struggles. They agreed not to bring his name into the electoral campaign. (By the same token, they also refrained from criticizing Benes.) In this manner, the democratic parties—especially the National Socialist Party, which had a legitimate claim to such benefits as might be derived from close association with Benes, who had been a member before 1938—were deprived of a major pillar of support. When the National Socialists attempted to suggest that they were Benes' party, in order to attract voters, the Communists immediately accused them, with righteous indignation, of violating the solemn agreement of the National Front.[31]

In addition to manipulating theoretical and real symbols, the Communists displayed a violent national chauvinism that no party could surpass. They carried the torch of Pan-Slavism higher than anyone. To some extent, their patriotism was genuine. It did not have to be artificially inculcated in the rank and file, and even the leaders could be reasonably expected to share in the general hatred of the national enemy. The same, perhaps in a more moderate fashion, held true of Pan-Slavism. But the Communists managed to make a special virtue of a sentiment common to the vast majority of the people. They, rather than other parties, identified land reform as "a final vindication of the indignities suffered by the Czechs after the Battle of the White Mountain [in 1620, when Czech independence was destroyed to stay under Austrian overlordship for 300 years.]"[32] Again, they coined such slogans as "Feierabend exported wheat [to Germany], we export Germans." (Feierabend was a former Agrarian leader who went abroad in 1940, having served briefly in the Czech puppet government set up by the Germans. He ultimately joined the National Socialists, and although he was not permitted to hold public office, he was singled out by the Communists as a living symbol of "the reaction" that allegedly held the National Socialists in its vise.)[33]

Meanwhile, the Communists painstakingly cultivated the non-proletarian strata, with whom they wished to remain in close alliance. The peasants were, by definition, a primary target. The general approach taken toward agricultural problems, which in itself was reassuring, was supplemented by subtle and persuasive propaganda to the effect that instead of reducing the kulaks to the status of agrarian laborers, the Communists were raising the agrarian proletariat to the level of the kulak.[34] A similar approach was used on tradesmen (artisans) and shopkeepers. Any design on nationalizing small trade establishments and shops was disavowed. Elaborate statistics were published, showing the vitality of small trade establishments and their importance for the country's economy. Rudolf Slansky proclaimed that "the Communists respect and will continue to respect the private property of all those who have come by it through hard work. . . . They will not only respect, but will defend such property. Any other assertion is a lie, and such lies are spread by those who would want to return to conditions in which cartels, with their pirating policy, were annihilating thousands of tradesmen and shopkeepers."[35]

Klement Gottwald, Antonin Zapotocky, Antonin Zmrhal (the Communist Minister of Internal Trade in 1946 and 1947), and Josef Horn, chairman of the trades commission in the Party's secretariat, gave repeated assurances that, under socialism, tradespeople would "obtain the same rights granted to all other working people"; they would at last know security in sickness and in old age and would have protection against the ravages of misfortune.[36]

Soothing words were found for the intelligentsia, despite some distressing overtones of intolerance. The official Communist cultural program admitted having a "strong Eastern orientation," but did not recommend apish imitation of the Soviet Union. It merely urged a better acquaintance with Soviet cultural achievements. It took issue with objective art and culture and claimed that all art is tendentious (utilitarian). It asked that the nation's culture "should be democratic, popular, socially progressive, and national in form as well as substance." It ruled out "socialist culture" for the moment, because "the time [for it was] not yet ripe."[37]

Finally, the Party professed to be for "freedom of conscience and religious belief, so long as religion is not used for political purposes."[38] Before the general election of 1946, the Communists actually obtained endorsements from Catholic priests; these were prominently featured in the Party press.[39]

The image of the Communist Party that was presented to the Czechoslovak public could not fail to allay suspicion and attract adherents. It is, of course, impossible to determine the exact share of propaganda in the Party's success at the polls in 1946. But both the National Socialist and People's parties commented plaintively that the Communists' electoral program was identical with theirs, and thus took the wind out of their sails.[40] Under circumstances in which other factors also favored the Communist Party, its political opponents were indeed hard pressed to find effective means of counteracting the appeal of the Communists.

Encroaching on premises traditionally reserved for liberal democratic or reform socialist parties was the outstanding feature of Communist propaganda before 1948. It was a distressing development. It constituted a successful invasion of the inner fort-

ress of democracy. Its implications transcended purely local interest. The tactics of appropriating liberal slogans and identifying
with popular and meaningful national symbols—tactics characteristic of Soviet foreign policy—have been adopted by Communist parties everywhere. By stealing the thunder of liberalism,
the Communists not only attract untold numbers of supporters,
but cheapen and undermine the integrity of liberal beliefs. In
either case, the cause of freedom suffers a serious setback.

10. THE REVOLUTION IN THE BALANCE: THE GENERAL ELECTION AND POLITICAL SKIRMISHING

THE GENERAL election, held on May 26, 1946, a little over a year after Czechoslovakia was liberated, attracted unusual interest. It was the first such test of public opinion in eleven years, and the first genuine opportunity the nation had to express itself freely, without fear of reprisals, on the many changes the postwar government had introduced. It was more than a mere contest among the political parties. Rightly or wrongly, politicians viewed it as a test of the government and the National Front, and looked expectantly to the election to clear a tense political atmosphere.

The electoral campaign was long and arduous. Although all parties agreed to make it a clean one, they could not desist from vituperation. The Communists mobilized the powerful means at their disposal to persuade the voters of an impending Communist landslide and thus to induce them to jump on the bandwagon.

The other parties fought vigorously, in spite of the more modest means at their disposal. While their chief opponent was the Communist Party, they did not fight it with equal zeal, nor did they reserve all their venom for it. The National Socialists and the Social Democrats were especially bitter rivals. At times it seemed that the chief issues were being fought out between these two contenders, with the result that nothing like a coherent anti-Communist electoral coalition developed.

The elections themselves were free and unfettered. An incident that threatened to cast a shadow over them was averted at the last minute. Shortly before election day, it became known that the Soviet command planned to execute large-scale troop movements from Austria to Poland, through Moravia, at the time of the Czechoslovak election. This projected maneuver bore the earmarks of intimidation. The government issued an urgent plea to the Russians to cancel or postpone the movement of troops. The plea was heeded.

The Results of the Election

The election results confirmed the leading role of the Communist Party and marked a high point in its popularity. The Party polled a commanding plurality, receiving 38 per cent of the national vote, or nearly double the amount of its nearest competitor, the National Socialist Party. (Tables 6, 7, 8, and 9.) A breakdown showed an uneven regional distribution in electoral support, making for even greater strength than the over-all results would have indicated. The Communists scored particularly heavily in Bohemia, the most Western, largest, most populous, and most densely industrialized province. Here, they received 43.3 per cent of the total vote and, together with the Social Democrats, had a commanding majority of 58 per cent. In three of thirteen electoral districts, the Communists had a clear majority, and in two others, a near majority. They carried Prague by a narrow margin over the National Socialists.

In Moravia, their strength dropped to 34.5 per cent of the total vote, with the People's Party in second place with 27.6 per cent. In Slovakia, they suffered a major defeat, polling only 30.4 per cent of the vote, whereas the Democratic Party obtained a majority of 62 per cent. Defeat in Slovakia must have surprised the Communist leadership, which undoubtedly counted on a heavy vote there to give it leverage against the central government. However, the strong showing of the Party in the Czech lands largely obviated the necessity for reserve strength in Slovakia, and by simply reducing their hypertrophied interest in Slovak autonomous administration in favor of greater centralization of power in Prague, the Communists managed to compensate for the damage they had suffered.

The pattern of voting by provinces showed declining Communist strength in proportion to a declining rate of industrialization. This suggests that they derived their greatest support from industrial workers. So simple an explanation, however, is deceptive. For they also scored heavily in some preponderantly agricultural districts (Ceske Budejovice, Jihlava), and achieved their greatest success in the border areas that had been cleared of Germans. In the three border districts—Karlovy Vary, Usti nad Labem, and Liberec—where the heaviest movement of population had taken place, the Communists obtained, respectively, 52.2, 56.5, and 48.3 per cent of the vote. These results seemed to bear eloquent testimony to the success of Communist handouts.

Their total of 38 per cent was within one percentage point of the support secured by the Social Democratic Party in the election that followed World War I. This time, however, Social Democrats captured an additional 13 per cent of the vote, raising the "Marxist" total to 51 per cent.

A comparison between Communist and Social Democratic electoral strength provides some foundation for estimating the radicalization of political sentiment and the attractiveness of the Communist Party to sundry nonproletarian elements. In round figures, the Communists outdistanced the Social Democrats by a margin of three to one. In fact, the Social Democratic Party was the only party that did not receive a substantially greater absolute number of votes, compared to prewar figures. In districts where no major change in population took place, the Social Democratic vote approximated the 1935 figures to within one or two thousand, indicating a remarkable constancy of support. In two highly industrialized districts (Kladno and Plzen), however, the signs of the times became obvious. The Social Democrats lost heavily, especially in Plzen, where they gathered only 66,819 votes, compared with 108,251 in 1935. The Communist vote, on the other hand, increased elevenfold—from 14,403 (in 1935) to 160,124. In Kladno, a traditional Communist stronghold, the Social Democrats lost about 20 per cent of their prewar support, whereas the Communist vote increased fourfold. In other industrialized areas, the Social Democrats held their own, or improved their position slightly. In Moravska Ostrava, they gained about 13 per cent (from 75,664 to 86,255); in Brno they did even better, increasing the total of their votes from 60,861 (in 1935) to 74,223. Communist gains, however, were far greater even in these districts. In

Moravska Ostrava, the Communist vote jumped from 61,173, in 1935, to 151,668, and in Brno it rose spectacularly, from 43,468 to 174,518.

The temptation to overinterpret election returns is always great, and the pitfalls presented thereby are not easily avoided. Nevertheless, the 1946 figures for Czechoslovakia lend themselves to interesting speculation. The constancy of the Social Democratic vote does not necessarily mean the absence of defection of prewar supporters and a failure to attract new groups. However, an inescapable conclusion is that, in the Social Democratic Party, only marginal changes took place. Some of its proletarian supporters deserted it in favor of the Communists and a small number of new adherents were acquired. But the hard core of party stalwarts seemed to stand intact and unmoved. If this was true of the Social Democrats, the enormous gains registered by the Communists were a result of the capture of the greatest portion of those voters who had supported the now banned rightist parties. The nature of the Communist vote therefore held interesting implications for the future, since a large percentage of this vote could be assumed to be motivated by something other than identification with the philosophical tenets of Communism.

The general election—although discouraging for many democrats who had hoped for a less decisive Communist show of strength—confirmed the *status quo*. The National Front continued without basic alteration in policy or composition. As had been expected, the election cleared the political atmosphere. The major test of strength among political parties was over. The time had come to settle down to the peaceful reconstruction of the country's economy.

The Revolution Recedes

By the summer of 1946, some of the initial enthusiasm for Communism and the Communist Party had dissipated. Excesses of local officials, many of whom were recent converts, had taken their toll in good will. But disillusionment grew only haltingly, and the losses the Communists might have sustained in popularity were counterbalanced by the vested interest so many people had in the welfare of the Party. The revolution, however, had definitely come to a stop. The major social and economic objectives had been achieved, and the ardor of the people had spent itself.

A return to normalcy was not conducive to further rapid strides toward socialism, nor did it augur well for a significant improvement in the Communist power position. To disturb the rapidly consolidating political situation, artificial issues would be necessary. For the time being, the Party seemed either uninterested in or unable to mount a sustained offensive against the democratic forces. For a full year, between the summers of 1946 and 1947, the Communist Party once more appeared to have fallen victim to the corrupting influence of its environment.

For its lack of revolutionary zeal, the Party was reportedly subjected to severe criticism from Marshal Tito, who—then still a member-in-good-standing of the Soviet satellite community—urged a more rapid pace toward political monolithism and socialism.[1] Whether or not the Russians disapproved of the slow progress is not known, but some time after the coup, Gottwald felt compelled to excuse the gradualism of the Party by pointing to the success which it engendered. He stressed the need for "almost three years" of schooling of the people, in order to make them realize "what stood behind Zenkl, and Sramek, and Lettrich and Majer, and other representatives of political parties and groups who gradually passed over to the camp of the reaction."[2] The excuse offered by Gottwald was lame, for, especially during the second half of 1946 and the first half of 1947, the Communists did little to expose their enemies as tools of the reaction. The Communist political campaign was not stepped up until the summer and fall of 1947, although the Party averted the onset of complete political apathy. It made a number of attempts to increase tension, to attack democratic strongholds, and to elicit class strife, by pitting the workers against the bourgeoisie. None of these attempts was forceful enough to bring tangible results. Moreover, the Party carefully let the trade unions serve as its mouthpiece for radical demands.

The Ministry of Justice Under Fire

An integral part of the class struggle, which the Party fostered under a cloak of moderation, was a sustained attack on the administration of justice. Although it fought a running battle against the Ministry of Justice from 1945 until the coup in 1948, the significance of its crusade against the Ministry and the courts stood out most clearly in this political lull. Under the able direction of Jaroslav Stransky and his successor, Prokop Drtina, both National Socialists, the Ministry and the entire judicial apparatus maintained a high standard of impartiality and integrity. Even the special courts set up to preside over cases concerning collaboration and war guilt did not succumb to pressure or temptation to interpret the letter of the law in the spirit of the times, on the basis of revenge and class consideration. Almost automatically, the courts appeared as embodiments of conservatism, favoring the old order, or, what was the same thing, bent on obstructing the achievement of a new one.

The Communists based their attack on two counts: leniency toward war criminals, and bias in favor of the bourgeoisie in ruling on the disposition of a number of industrial plants confiscated by the state.

They showed concern over the implementation of the national purge, because they regarded it—and intended to use it—as an instrument of class warfare, serving to eliminate all manner of exponents of the old order. They were dismayed, therefore, at the large number of collaborationist charges (turned in by the Communist-controlled security organs) dismissed by the courts, and the light sentences imposed on even major offenders. The trial of the cabinet members of the Protectorate government brought the situation to a climax. The ministers were tried before the National Tribunal, and although they were found guilty, extenuating circumstances caused the court to impose relatively minor sentences. Three defendants were acquitted, two received suspended sentences, and four were given jail terms ranging from three years to life imprisonment.[3] (Unfortunately for the Communists, the puppet President, Emil Hacha, died long before the trial, and Emanuel Moravec, the only Minister in the collaborationist cabinet who was universally hated and who, therefore, might have been sentenced to death, escaped trial by committing suicide.)

The Communists tried to use this occasion to arouse public anger. Mass meetings of workers and partisans were organized, demonstrations were staged, and the government was deluged with telegrams and petitions demanding a review of the verdict.[4] The government, however, refused to overrule the court, and the synthetic nature of public expressions of indignation soon became apparent. The people were not inclined to act harshly against collaborators. The line between collaboration and opposition was at best a fuzzy one, and the majority of the nation was content to let well enough alone.[5]

The second issue that served as a platform for attacks against the judiciary concerned the adjudication of disputed property cases. The disposition of such property as was subject to nationalization was not questionable, but among the confiscates there were several hundred smaller industrial plants that were exempt. The Communist Party, through the intermediary of the trade unions, fought against returning these plants to their rightful owners, their heirs, or other claimants. But the courts insisted on investigating on its merits every case that came before them, and in a number of instances they ruled in favor of the individual claimant. Vigorous protest came from the trade unions, which averred that the interests of the working people were being crassly violated, but the verdict held, and the Communists were not yet ready to force the issue.

The Communists in Retreat

If the Communists scored no noticeable gains during this period, their power position also remained unchallenged. Ideally, the democratic parties should have utilized the relaxation in pressure to consolidate their positions, to agree on a common platform, and to press the attack on the Communists. They did none of these things. Their attitude was influenced by the illusions besetting many democratic politicians, that the Communists believed in parliamentary democracy.

In this period, too, Czech-Slovak relations became strained, and this development retarded—if it did not altogether prevent—efforts by democratic parties to work out a joint comprehensive program of action. The immediate cause of tension was the refusal of the government and the President to commute the death sentence imposed on Msgr. Jozef Tiso, the puppet President of the Slovak Republic, by a regional tribunal in Bratislava presided over by Igor Daxner. The verdict of the Slovak court was in sharp contrast with the leniency that a similar tribunal had shown toward members of the Protectorate government. Although Tiso's guilt was not in dispute, his status as a priest who had never been defrocked commended him for pardon. The Democratic Party was under great pressure from its numerous Catholic supporters to appeal to the authorities in Prague. But its pleas fell on deaf ears. The Czech parties stood together on this issue, regardless of their ideological differences, and the President was not inclined to show any clemency either. Msgr. Tiso was hanged on April 18, 1947.

The democrats could hardly be blamed for their failure to challenge the Communist Party successfully by parliamentary means. The parliamentary process is not well suited—as, indeed, it is not designed—to wrest power from a party that controls the physical instruments of repression and abides by the rule of law only conditionally. In this sense, the fate of the democratic parties was sealed from the very beginning of the revolution. Their negligence to do their utmost to mobilize public opinion in their behalf and to clarify the moral issues in the struggle between Communism and democracy is far more susceptible to censure.

Until the eve of the coup d'état, in February, 1948, the democratic parties concealed the seriousness of the underlying conflict between themselves and the Communists and conveyed an impression of over-all harmony, which did not exist. They were also given to periodic affirmations of their loyalty to the U.S.S.R. In this manner, they misled public opinion abroad and their followers at home. The democratic parties seemed to be fighting the Communists on individual rather than fundamental issues and thereby undermined themselves.

The Communist Party reached the nadir in its retreat early in July, 1947, when, along with other parties, it approved the acceptance of an Anglo-French invitation to attend preliminary discussions on the Marshall Plan. The government's affirmative decision was reversed at the direct request of Joseph Stalin. This incident effectively destroyed the fiction of the preferential treatment that many Czechs thought they were receiving from the U.S.S.R. It also marked a turning point in political developments in Czechoslovakia, leading, as it did, to increased activity on the part of the Communists and to a proliferation of anti-Communist actions as well.[6]

In Search of New Issues

It is impossible for an outside observer to know whether Stalin, in his talk with Gottwald—which preceded a formal meeting with the delegation of the Czechoslovak Government in Moscow, on July 8—admonished the Czechoslovak Communists for their lack of revolutionary zeal. At any rate, on Gottwald's return from Moscow, Communist propaganda shifted into a higher gear and adopted a more belligerent tone. This was surprising, as the summer months, during which the National Assembly was in recess, were usually marked by political inactivity. The purpose of increased propaganda efforts might have been merely to counteract the damaging effect of the rebuke suffered in Moscow. However, the end of the summer found the Party mounting a major political offensive. Matters were complicated by genuine economic difficulties then afflicting Czechoslovakia. A terrible drought caused widespread damage to crops and threatened famine. While the obvious and only practical solution was to acquire foodstuffs from the Soviet Union—which was done—the Communists seized the opportunity to focus attention on the country's class inequalities. They proposed a millionaire's levy to alleviate the plight of the peasants.* The plan was to impose a heavy surtax on all individuals with a salary or net worth of over 1 million Kcs. ($20,000 at the official rate of exchange). This proposal met with unanimous opposition in the cabinet and was defeated, whereupon the Communists set about mending some political fences. Their first target was the Social Democratic Party, with whom they renewed a formal working alliance.

Communists and Social Democrats

Publication, on September 12, 1947, of a document signed by three Communists and three Social Democrats (Fierlinger, Tymes, and Vilim), pledging a common approach of their respective parties to all significant political problems, struck the nation like a bombshell. The deal was negotiated surreptitiously —not even the executive committee of the Social Democratic Party was informed in advance. Like some other historic bombshells, the agreement backfired. It aroused the anger of the Social Democratic membership and stiffened the backbone of old, mod-

---

* Total loss in revenue was estimated at 10 billion Kcs.

erate party wheel horses, who had been pushed into the background. At the party's congress in November, an indignant and wrathful old guard, stirred to making fiery speeches from the rostrum abandoned three years before, pointed an accusing finger at Fierlinger and his young Slovak colleagues who had hurried to merge with the Communists in 1944.[7] The upshot was a resounding defeat for Fierlinger, and the elevation of Bohumil Lausman to the chairmanship of the party. Lausman himself was no moderate. His former behavior and close association with Fierlinger proved that. But he had apparently had second thoughts on political questions, as well as on issues involving fundamental tenets of human rights and freedom; as a result, he was more and more frequently associated with a moderate viewpoint. This made him acceptable to the old guard which did not feel it proper to turn back the clock entirely to the prewar era by proposing one of its own members for the chairmanship. While Lausman's election was not an irretrievable loss for the Communists (the problems of the Social Democratic Party were far from solved), it definitely meant that the partnership of the Marxist parties had deteriorated.

On political issues, the new Social Democratic leadership found itself increasingly in agreement with the democratic parties and ready to join forces with them. On social and economic issues, however, the Social Democrats could not relax their radical policies. They continued to cooperate closely with the Communists, and they concluded a number of specific agreements to that effect in the winter of 1947–48. Nor was the Social Democratic left wing content to accept its defeat. It retained considerable strength which it used to keep the duly elected leadership in check. It also began organizing within the party, in order to consolidate its position and to mount an attack to recapture control. The "left" created a six-member political directorate, a three-member political secretariat, and a three-member organizational secretariat, a separate faction in the executive committee of the party and in its parliamentary club. In January, 1948, the "left" began issuing a periodical, *Smer,* and formed a separate Social Democratic Club to provide itself with an institutional outlet.

Trouble in Slovakia

Meanwhile, the Communists were probing for weak points in

their opponents' armor. They soon found one, in the Slovak Democratic Party. Through the probing of the secret police, subversive activities were traced to the office of Jan Ursiny, Vice-Premier of the Slovak Democratic Party. Whatever Ursiny's personal guilt was, he had been imprudent, to say the least, in employing as personal secretary one Otto Obuch, who had been an assistant of the propaganda chief of the Slovak puppet government during the war and was still in contact with reactionary die-hards abroad.* Working in Ursiny's office, Obuch had easy access to secret state papers and, according to the charge against him, availed himself of this opportunity. The disclosure of such irregularities led to his arrest and to Ursiny's resignation.

This rift was widened by the discovery of an extensive espionage ring in Slovakia, financed by these same reactionary die-hards.[8] Two of the three Secretaries-General of the Slovak Democratic Party, Jan Kempny and Milos Bugar, were allegedly implicated in the plot. Conveniently, both were Catholics, and the purpose of centering the attack on them appeared to be to split the Catholic and Protestant components of the Democratic Party, thus weakening and discrediting it. Kempny's and Bugar's parliamentary immunity was suspended and proceedings against them were under way when other events intervened. This approach held out promising prospects, however, for at a meeting of the full executive committee of the Democratic Party, on November 22, 1947, the agreement that had been reached with representatives of Catholic interests in March, 1946, was voided, and a serious breach in the party seemed unavoidable.

In addition to these attacks on the Democratic Party, the Communists sought directly to reduce its influence in the Slovak provincial administration. In response to demands by impatient organizations of partisans (headed by the Communist Karol Smidke) and by the trade unions, a reorganization of the Slovak Board of Commissioners, in which the Democrats had a majority, was undertaken. So intent were the Communists on whittling down their opponents in Slovakia, that Gottwald himself, in his capacity as Premier, went to Bratislava, the capital, to settle the matter. He was only partially successful, for the Czech democratic parties, which really favored the general idea of cutting the Slo-

---

*Primarily Ferdinand Durcansky, a former high official in the Tiso government.

vak Democratic Party down to size, nevertheless could not associate themselves with its complete destruction. The Board of Commissioners was reorganized. The Democrats lost their majority, but the gains made by the Communists were not sufficient to put them in commanding position.

Finally, the Communists sought to alter the composition of the National Front by urging the formal admission of professional and interest groups. This effort, too, encountered resolute opposition from the democratic parties, and nothing came of it.

The stepped-up tempo of Communist attacks on their partners paralleled the sharp deterioration in East-West relations resulting from the decisively negative stand taken by the Soviet Government on the Marshall Plan. It is possible that there was a causal relationship between the deterioration of international relations and the worsening of political conditions in Czechoslovakia. Czechoslovakia was in an exposed position, vulnerable to Western influence and, as was demonstrated in July, 1947, its government was not unmindful of the true economic interests of the country. The founding meeting of the Cominform, held at Szklarska Poreba, Poland, in September, 1947, at which the spirit of the Communist international was revived at least in modified form, also spurred the Czech Communists to greater radicalism.[9]

At the same time, purely domestic considerations cannot be dismissed as the immediate causes of mounting Communist belligerence. Although the danger of an effective and solid anti-Communist front was remote, the possibilities for Communist maneuvering within the limits of parliamentary government were curtailed. To advance the cause of the Communist Party further, some new approach would have to be found. Only two alternatives seemed to be available: to gain a majority by constitutional means, or to prepare for a seizure of power. The tactics of the early fall of 1947 indicated that the first alternative, if not actually favored, had not been discarded by the Party leadership. As evidence, one can cite the nature of the campaign against the Slovak Democrats and a renewed Communist membership drive, intended to raise Party rolls to 1.5 million.

If domestic considerations were paramount in dictating the pace of Communist preparations, the late spring of 1948 loomed as a likely date for action. The term of the Constituent Assembly would then expire. With little more than half a year to go, the Constitution was not at all ready for presentation to the Assembly. The parties were still dickering about fundamental principles and preliminary clauses. A number of basic social and economic measures, which the Communists hoped to embody in the Constitution, were still tied up in committee. It was time to make haste. It is possible that the Communist high command, or at least a faction in it, became unduly sensitive to incipient changes in political alignments. This would explain the violent reaction of the Communist press to the outcome of the Social Democratic Congress.[10] Some Communists might have doubted the Party's ability to attain its avowed goal of winning the majority of the nation by constitutional means. Others might have been apprehensive lest the Party prove unable to carry out a coup d'état. In an atmosphere of mounting tension, the Communist Central Committee convened, on November 29, 1947, for its regular quarterly meeting to hear the reports of its chiefs.

11. THE COUP D'ÉTAT AND ITS ANTECEDENTS

THE KEYNOTE of the Communist Central Committee meeting was struck by Gottwald, who observed that the internal situation had become aggravated and warned that the Communists would not stand by idly, watching the "obstructionist tactics" of the other political parties, which had come under the sway of "reactionary elements."[1]

The battle lines drawn by Gottwald were clear, and his main argument was simple. The influence of the reaction in all non-Communist parties, including the Social Democratic, was growing. The National Socialist and People's parties were joining forces with the Slovak Democrats to protect subversive elements uncovered by the secret police. Moreover, the three non-Marxist parties were trying to exclude the broad strata of the population from the National Front. This, in Gottwald's interpretation, amounted to preventing the people from the exercise of their rightful prerogative to participate in deliberations of vital interest to them. The democratic parties were also declared guilty of violating the principles to which they had solemnly subscribed in 1945. By contrast, the Communist Party stood for honest constructive work and aimed to "win a majority of the nation in order to overcome all obstacles barring the way to permanent progress toward economic growth and a tranquil development of the Republic."[2]

According to Gottwald, the "reaction" sought to undermine the work of the government in order to precipitate a crisis, "which would lead to the creation of a government of experts." Such a move, he said, "would have to be evaluated as an attempt at a coup, an attempt for a reactionary overthrow of the government. It would be necessary to answer it appropriately, by smashing the reaction completely."[3] His detailed analysis of the plans of the reaction, and of the necessary response to it, strongly suggested the direction in which the Communist high command sought to steer events. This passage in the speech stands out because it appeared to be the signal for the opening of the final drive against the reaction. Two days before the coup, when a government crisis was an unavoidable certainty, the Communist Party's presidium issued a proclamation accusing the leaders of "some political parties" of plotting to "establish by antidemocratic and anticonstitutional means a nonparliamentary government of experts, which would wrest power from the people and would prepare antidemocratic elections in an atmosphere of political and economic chaos."[4] The wording of the announcement could not have been accidental. Its meaning was unmistakable. It called for the mobilization of the Communist apparatus to "give the necessary response."

Communists on the Attack

After the meeting of the Central Committee, the Party's more prominent spokesmen toured the country, repeating the essence of Gottwald's remarks. The Christmas holidays provided a temporary relaxation. But in January, 1948, the Communist offensive regained momentum. The Party, with an eye on the rapidly approaching general election, was vigorously recruiting members and giving much publicity to reported switches of allegiance to it from the National Socialist and People's parties. The Communist press became more belligerent. The activities of Communist *agents provocateurs* increased, and the Ministry of the Interior announced the discovery of a subversive reactionary plot at Most, in northwestern Bohemia.

The discovery of plots is standard procedure with the Communists. In this particular instance, it served a variety of purposes. It dramatized the "real danger" that threatened the "people's democratic regime." It helped to incriminate the National Socialist Party, the most formidable foe of the Communists in the Czech lands, and provided the Communists with ammunition to counteract a probable assault by the National Socialists, who had gathered imposing evidence about widespread use of Communist *agents provocateurs* and had managed to ascertain that several Communists had been involved in the preparation of a bomb plot against Ministers Zenkl, Drtina, and Masaryk, in September, 1947.

Late in January, Communist maneuvers conveyed an added sense of urgency. Just what caused a further acceleration of an already vehement campaign is not clear. It is possible that instructions were received from Moscow to bring Czechoslovakia safely into the Communist fold in the shortest possible time. These instructions might have been in causal relation to the Tito affair, which was then coming to a head. That the Czechoslovak Communists felt under pressure to make more rapid progress toward socialism was evident from statements made at Party gatherings, where it was pointed out that "Czechoslovakia lags behind other people's democratic countries both economically and politically, and it is necessary to catch up with them."[5] But Communist strategy might have been affected by a poll the Institute of Public Opinion had conducted at the Party's request.[6] (The Institute's pre-election poll in 1946 had been correct to within 0.5 per cent of the actual results.) The poll allegedly indicated a 10 per cent decrease in Communist electoral support, as compared with 1946.[7] This, of course, was a serious matter; proper measures were required to counteract the loss of popular support. The tactics adopted called for a pincer move against the opposition. The Communists moved to consolidate their control over the security police. Colonel Dybal, the police commander of Bohemia, ordered the replacement of eight non-Communist district commanders in Prague, and other personnel shifts, involving approximately sixty additional officials, were carried out throughout Bohemia. They touched off a chain of events that finally culminated in the resignation of twelve non-Communist ministers.

Simultaneously, the Communists launched a large-scale propaganda campaign, built around still unsolved or artificially exaggerated social and economic issues. Its purpose was to arouse the working people against the reaction, in order to build up pressure for the implementation of additional reforms. If the opposition succumbed, the electoral campaign would be fought on dead issues. If it resisted, the Communists could conceivably create sufficient indignation to bring about a defeat of their enemies at the polls or, if necessary, could use the recalcitrant attitude of their opponents as a pretext for a "justified" coup d'état.

The crisis, which culminated on February 20, actually began to unfold on February 5, when the National Front met in an attempt to break a serious deadlock that had retarded the writing of a new Constitution. The country's new organic law was due to be enacted before the expiration of the National Assembly's term, in May, 1948. The likelihood of accomplishing this task diminished with every passing day. Concomitantly, the time for setting a date for new elections was coming closer.

No agreement was reached at this meeting on the Constitution, and the National Socialist Party proposed to set a ten-day limit for settling the differences among the parties. If they failed to agree, new elections should be held without delay. The National Socialists' proposal was voted down by a slim majority of Communists and Social Democrats, who suggested May 23 as a suitable date for the election.[8]

The National Socialists then introduced a resolution calling for the appointment of a special cabinet committee to investigate recent developments in the police. Their motion was carried over Communist opposition, and they announced that they would introduce their resolution at the next cabinet meeting.[9]

Their haste to hold elections was based on the premise and fear that the longer the electoral campaign, the better would be the chances of the Communist Party to improve its position, by using the police and the media of communication for partisan purposes.[10]

Five days later, the Communists introduced one of the issues they had chosen as a campaign platform. A pending adjustment of the pay scale of civil servants was before the government. The trade unions had worked out one proposal, and the rightist Social Democratic Minister, Vaclav Majer, another. The two differed in that the former specified modest across-the-board increases for all employees (favoring the lower paid employees), whereas the latter suggested somewhat larger graduated increases, in percentages of actual salaries (favoring the higher brackets). The significance of the salary raise was overshadowed by the broader political considerations with which the Communists endowed this issue. They made it a test of strength between the trade unions and themselves on the one hand, and the opposition on the other hand, and when the opposition came out victorious in the government, the Communists took the matter to the people.

Although the Communists and the trade unions pretended bitter disappointment at their defeat, their displeasure could not have been as great as they indicated, for they now had a ready-made pretext to present the issue of civil servants' salaries in its "proper" light—as a symbol of unsettled economic questions requiring the people's urgent attention. Immediately after the government's vote, Antonin Zapotocky, who had attended the cabinet meeting in an advisory capacity, strongly chided it for overriding the "carefully worked-out plan of the unions" and warned that its decision "seriously threatens the peace of the country."[11] URO also announced that it had decided to call a congress of works-council and trade-union representatives for February 22, in order to determine the future policy of the unions. The union leadership made no secret of the fact that the decision to hold a congress had been reached on January 22, before the crisis over civil-service pay increases had developed. The public announcement, however, was cleverly timed to coincide with the clash between the unions and the non-Communist parties, thus imparting to the congress a greater sense of importance and urgency.

During the following ten days, preparations for the works-council congress were the main topic of the Communist propaganda campaign. One of the outstanding features was the playing down of the connection between the Party and the trade-union leadership. Even the obvious identity of interest was conveyed implicitly rather than explicitly. The issues were presented to the public in the simplest terms. The antagonists were the unions, as representatives of the working people, and the "reaction," which was trying to raise its ugly head and turn back the clock. The alternative choices put before the people were progress toward greater social benefits and a more secure economic future, as opposed to social and economic obscurantism that threatened to deprive them of their hard-won achievements and to plunge the country into political chaos.

The significance of the campaign lay not so much in its aim to mobilize public opinion as in the skillful manner in which it isolated the political opposition and catered to the basic material aspirations of the working people. It also sought to imbue the workers with a feeling of importance and power, in order to spur them to act and to display a belligerence, which, under the circumstances, was highly desirable from the Communist point of view. The works-council congress was flatteringly described as "a parliament of the working people" that would pass on vital questions affecting the welfare of the great majority of the nation, "the workers, peasants, small tradesmen, and the working intelligentsia."[12] The trade unions were praised for the wisdom, circumspection, and moderation of their policies, which were largely responsible for the "rapid and peaceful reconstruction of Czechoslovakia" and the "notable progress to a better future."[13] They were identified as the "greatest organized power in the country," capable of giving the ship of state its proper direction. Antonin Zapotocky who acted as the chief spokesman of the "working people," gravely but confidently proclaimed that the "decisions reached at the congress would be submitted publicly to the political parties and the government, and to give greater weight to the workers' demands, a short strike would be held as a token of the unions' willingness to fight for their demands if necessary."[14] However, Zapotocky said that he did not think it would be necessary to fight.[15]

Complementing this campaign, meetings were held in all factories and workshops. Their purpose was to choose delegates to the congress and to endorse the stand taken by the trade-union leadership. Communist trade-union organizers exerted a tremendous effort to create an atmosphere of solidarity and militance at these meetings, in order to silence any possible opposition. The result was hundreds of telegrams dispatched to the trade-union headquarters in Prague, urging the implementation of the "just demands" of the workers.

As the appointed day approached, the Communist-controlled press, without breaking its stride, almost insensibly enlarged the area of "just demands" to include not only previously publicized measures, such as a national insurance law and other social legislation, but also the nationalization of export and import firms, department stores, and some privately owned small industrial enterprises. On February 18, *Rude Pravo* bluntly proclaimed that "the factories are prepared to enforce their demands." At the same time, an innocuous announcement revealed that, at the works-council congress, uniformed members of the police would serve as ushers. Ostensibly, this was a symbolic gesture to indicate the unbreakable solidarity between the working people and the police (who were organized in the unions) and to point up the difference between the "people's democratic regime" and the pre-Munich bourgeois Republic, in which the police, instead of serving the interests of the workers, were used to crush them. Although the congress was rigged, in the sense that the choice of delegates assured the Communists of an overwhelming majority of sympathetic representatives, the chances of mishaps were being minimized in every possible way.

The democratic parties protested against the calling of a congress of works councils, as well as against the tactics used in its preparation. But their protest was meek and wholly ineffective. It could not be different, for these parties were not powerful enough to challenge the Communists in the trade-union movement, or to appeal to the workers in anything but subdued tones.

Simultaneously with their attack on the industrial front, the Communists launched an assault against the democratic positions in the agricultural sector. The pattern was the same. The Ministry of Agriculture introduced six new draft decrees in the government, reflecting the principle, later adopted by the Communist regime, that "the land belongs to those who work it." The decrees called for limiting land tenure to fifty hectares and provided for the redistribution of all agricultural property over and above that figure to the remaining landless peasants. They also introduced a system of discriminatory taxation. The Communists urged the adoption of the decrees before the elections, and, if possible, even before completion of the new Constitution, so that the guiding principles of the decrees could be included in it.

In their drive to force the adoption of the agricultural decrees, the Communists once more invoked President Benes' support, citing his alleged concurrence with a 50-hectare limit on agricultural holdings. The representatives of all the other parties opposed the decrees as unnecessary and resorted to delaying tactics in the agricultural committee of the National Assembly. They clashed openly with the Communist Minister of Agriculture, whom they took to task for his irregular handling of the decrees, inasmuch as these had been distributed in draft to peasant organizations even before the Assembly had had a chance to study them, in order to create popular pressure for their adoption. The clashes between Julius Duris, the Minister, and his parliamentary opponents were given wide publicity by the Communist press and, on February 15, the Minister announced the convocation of a congress of farmers' commissions for February 29. This congress was to serve the same purpose in the field of agriculture as did the works-council congress in the field of industry.

The non-Communist parties protested more vigorously in this case, because they had greater support in the official peasant organization, the JSCZ, and because they had a valid reason to object. The democratic parties in effect told the Minister that he had no right to call a congress of farmers' commissions to speak on behalf of peasant interests, for the commissions were merely auxiliary organs, limited in scope to the implementation of land reform (and in social composition to landless peasants), whereas the JSCZ was the authorized spokesman of all peasants. Leading non-Communist officials of the JSCZ, among them its president, Vaclav Mikulas, condemned the congress as illegal. The protests, however, were to no avail. Preparations for the congress could not be stopped.

While Communist propaganda efforts concentrated on social and economic issues, subsidiary topics were not forgotten. The public was kept abreast of new discoveries of "subversive plots," and the police was carefully built up as a friend and guardian of the people. Communist journals gave extensive coverage to interviews with members of the police and with the Minister of the Interior, in which the solidarity of the police with the people was emphasized. Assurances were given that the police "would never betray its duty to the nation."[16] It was important for the Communists to allay any apprehension concerning the possible uses of the police for partisan or terroristic purposes, especially since the democratic parties were playing up the police issue, making it the subject of their do or die stand in the government.

Meanwhile, a crisis in the government was maturing. On February 12, seven days after his party had raised the police issue in the National Front, Vladimir Krajina, Secretary-General of the National Socialist Party, introduced it in the National Assembly's security committee.[17] Vaclav Nosek, the Minister of the Interior, was requested to stop all transfers in the police until further notice and to appear before the committee for questioning.

On the following day, the National Socialists brought the matter before the cabinet. Backed by all the non-Communist ministers present (including the Social Democrats), they ordered Nosek to rescind an order of the commander of the security police for Bohemia, calling for the replacement of regional police officers by Communists. The National Socialists made all future cooperation in the government dependent on the implementation of the cabinet's decision.[18] At the next meeting of the cabinet, on February 17, Prime Minister Gottwald explained that Nosek's illness prevented a discussion of the police issue. However, he placed it on the agenda for the following meeting, scheduled for February 20.

On February 18, a subcommission of the National Front met to discuss major issues pertaining to the Constitution. The subcommission had been appointed only a short time before to speed the writing of the Constitution. Jaroslav Stransky, the National Socialist representative, again attempted to raise the police issue, but Gottwald refused to discuss it, since, he claimed, it was not within the competence of that body to do so. The meeting was then adjourned and the National Socialists intimated that they might not attend the next session of the cabinet, since they saw no sense in participating in a government that could not carry out its own orders.[19]

The Crisis Breaks

On February 20, just before the opening of the cabinet meeting, Petr Zenkl, the Chairman of the National Socialist Party and a Deputy Premier, inquired of Gottwald whether the police order that was at the root of the difficulties had been rescinded. Gottwald gave an evasive answer, but he indicated that Ministers Svoboda and Nosek would have important information to impart to the cabinet on an espionage ring uncovered at Most. Thereupon, the ministers of the National Socialist Party resigned from the government. The People's and Slovak Democratic parties followed suit.* The Social Democrats did not resign, nor did Jan Masaryk and General Ludvik Svoboda, the two ministers without party affiliation.

The precipitous action of the democratic ministers took the country by surprise. Although the National Socialists had implied that they might resign, no one had seriously believed it. If the population was surprised and bewildered by the cataclysmic developments in Prague, the Communist Party was not. Its forces had been mobilized and alerted to battle readiness. During the closing stages of the government crisis, Communist cadres had been thoroughly briefed on the internal situation. They had been urged to maintain constant vigilance. They had been instructed on the possible ways and means of action in quest of the Communist objective to gain an absolute majority, i.e., the right to rule unshackled by a coalition government. The economic situation had been painstakingly outlined to them. They had been apprised of the vital necessity of extending the "public sector" of the economy, by nationalizing those branches of the economy that had so far remained in private hands. They were told that "on the road to socialism, the private capitalist sector of the economy will have to be progressively curtailed and, finally, completely eliminated."[20] Moreover, they were advised that the measures necessary to insure further nationalization would not have to be postponed until after the elections; they "could be put across even before the elections, if sufficiently great pressure were exerted."[21]

These instructions, of course, were confined to closed Party meetings; news of them did not leak out until after the coup. There were, however, other gatherings, which were widely publicized. For example, on Tuesday, February 17, the Communist factory secretaries of the Prague region were briefed by Rudolf Slansky, who alerted them to "be on guard to parry every effort of the reaction to turn back the clock."[22] Similar meetings took place in other large cities. On the same evening, the Communist

---

* The Ministers who resigned were Zenkl, Stransky, Drtina, and Ripka for the National Socialist Party, Msgr. Sramek, Msgr. Hala, Kopecky, and Prochazka for the People's Party, and Kocvara, Pietor, Franek, and Lichner for the Slovak Democratic Party.

Central Committee sounded the alarm. It issued a dramatic proclamation, baring the danger of a reactionary coup.[23]

In accordance with Slansky's instructions, factories in and around Prague were placed on a twenty-four-hour alert against alleged threats of sabotage. The regular factory guards maintained by the trade unions were augmented by security patrols (strazni hlidka) made up of the most reliable Communist workers. In great centers, where the working class was concentrated, a state of readiness and semimobilization was created.[24] The vast machinery of the Communist Party was primed for instantaneous action.

Democrats in Isolation

The democrats had shot their one and only bolt by resigning and were now passively awaiting the result. The record of their activities shows immediate relinquishment of the initiative they had momentarily seized by precipitating a government crisis. They did not establish contact with Benes, on whom the entire success of their scheme depended. They saw him but once, three days after their resignation, and then only briefly. The rest of the time, information of the President's disposition came indirectly and intermittently by one of his personal secretaries. They did not exhort their party followers to a determined stand. They disappeared from the public scene and kept in touch with one another privately, meeting for the most part on "neutral ground" such as the home of Bohumil Lausman, where they bemoaned the fate that was about to overtake them. Several of the ministers quickly recognized the untenable nature of the position in which their rash action had placed them. They admitted to each other that even if Benes succeeded in solving the crisis and in reconstituting the government on a democratic basis, there would be no place for them in the new cabinet.[25]

In vivid contrast, the Communist leaders were seemingly ubiquitous and tireless. "Strike while the iron is hot," was Gottwald's advice to his followers, and that is exactly what they did. Far from permitting events to take their course, the Party exerted every effort within its means to force the issues and turn the government crisis into a rout of its opponents.

The situation remained fluid for five days, but the outcome

was never in doubt. The supremacy of the Communists was complete. They were masters of the instruments of power and of the media of communications, and they controlled the regimented masses. The only thing that delayed victory for five days was Benes' refusal to accept the resignation of the twelve democratic ministers, or to permit the formation of a new government reflecting Gottwald's idea of a "regenerated, people's National Front." Even while Benes held fast, however, the Communists, on the chance that he might not capitulate, proceeded to resolve the crisis unilaterally.

The Role of the Government

The cabinet as a collective body was inactive, but the Communist-held Ministries, especially Interior and Information, became important operational bases. The Ministry of the Interior deployed police regiments to sensitive areas and directed the police, who began making arrests on the third day of the crisis and searched the secretariat of the National Socialist Party on the trumped-up charge that it was preparing an armed uprising.[26]

In addition, the Ministry of the Interior was instrumental in organizing and equipping the workers' militia, an auxiliary armed formation created by the Communist Party and directly subordinated to its Presidium. The Minister, Vaclav Nosek, and other high-ranking officials such as Jindrich Vesely, were particularly helpful in the initial stages of organization. Josef Pavel, a senior member of the security police, was appointed chief of staff, and two more officers of the SNB (Majors Duda and Paducha) were attached to the staff to lend it professional competence and to act as liaison with the SNB, should the need for close coordination between the two organizations arise.[27]

The Ministry of Information secured for the Communists a monopoly over the media of communications, with the exception of the press of the non-Communist parties. These were taken care of by the workers.[28] On the day following the resignation of the democratic ministers, non-Communist employees of the Ministry of Information were not permitted to occupy their desks. Moreover, the Ministry refused broadcasting time to non-Communist officials. Among others, it canceled a scheduled broadcast of the right-wing Social Democrat, Vaclav Majer.[29]

While Communist-held Ministries became operational bases, the Ministries held by the democratic parties were "secured" by Communist "action committees." Several of the ministers who had resigned were barred from their offices by action committees, although the President had not yet accepted their resignations. For example, in the forenoon of February 23, the Minister of Transportation, Jan Pietor, a Slovak Democrat, was asked by the action committee composed of leading Communists of the Ministry's staff to leave his office "because of the distrust of the employees toward him."[30] Simultaneously, three of his associates, Sillinger, Preis, and Velimsky were requested to leave. They were given until 1 P.M. to vacate the premises, an ultimatum with which they meekly complied.[31] A similar situation developed in the Ministry of Foreign Trade, whose action committee was headed by Eugene Lobl. It included other Communists and Social Democrats (e.g., Mrs. Souckova and Jan Fierlinger).[32] The Minister of Foreign Trade, Hubert Ripka, also heeded the demand to abandon his office.

A National Assembly meeting, scheduled for February 24, was postponed *sine die* on the initiative of the Communists. The Assembly did not convene before the government crisis was resolved in favor of the Communists.

Extralegal Measures

Important as the government was in the coup d'état, the most significant developments took place outside the formal channels of authority. The Communists moved deliberately to create a situation of "dual power" in the state, adding a complete and effective power structure to the one in existence. By manipulating both structures, they ran little risk of not winning their point. In rapid succession after the crisis broke out, the Party undertook to form an armed workers' militia, acted to "rejuvenate" the National Front by including mass organizations in it, and called for the establishment of revolutionary action committees not only in the ministries held by democrats but also in the National Committees on every operational level, and in all organizations, institutions, and industrial and commercial installations, with the exception of the Communist Party, its affiliates, and the trade unions.[33]

THE WORKERS' MILITIA. The formation of security patrols in factories before the outbreak of the crisis constituted the first step toward the organization of a workers' militia. On February 20, the membership of the security patrols was greatly increased and they were renamed "alert squads" (*pohotovostni oddil*). They were responsible for the safety of the factories' key installations—the main gate, the telephone switchboard, the intercommunications system, the motor pool and garage, and the electric power plant. Their sphere of activity did not extend outside their respective places of employment.

The next day, the Party transformed the network of alert squads into a workers' militia under centralized leadership. Overall direction was in the hands of the Party Presidium, while organizational matters were in the charge of the regional secretariat for Prague. A general staff was created, and Prague was divided into seven regions, with a commander at the head of each one. In this manner, a system of "revolutionary fighting units of the working class and the Communist Party" was rapidly developed.[34]

Even in the preparatory stages, unarmed members of the militia assisted in the "maintenance of peace" in the capital and in the organization of rallies sponsored by the Party and the trade unions. During the night of February 23, a convoy of trucks, escorted by units of the SNB, delivered to Prague 10,000 rifles and 2,000 submachine guns from the Zbrojovka factory in Brno. On February 24, the militia was increasingly in evidence. Unarmed members patrolled the main thoroughfares and for a time occupied all the bridges connecting the two parts of the city. That evening, they led a massive workers' demonstration in the heart of the city to counter a march of university students on the President's quarters at the Castle. On February 25, the terminal date set by the Party for a peaceful resolution of the crisis on its terms, arms were distributed to 6,550 militiamen in major factories serving as fortified operational bases. In the meantime, an undisclosed number without arms kept the center of town under surveillance and, in St. Wenceslas Square, participated in a monster rally that was awaiting the result of the ultimatum, given to the President, to accept the resignation of the democratic ministers and to appoint a new government. The President's capitulation made the use of force unnecessary, except against a group of stu-

dents who, in a last desperate effort, tried to reach Benes to im-
plore him to hold firm. They were dispersed by gunfire from
combined units of the SNB and the workers' militia. Otherwise,
the militia was not needed, but once armed, it was called out to
give a demonstration of its might before the citizenry of the capital. Units were taken to predetermined assembly points, whence
they paraded in formation, led by several platoons of the SNB's
border guard.

ACTION COMMITTEES. An appeal to the nation to begin creating
action committees in "every village, town, and district"[35] was issued by Gottwald on February 21, one day after the resignation
of the democratic ministers. The people were urged to fill "the
vacancies created by the resignations with new men who had remained loyal to the original spirit of the National Front." The
appeal was directed at "all honest democrats," and it did not go
unheeded. At the initiative of trusted Communist officials, action
committees mushroomed throughout the country. They began
purging undesirable elements in advance of any legally valid
sanction to do so.

On February 23, a preparatory committee of the Central Action Committee of the National Front (Ustredni Akcni Vybor—
UAV) met at the suggestion of the trade unions. Antonin Zapotocky was appointed Chairman, and Alexei Cepicka, the Party's
rapidly rising young trouble shooter, became Secretary-General.
The meeting was attended by dissidents from the democratic
parties and representatives of the Communist-dominated mass
organizations;[36] it signaled the successful "rejuvenation" of the
National Front. In the Central Action Committee, the fast-grow-
ing hierarchy of action committees acquired a directing body possessing the necessary attributes of a national executive. At this
juncture, even if it had proved possible, by some miracle, to restore the government, a second rival center of power was in existence, ready and able to challenge the prerogatives of the cabinet.

The Role of the Trade Unions

The Communist Party took every precaution to retain the direction of all affairs connected with the government crisis; it did
not permit even the Revolutionary Trade Unions to exercise any
independence of action. Strategy consisted in the application of

graduated pressure, for which it relied particularly on the workers and their social and economic demands. The trade unions were instrumental in mobilizing the masses and turning the "street" into a Communist fortress. On February 21, the unions helped to fill Old Town Square with a milling mass, 100,000 strong, to hear exalted harangues by Communist spokesmen. The works-council congress, scheduled for February 22, was one of the highlights of the crisis. It served as a platform for advancing new social and economic demands and for urging the President, as well as the people, to hasten a "just solution" of the crisis. The congress adopted a strongly worded resolution demanding "further nationalization" and a "clean-up" in the country's political life.[37] On February 23, Communist-led workers refused to manufacture newsprint for the democratic press, and transportation workers refused to load paper for these journals.[38] On February 24, the unions—at the instigation of the Communist Party—organized a token one-hour general strike, from noon to one o'clock, to demonstrate the solidarity of the working class and its paralyzing power. The strike was an impressive and solemn show of strength. It gave notice that the Communists could and, if necessary, would use this weapon to cow their opponents into submission. On February 25, the workers were used once again, in the final triumphant mass rally of the coup.

In addition to the use of workers in large numbers, small groups of militia and goon squads were employed in several instances—to secure a printing shop, or occupy a building belonging to a non-Communist political party.

None of the demonstrations was of spontaneous character. Each was planned by the Communists and carefully controlled by reliable members of the workers' militia, who also helped to round up and dispatch the participants to their designated places. This does not mean that the workers went against their wishes. In so far as it is possible to tell, they were in sympathy with the avowed objective of the Communists and the trade unions. But they did not fully comprehend the gravity of the situation. They believed that the question at issue was a change of government, not the completion of a revolutionary overturn that would usher in an entirely new historic phase, with profound and disagreeable consequences for themselves as well as other strata of the population. Their enthusiasm was at best lukewarm; at no time did an electric and vibrant atmosphere permeate Prague, or any other city. The synthetic nature of the excitement that was generated here and there contributed to the general sense of normalcy that persisted throughout the crisis. The Communists probably preferred it this way. Regimented and partially apathetic demonstrations have their own special virtue. They are safer than uncontrolled stirrings of the masses, which can take unpredictable and dangerous turns.

The Break Through Enemy Lines

The Communist break through enemy lines was completed on February 24. Two dissidents in the People's Party, Josef Plojhar and Dyonisius Polansky, armed with a writ of authority from the Minister of the Interior, moved to take over their party's printing press. They stopped publication of *Obzory* and *Vyvoj*, two periodicals best known for opposition to the Communists.[39] On the same day, National Socialist dissidents, responding to Communist appeals, offered to work against the duly elected leadership of their party. In the evening, the Social Democratic "left" finally won control of the executive committee of its party, forcibly unified it, and announced its solidarity with the Communists. Until then, the Social Democrats, who had not resigned, attempted to straddle the fence and to find a compromise. The Communists earnestly sought the support of the Social Democrats, in order to safeguard their claim to a "constitutional solution" of the crisis and to avoid political isolation.

As an inducement to the founding of a two-party government, the Communists allegedly offered the Social Democrats "incredible advantages"—among other things two-fifths of the cabinet posts. Although their offer was rejected, they continued to urge the Social Democrats to agree to a common course of action. "It is essential," they said, "that our parties . . . provide a firm socialist nucleus around which all democratic and socialist forces in the country can rally."[40]They expressed hope that "the Czechoslovak Social Democratic Party will, together with us and on a basis of cooperation as equals, take its place resolutely on the side of peace, order, and the further consolidation of the state."[41] Their desire not to alienate the Social Democrats, nor even to split the ranks of the party, was revealed in a warning to over-zealous action committees that might have been inclined to proceed against "right-wing" Social Democrats in the same manner as against other "reactionaries."

"We will behave toward the Social Democrats in exactly the same manner as they will behave toward us," the warning read. "If they join the reaction, we will treat them as we would any of the other parties. But as long as they have not made up their minds and there is a chance that they will go with us in this phase of our struggle, it would be unwise to fight against them."[42] This did not prevent the Communist-controlled militia from lending "left-wing" Social Democrats a helping hand in invading the printing press of the party. But the Party command ordered the armed detachments to withdraw and left the Social Democrats to settle their own quarrels.*

Benes Capitulates

The morning after the victory of the Fierlinger faction in the Social Democratic Party, the last turn of the screw was applied to Benes, who accepted the resignations of the Ministers at noon, and approved the composition of the new cabinet later in the day.

For the President the government crisis was an excruciating ordeal. It is possible that he had known the intentions of the resigning Ministers and that he had even expressed vague approval. But no firm commitments had been made, either by the Ministers or by Benes, for a concerted approach to current political problems, and he was obviously stunned when informed of their deed by telephone. The constitutional resolution of the conflict rested with him, but he had no plan of action and little leeway in what

---

*The full story of the struggle within the Social Democratic Party and of the role played by the Social Democrats in the coup is deeply dramatic and deserves detailed treatment, for which there is no space here. It might suffice to say that some right-wing and moderate Social Democratic leaders showed real courage in the crisis, although they were unable to act decisively on behalf of the party, and that, although they were not directly involved in the resignation of the democratic ministers, they showed far greater agility than their democratic colleagues, at least in attempting to communicate with the President. See B. Lausman, *Kdo Byl Vinen? (Who Was Responsible?)* (Vienna: Vorwarts, 1953), *passim*.

he could do. The Ministers wanted him to refuse to accept their resignations and to dissolve the entire government instead. The Communists, in turn, wanted him to accept the resignations and to approve drastic changes in the composition of the government. It must have been clear to the President that to accede to the Communists' wishes would entail more than a routine reorganization of the government, although it is unlikely that he could have fully anticipated the dimensions of change that would follow. The question was what would happen if he refused. Would this enhance a peaceful and satisfactory solution of differences, or would it increase the danger of civil strife, or even international conflict? Whatever the reality of the situation, especially with respect to intervention from the outside, Benes must have found the alternatives awesome, and he grappled with them courageously for several days—a pathetic and forlorn figure, isolated from the people and the democratic parties, and relentlessly besieged by the Communists.

To some extent his isolation was self-imposed. He wanted to deny the Communists any pretext for accusing him of collusion, and for this reason he shunned the democratic ministers, allowing them only one brief audience three days after the beginning of the crisis. He gave neither guidance nor encouragement to the democratic parties and to the nation, which had become accustomed to look to him for its cue. His most forceful statement was to a workers' delegation, on February 21; he assured them that he would seek a parliamentary solution for the crisis and that he would not consider asking anyone but Gottwald to form a new government. The only communiqué from his chancery was issued on Monday night, February 23. In it, he promised to acquaint the nation with his viewpoint "in the next few days" and bade the population to remain calm and work peacefully.[43]

The Communists knew Benes well and judged him by the consistency of his past behavior. Cogently, they did not attack him in public. They made no derogatory references to him, and they let the crowds cheer him at will. But they kept him under constant pressure.

Immediately after the ministers resigned, a five-man delegation including Gottwald, Nosek, General Svoboda, the Minister of National Defense, and two of his officers in the counterintelligence section, Reicin and Janda, visited Benes and remained closeted with him for four and a half hours. The following morning, Gottwald again called on him. Then came a delegation of fifty-five workers—from the mass rally in Old Town Square—to urge acceptance of the resignations. That Saturday afternoon, Benes, exhausted and confused, left for his country home, where he remained out of touch with the political leaders, with the radio as his only source of information. What he heard on the radio did not cheer him. He returned to Prague on Sunday night, and on Monday morning, his first visitor was again Gottwald, who was later joined by Nosek bearing news of the armed plot his agents allegedly had discovered. These visits were interspersed with exchanges of letters.[44] From Monday noon until Wednesday morning, the Communists left Benes alone. Meanwhile, the President, responding to an earlier letter of the Communist Presidium, made a moving plea for "agreement and successful cooperation in a parliamentary manner and through the National Front." He said:

> It is clear to me that the Prime Minister will be the chairman of the strongest party, Mr. Klement Gottwald. It is also clear to me that Socialism is a way of life which the majority of our nation desires. I believe that a certain measure of freedom and harmony [unity], those essential principles of our whole national life, are compatible with Socialism. During its entire history our nation has always fought passionately for freedom. History has also shown where discord leads. I beg you, therefore, to remember these facts and to make them the starting point of our negotiations. Let us all again begin jointly to agree on further permanent cooperation, and let us not prolong the division of the nation into two conflicting camps. I believe that reasonable agreement is possible because it is absolutely essential.

The plea fell on deaf ears. The Communists restated familiar accusations against the three democratic parties, which had "ceased to represent the interests of the working people of town and country" and whose leadership "betrayed the fundamental principles of the people's democracy . . . and took an attitude of subversive opposition." Cooperation with these parties was thus out of the question, and the "peaceable development of the Republic" could be guaranteed only by a constitutional and parliamentary procedure proposed by Gottwald. The Communists emphasized, however, that the reconstructed government—in which vacancies would be filled by (hand-picked) representatives of all parties and vital national organizations—"in accordance with the principles of parliamentary democracy, will present itself to the Constituent National Assembly, present its program, and ask for approval."

Bringing this answer, a group of Communist leaders visited Benes on Wednesday forenoon, February 25. With the coup as good as won, they indicated that their patience had run out, and they gave the President an ultimatum. After a brief delay, he complied. The arguments used to convince him are not reliably known. The threat of Soviet intervention, the prospect of bloodshed, the menace of a general strike, and possibly the suggestion that, in the final analysis, the Communists could muster a parliamentary majority, might have contributed to his surrender.

His final act was of little practical importance. However, adherence to the formal amenities attendant upon the appointment of a new government bestowed on the coup a moral approbation that was clearly out of order, and helped to maintain the fiction of a legal transfer of power.

The Coup in Slovakia

Although Prague was the center of the crisis, a side show also took place in Bratislava. The resignation of the Slovak Democratic ministers did not automatically entail the resignation of Democratic officeholders from the Slovak National Council and the Board of Commissioners. Nevertheless, Gustav Husak, the Communist chairman of the board, notified the Democratic representatives of their dismissal and appointed Communists in their place.[45] No resistance was offered to this forcible change. In quick order, Democrats were purged from other public institutions as well.

Communist Advantages

The denouement of the government crisis demonstrated the advantages of the Communists. Their firm hold on key govern-

ment departments and important mass organizations alone would
have enabled them to score a decisive victory. But they held more
than the salient political and economic heights. They were entrenched in thousands of positions in government offices, in public administration, and in industry. They could seize power at the
top and annihilate their opponents throughout the country. The
breadth and depth of the Communist victory was used as a justification for the three-year period of preparation preceding the
seizure of power, which had been regarded as unnecessarily waste-
ful by some of the more impatient members of the Party.[46]

The Party's superiority was bolstered by a favorable alignment
of international forces. Although the danger of intervention by
the Soviet Union was more apparent than real, few Czechs cared
to test their protector's intentions. The oddly coincidental appearance in Prague of Valerian Zorin on the eve of the coup had
a psychological impact. Zorin had served as Soviet Ambassador in
Czechoslovakia until the fall of 1947, when he was recalled to
Moscow to become a Deputy Minister of Foreign Affairs. He arrived in Prague on February 19, without advance warning, ostensibly to supervise the delivery of Soviet wheat.[47] His movements in the capital remained well concealed, although he paid
courtesy visits to Foreign Minister Jan Masaryk, and to Jan
Pietor, the Minister of Transportation.*

The Communists made the most of Soviet press comments,
which conveyed unmistakable support of their position against
the democratic parties. At the height of the crisis, on February
23, they distributed, free of charge, a special edition of their daily,
which prominently featured an article from the Soviet newspaper *Izvestia*. On the following day, their papers presented a long
Tass dispatch from *Pravda*, roundly condemning the "three par-

---

*By an equally odd coincidence, U.S. Ambassador Lawrence Steinhardt, re-
turning from a lengthy visit in Washington, also arrived in Prague just in
time to witness the coup. The Communists made much of this, accusing him
of triggering the reactionary attempt at a coup. The accusation was completely false. Steinhardt returned to Czechoslovakia hopeful of the ability of
the democratic parties to score an electoral victory in the spring of 1948. He
had no idea of the serious deterioration in the political situation that had
taken place in his absence, and he believed, quite naïvely, in the staying powers of Czech democracy. His presence was no stimulus to the democratic leaders, since he was unable to promise the opponents of Communism any tangible
assistance at all.

ties—the National Socialist, People's, and Slovak Democratic parties—which have conspired against the National Front in Czechoslovakia," and asserting that, if these three parties seek to
implement a "policy aimed against the people, there cannot be
and must not be a compromise."[48]

Against such odds, the democratic parties had no chance. They
were crushed by forces stronger than their own and outmaneuvered by the greater political skill of the Communists.

Democratic Errors

The police issue, chosen by the democrats as a pretext for a
showdown with the Communists, was probably the best available.
A determined stand on social and economic matters would have
been impossible. Nevertheless, the police issue, on its intrinsic
merits, without careful propaganda, was not one that could easily
arouse the people to rally around the democratic parties.
There was no real police terror in Czechoslovakia; to become
aroused over future prospects of terror required more sophistica-
tion than the Czech public could be assumed to possess. The democratic parties in general, and the National Socialists in particular, did not give the police issue the necessary build-up. They
did not make it a clear symbol of the threat to political freedom,
nor did they exploit the issue of political freedom with sufficient
vigor. They handled it gingerly and only a day or so before the
ministers resigned did cries of "police regime" emanate from the
democratic ranks. It was then too late.

The tactics and the timing of the democratic forces were disastrous. The National Socialists, who spearheaded the attack
against the Communists in the government, tipped their hand on
February 5, when they revealed great interest in holding early
elections. They exposed themselves to deliberate provocation by
repeatedly intimating that they might consider the police issue
a sufficient cause for boycotting meetings. Deliberate provocation
of the anti-Communist forces was a facet of Communist strategy,
and the intransigent attitude of the National Socialists aided
in its execution. By proper maneuvering in the government—i.e.,
refusing to make the slightest, even sham, concessions on the police issue, and at the same time delaying a showdown by the use
of Nosek's feigned illness as an excuse for not discussing the ques-

tion in the cabinet—the Communists could hope to influence the moves of their opponents in two ways. They could make certain that the National Socialists would resign from the government, thereby appearing to take the offensive, and the responsibility for breaking up the National Front. They could also pinpoint the National Socialists' decisive move to make it coincide with an optimum concentration of Communist strength. The National Socialists and their comrades-in-arms were not astute enough to avoid the trap. The timing of the resignations, on February 20—two days before the scheduled congress of works councils, when excitement was certain to be at a high pitch and Prague would be swarming with Communist workers—was an invitation to disaster.

The democratic leaders committed other strategic and tactical errors. They did not acquaint the nation with their plans and the motivations for them, thus leaving even their own supporters in doubt as to the significance of their actions. They did not pay sufficient attention to the erection of a strong moral platform in support of their case. They did not enlighten the people about the seriousness of the situation and did not point out the very high stakes for which the struggle was conducted. Public airing of the issues was one of the few weapons left to the democrats. They did not avail themselves of it, leaving the molding of public opinion almost entirely to the Communists. Coupled with the absence of a well developed plan of action to follow up their withdrawal from the government, this was a blunder of gigantic proportions. The public, surprised at the democrats' sudden and ill-substantiated resignation, was totally abandoned to the leadership of the Communist Party.

The followers of the democratic parties received no instructions from their leaders beyond exhortations to remain calm and await a peaceful solution of the government crisis. The Communists were quick to exploit the possibilities opened by the furtive manner in which the democratic leaders went about their business. Gottwald promptly accused "the ministers who resigned" of "deserting the idea and program of the National Front" and of "acting without consultation and behind the backs of their own party members."[49] The target was narrowed to twelve individuals, and Gottwald's appeal to clean house was directed as well at the members of the democratic parties, who were asked to repudiate their errant leaders and replace them with "good Czech and Slovak men and women," of whom there was a sufficient number "in all political parties and in all national organizations."[50] It is impossible to determine how effective the Communist appeal was. Incontestably, the democratic leaders contributed to their own isolation and, in that respect, facilitated the task of the Communist Party.

Another serious mistake was their failure to ascertain exactly what course the Social Democratic Party intended to take. They knew that they could count on the support of the Social Democratic Party on the police matter, but not on social and economic issues. They should have known that the Social Democratic Party would have great difficulty in taking drastic steps against the Communists, even on the police issue, as soon as it transcended the bounds of cabinet discussions. They should have known that the threat of a split within its own ranks would prevent the Social Democratic Party from aligning itself with the democrats in an open crisis. Under these circumstances, the resignation of the democratic Ministers left the cabinet and the National Assembly with small working majorities, constitutionally sufficient to assure their bodies of continuous existence without the Ministers who voluntarily withdrew. Once again the Communists were gratuitously provided with an argument that bolstered their cause, and they reportedly used it with Benes.

Finally, the democratic leaders failed to come to a clear understanding with President Benes about the methods and means of implementing their plan. They have since claimed that he had been informed of their intentions and had approved the resignation of the Ministers as a suitable means of carrying the fight to the Communists.[51] They have not revealed how explicit Benes' approval was and to what extent he understood his role in the crisis. For whether or not he liked it (or knew it), the democrats regarded him as the repository of all their hopes from the moment they resigned. Their expectations can be reconstructed as follows: by resigning, they would precipitate a government crisis, the President would refuse to accept their resignation, but would declare the government incapable of performing its functions, and call for new elections. Elections could not be held immediately, because of a legal provision imposing a sixty-day waiting period, but in view of the inability of the old government to operate efficiently, the President would appoint a caretaker cabinet which—regardless of its composition—would not transact any serious business because of its purely temporary character. In this manner, the democrats hoped to escape the trap the Communists were setting for them in the form of demands for new social and economic legislation before the electoral contest.

The success of the maneuver hinged entirely on two conditions: the Communists' willingness to abide by the rules of parliamentary procedure, and the President's ability to resist Communist demands, in the event that the latter did not acquiesce in a parliamentary solution of the crisis. The hopes of the democrats were built on shaky foundations. The Communists had no intention of limiting themselves to parliamentary methods, and the President was unable to withstand their onslaught.

Knowing that the President was given to hesitation in a time of crisis, and that he was not at the peak of physical fitness—he had suffered a stroke in the fall of 1947—the democratic parties should have been prepared to give him the strongest possible moral support. They should have been in constant touch with him, urging him to go through with the scheme he had reportedly approved. But they did none of this. They remained at a respectful distance, showing their customary deference to him.

The passivity of the democratic leaders cannot be explained except by assuming that they were the victims of their own fallacious logic and prisoners of their unwavering belief in parliamentary democracy. Although the rationale for their resignation was to avert a possible Communist coup, implicitly they could not face up to the political realities surrounding them, nor imagine that the Czechoslovak Communists were ready to dispense with parliamentary niceties. Their resignation was manifestly a parliamentary maneuver, not an attempt at a *coup de force*. Their behavior during the crisis eloquently supports this belief. They offered only perfunctory resistance to the use of extralegal methods against them.

The resigning Ministers abided by the decisions of action committees depriving them of the use of their offices. They made no attempt, belated and futile though it would have been, to stage

public rallies, and instead of permitting some of the more san-
guine members of their parties to fight fire with fire, they exerted
every effort within their means to keep the population calm and
to prevent disturbances, even in closed meetings. One example
will illustrate their frame of mind. On Tuesday, February 24, the
National Socialist Party called a meeting of its executive committee to give *post factum* approval to the Ministers' action. At this
meeting, the chairman of the party inquired whether anyone
among those present had received an offer from Gottwald to collaborate with the Communists. Alois Neumann, a member of the
executive committee, indicated that he had been approached and
had accepted their offer. He was then asked to leave the meeting,
and the leadership used all of its authority to prevent several hot-
headed members from venting their anger on Neumann.[52]

The absence of violence—with the exception of a few minor in-
cidents—was an outstanding characteristic of the Czechoslovak
coup. Even the Communists showed a somewhat exaggerated
concern for the observance of legal niceties and demonstrated
that they were not unmindful of the Czech people's general
aversion to gross violence. They were plainly anxious not to be
stigmatized with having engineered a coup. (To this day, they
keep referring to the coup euphemistically as "February" or "the
February events.") They sought legal and moral approval for
their actions. They insisted that Benes confirm the formal changes
in the government, whereas they easily could have disregarded
him. They emphasized the fact that they had a sufficient parliamentary majority to reconstitute the government, and tried, in
several ways, to soften the impact of the extralegal measures they
were taking.

The workers were told that they should not hesitate to secure
plants with fifty or more employees by placing them under national administrators, invoking decree No. 5 (of 1945) which made
such a move possible in plants where normal production was
threatened.[53] It was of no concern to the Communists that decree No. 5 was meant to apply only to the immediate postwar
situation. But urging the dismissal of unreliable managers, su-
pervisors, and employees, the Communists suggested a genteel
approach:

It is not always necessary to fire someone who is unreliable or to transfer him. Why not send him on an official trip to Slovakia? Why not give him some project to work on? For that, it is enough to provide him with an office and a secretary. Why not suggest that he take a paid vacation?[54]

The soft approach did not alter the Communists' objectives. It merely made their tactics conform to the placid environment in which they operated, and facilitated their victory. It helped to prevent major social disturbances and economic dislocations, which were neither desirable nor necessary.

The coup d'état terminated the coalition that had governed Czechoslovakia for nearly three years. It lent emphatic point to the incompatibility of the Communist and democratic viewpoints concerning the role and purposes of coalition government. The democratic parties regarded the coalition as a *conditio sine qua non* of their country's continued independence. Far from wanting to exclude the Communists from the government, they sought only to dull the cutting edge of Communist power in order to improve the chances for compromise. They hoped that, in coalition with the Communists, they could stabilize Czechoslovakia's political and economic structures as a self-styled socialist system. But the Communists had different ideas. To them the coalition was at best a temporary expedient whose primary tactical justification was "to avoid unnecessary sacrifices on the road to socialism, but not socialism [as understood by the Communists] itself."

The coalition was useful in tearing the old society, whose fabric had been much weakened by the war, from its moorings. Sooner or later, however, it was bound to outlive its usefulness. Instead of advancing Communist goals, it would impede them. At such a time, the liquidation of the democratic parties would become an indispensable prerequisite for further progress toward "socialism." In February, 1948, that time had arrived.

EPILOGUE

THEIR CRUSHING victory enabled the Communists to consolidate their gains without any loss of momentum or disturbance of the rhythm of daily life.

In the aftermath of the coup, formal political opposition collapsed precipitously. The National Socialist, Slovak Democratic, and People's parties, shorn of their duly elected leaders, simply disintegrated.* They were permitted to continue under somewhat changed names—Czechoslovak Socialist Party instead of National Socialist, Slovak Party of Revival instead of Democratic—but they were hollow shells of their former selves. They had no independence, and many of their adherents deserted to join the Communist Party, in a desperate act of self-protection. Their ranks were purged by action committees appointed by the National Front. These committees had veto power over all new personnel appointments and organizational changes.

The disintegration of the democratic opposition was accompanied by the integration of the "Marxist left." Proposals for the merger of the Social Democratic and Communist parties were made public on April 18, 1948. Coordinating committees were immediately established to eliminate unreliable Social Democrats from the roster and to ensure an orderly absorption by the Communist Party. The formal merger took place on June 27. Three months later, the Slovak Communist Party was formally

---

*The leaders sought to escape from Czechoslovakia, and most of them succeeded. Thus, Zenkl, Krajina, Ripka, and Stransky of the National Socialist Party, Prochazka and Duchacek of the People's Party, Lettrich, Hodza, and Kocvara of the Slovak Democratic Party—to name only a few—soon made their way to the West. Prokop Drtina, the courageous National Socialist Minister of Justice, attempted to commit suicide by jumping from a window. He was taken to a prison hospital, where he survived. Msgrs. Sramek and Hala had the misfortune of being apprehended in flight and were interned in monasteries.

incorporated in the Czechoslovak Communist Party. The tactical necessity for two separate Communist parties had passed. From then on, the relationship between the Czechoslovak Party and its Slovak branch was similar to that existing between the All Union Party and the Republic parties in the Soviet Union.

In the meantime, the remaining personal symbols of democracy, Jan Masaryk and Eduard Benes, also disappeared. Jan Masaryk, confused and bewildered by the tumultuous events, retained his ministerial post in the cabinet, but he did not stay long. On March 5, he vowed in a newspaper interview "always to go with the people." This was his last public utterance. Five days later, at dawn, he was found dead under his apartment window in the courtyard of the Ministry of Foreign Affairs.*

Benes retained the presidency until June 7, although he retired to his country home immediately after the coup, returning to Prague only twice—to attend a celebration of the six-hundredth anniversary of the founding of Charles University, and to resign. His resignation was prompted by the passage of a new Constitution, to which he could not in good conscience affix his signature, even if the Communists had asked him to. It is doubtful that they made such a request, since by this time he had outlived his usefulness to them, and they probably preferred to have one of their own members sign the country's organic law, heralding the onset of a new era.** After resigning, Benes returned to his country residence, where he died less than three months later.

Klement Gottwald was elected President on June 14, complet-

---

*His death elicited much speculation, and many of his friends in the West, as well as some Czechoslovak refugees, suggested that he was murdered. It seems more likely that he killed himself in a fit of melancholy, precipitated by a visit to his father's grave on the anniversary of his birth, March 7.

**The circumstances surrounding Benes' resignation remain obscure. The President apparently tried to resign some time between May 9, when the National Assembly approved the new Constitution, and May 30, the date of the general election. The Communists, however, interpreted his intentions as a political provocation, designed to influence the outcome of the election. They insisted that he refrain from carrying out his plan until after the election, at which time he would have a leeway of nine days for resigning, since the Constitution had to be signed by the chief executive within thirty days of its approval by Parliament. He chose June 7, and on the following day, Gottwald who, as Prime Minister, was empowered to act under such circumstances, signed the document.

ing the domination of the organs of government by Communists.

The cabinet, after the death of Masaryk and the merger of the Marxist parties, contained eighteen Communists and six hand-picked representatives of non-Communist splinter parties.

The National Assembly, duly purged of eighty-two recalcitrant members (out of a total of 300), approved a new Constitution, with time to spare before its term expired. The elections of May 30 featured a single electoral list of the National Front, although a "blank" or white ballot was provided for registering dissent. In most places, voting was done openly for the first time in the con-stitutional history of the country. The official results showed that 89 per cent of the electorate endorsed the single list of candidates, among whom were 214 Communists and 86 representatives of other parties.

Simultaneously with the streamlining of political institutions, rapid strides were made toward "the curtailment of isolation" of capitalist elements in the economy. The six-point agricultural program, which had been vigorously opposed by the democrats, was enacted into law on March 21. The major stated objectives of this program were the limitation of landholdings to fifty hectares, and the elimination of absentee ownership (in order to imple-ment the principle that "the land belongs to those who till it"). Additional objectives included a unified system of taxation that favored small farmers owning less than fifteen hectares of land, and adjustment of other financial and technical questions. The purpose of limiting landholdings was not to satisfy a hunger for land, but to break the back of a very small number of big farm-ers, to deprive the Catholic Church of the landholdings consti-tuting one of the more important sources of its economic power, and to create a land pool suitable as a jumping-off point for collectivization.*

In the industrial and commercial fields, a series of decrees of nationalization were passed, reducing the capitalist sectors to im-potence and leading to drastic changes in the class structure. The need for additional nationalization was explained in economic and political terms. The relatively large sector of the economy

---

*Agricultural enterprises of more than fifty hectares numbered 7,000, and the total amount of land expropriated under the new legislation was approxi-mately 800,000 hectares, or 10 per cent of the country's agricultural area.

controlled by capitalists hampered planned economic development, damaged the best interests of the public—primarily through illegal profits and transfer of money abroad—and served as a reservoir of political strength of the "reaction." To support their argument, Communist economists pointed to production statistics showing that the Two-Year Plan was most severely underfulfilled in the building trade and in food production, in which, respectively, 76 per cent and 47 per cent of the enterprises were in private hands.[1]

In addition, they charged that wholesale trade and export-import firms, which were 75 per cent privately owned, accounted for yearly profits of 2.6 billion Kcs., which went into the pockets of private owners instead of the public treasury, while an additional 3 billion Kcs. in illegal profits were transferred abroad. Profits in the capitalist sector of industry allegedly amounted to 4.6 billion Kcs. Moreover, the rate of investment in privately owned enterprises was 70 per cent higher (measured in terms of investment per number of employees) than in nationalized plants. The capitalist sector, therefore, tended to grow at the expense of nationalized industries, especially since investment in privately owned enterprises was said to be spent mainly on expansion and improvement, whereas in nationalized plants the bulk of investment went toward restoring production facilities damaged in the war.[2]

Nationalization exceeded the scope foreseen by Communists immediately before the coup. The total share of private ownership in industry was reduced from 20 to 5 per cent. In wholesale and foreign trade, private ownership was abolished altogether. Moreover, nationalization was extended to retail stores and artisan shops. It was suddenly "discovered" that even the retail trade harbored a capitalist sector, with 23.1 per cent of the stores (19,000 stores) employing 50 per cent of the labor force (78,000) and doing 55.6 per cent of the total volume of business (30 billion Kcs.).[3]

To arrive at these figures, the term "capitalist enterprise" was applied to all stores with three or more employees. To be sure, only stores with fifty or more employees were nationalized at once. The same held true for the small trades, in which 252 enterprises (less than 1 per cent of the total) with more than 50 employees were immediately nationalized. Only an insignificant number of industrial enterprises remained in private hands, as did some 80,000 retail stores and 170,000 artisan shops, which, on the average, had fewer than 3 employees. The way was clear for the implementation of a Five-Year Economic Plan, the blueprint of which was rushed to completion in order to enact it into law on October 28, 1948.[4]

Thus, the coup d'état terminated the national and democratic revolution and opened a phase of socialist construction qualitatively different from the preceding one, exposing Czechoslovakia to the rigors attending the forcible transformation of its institutions, its social relations, and its values under the aegis of a proletarian dictatorship patterned on the Soviet model.

The Party itself for some time persisted in minimizing the seriousness of the overturn and maintained the fiction of a constitutional change of government. Given the socialist bias of large segments of the Czechoslovak population, it was not difficult to play down the extralegal aspects of the coup and to present it as insurance against the resurgence of reactionary capitalism, allowing the people to form their own image of the future—an image which, in surprisingly many cases, appeared to be one of unfettered progress toward an idealized form of socialism.

The alleged threat to the welfare of the working people was wholly imaginary. No democratic party wanted to curtail the rights of the workers. But the genuine gains made since World War II were undermined by the Communist-installed system of power. Illusions of an idealized form of socialism were quickly shattered. However, the monopolistic control of the Communists could not be broken. They reaped the full benefit of the transition they had engineered—a transition from one revolutionary phase to another, free of convulsive outbursts. This was a luxury not enjoyed by any other Communist Party.

Soviet spokesmen have since pointed to Czechoslovakia as an outstanding example of the success of peaceful methods of power seizure.[5] Undeniably, the Communist victory was achieved with a minimum of social dislocation and political unrest. But it was not a parliamentary transfer of governmental responsibility within a constitutional framework, in the normal meaning of these terms. The Communists used parliamentary institutions and had recourse to such constitutional forms as suited their purposes. Of all the institutions involved in the protracted process of power seizure, the National Assembly was least helpful to them, despite a tradition of pliancy to the wishes of the executive and a very strong leftist bloc in it as a result of the returns of the electoral contest. The observance of constitutional amenities during the coup d'état was a deliberate choice. In actuality, the Communists did not rely on constitutional procedures to settle the crisis in their own favor.

The absence of overt violence did not imply abandonment of the use of force as that appeared necessary, nor of the application of time-honored concepts of power to every possible means of political struggle. The ease with which the Communists achieved their objectives stemmed from several circumstances, including a benign international environment and favorable internal conditions.

Much has been made of the assistance rendered by the Soviet Union to Communists in Czechoslovakia and elsewhere in Eastern Europe. For a time the Communists themselves, in deference to Stalin, exaggerated the "fraternal help" given them by Russia. In Czechoslovakia, direct assistance was marginal. The preponderance of Soviet power in Eastern Europe filled the Communists with confidence and gave them a strong guarantee against failure. But they were not alone in rejoicing over Russia's domination, and few people thought that Soviet might was a handicap to the free and untrammeled internal development of their country. To assert that the threat of Soviet intervention, possibly of a military character, decided the outcome of the clash in 1948 is *ex post facto* rationalization on the part of those who lost the struggle.* There is no certainty that Russian troops would have moved across the

---

*The failure of American military forces to occupy Prague at the end of World War II has also been cited as a source of the democrats' woes. It seems to me that although the wisdom of the decision not to occupy Prague could be questioned, the effect of such an occupation is not open to second guessing. The prevailing mood of the Czechoslovak people and the existence of a Communist-dominated government were certain to nullify any tangible political expression of the strong residue of empathy with America. The presence of United States troops in Plzen, in 1945, had no appreciable effect on the voting preference of the citizenry of that town in 1946. They endorsed the Communist Party by an overwhelming margin.

border, and there were none inside the country. In any event, the intentions of the Soviet Union were never tested. The significance of the threat consisted in a largely self-induced psychological effect rather than in any real danger it held for the population.

The consequences of this implied or imagined threat draw attention to the general problem of the interdependence of national and international politics. No country's politics, especially not those of a small one in the neighborhood of a great power, can be free of interference from influences that prevail outside national borders. Frontiers have lost their erstwhile magical significance, and it is false comfort to say that the power seizure in Czechoslovakia took place in an area of high Soviet military potential. Such protection as was afforded the Communists can now be extended much further, and emphasizing its military aspect is bound to lead to a paralysis of will and a loss of morale, which, in the end, are likely to be decisive in determining the outcome of a struggle for power within the borders of any nation, regardless of its location. One can say only that, in Czechoslovakia, Communists knew how to turn a generally favorable situation to specific and decisive advantage.

Among the internal conditions aiding the Communists, the alignment of class forces and the ineptitude of potential and actual rivals stand out significantly. There is no question that the working class was in a favored position in the postwar period. For one thing, it was very large in comparison with other social classes. It was highly self-conscious and possessed an internal cohesiveness that no other social group had. Secondly, its claims to political representation and to social and economic rights were generally recognized as valid. No one dared to oppose the wishes of the working class, or even those advanced in its name. The workers, in turn, overwhelmingly favored the Communist Party as the best guarantee, under existing circumstances, of the fulfillment and preservation of their just demands. The Communists were able to use working-class support as a powerful lever against all other parties; at the same time, they could seize control of the unified trade-union machinery that assured them of a strangle hold on the workers themselves, should they ever falter in their allegiance to the Party.

The ineptitude of the democratic parties that entered into coalition with the Communist Party in 1945—to be defeated ignominiously by it in 1948—was the result of many factors, some of which they could not control. Their situation was difficult. But it was not hopeless from the beginning; at least they did not assess it in that light. There was no sense of doom over their activities. They behaved as though they were operating within a stable parliamentary system and consciously perpetuated an illusion of normalcy, instead of boldly pointing to issues on which they opposed the Communists. They did not mobilize the efforts of their followers to safeguard fundamental principles, in which they professed to believe, and which were threatened. Perhaps to do so would have been futile. The purpose here is not to pass judgment, but simply to note that the effort was not made.

For various reasons, Czechoslovakia was highly susceptible to Communist penetration. Its tradition of democracy did not provide an adequate bulwark of defense, while its industrial maturity lowered the threshold of resistance against the type of assault mounted by the Communists.

The situation that prevailed in Czechoslovakia was unique in many respects; in other ways, it was similar to that which has led to successful revolutionary overturn elsewhere:

1) The collapse of the old social and political order was a precondition of Communist power seizure. The Communists themselves did not create this condition and the attitude accompanying it; their benefit accrued from understanding how to turn it to their advantage.

2) National revolutionary and social emancipatory aspirations coincided and mutually reinforced each other. Although national revolutionary strivings were paramount, they obscured subtle distinctions between national and social goals, facilitated the implementation of social measures under the aegis of national objectives that could not be easily opposed, and sustained a mood of radicalism.

3) The image of the Communist Party was not that of an alien, antidemocratic instrument, but rather that of a native popular force, capable of engaging the imagination of the most dynamic

portion of the population, attracting fierce loyalties, imbuing people with purpose, and providing them with the best leadership available.

The techniques demonstrated by the Communists are applicable everywhere, under remotely similar conditions. For success, it is not necessary that the circumstances be duplicated in minute detail. In Czechoslovakia, the Communists had a plan for the seizure of power and acted on it systematically, yet flexibly, in accordance with the fluctuating situation. This plan was based on Marxist-Leninist precepts of social analysis; its implementation was derived from Leninist-Stalinist principles of political struggle.

Marx outlined the Communist revolutionary design a hundred years ago:

> The democratic petty bourgeois, far from desiring to revolutionize all society for the revolutionary proletarians, strive for a change in social conditions by means of which existing society will be made as tolerable and comfortable as possible for them. . . . While the democratic petty bourgeois wish to bring the revolution to a conclusion as quickly as possible . . . it is our interest and our task to make the revolution permanent, until all more or less possessing classes have been displaced from domination, until the proletariat has conquered state power . . . and at least the decisive productive forces are concentrated in the hands of the proletarians.
>
> For us the issue cannot be the alteration of private property but only its abolition, not the smoothing over of class antagonisms but abolition of classes, not the improvement of existing society but the foundation of a new one.[6]

The strategy and tactics of the Czechoslovak Communist Party conformed remarkably to Marx's dictum.

NOTES

Chapter 1: The Political Character of Czechoslovakia

1. The subject matter covered in this chapter is exhaustively and authoritatively treated in the following general works:

   Eduard Benes, *Svetova Valka a Nase Revoluce* (*The World War and Our Revolution*) (3 vols.; Prague, 1927–28). The memoirs of one of the founders of the Republic.

   Ceskoslovenska Vlastiveda (*Czechoslovak History*) (Prague: Sfinx, 1932–33), Part IV. An encyclopedic work of high quality covering the period up to 1918.

   Deset let Ceskoslovenske Republiky (*Ten Years of the Czechoslovak Republic*) (Prague, 1928). A three-volume *magnum opus* sponsored by the National Assembly in commemoration of ten years of independence. It reviews every aspect of national life between 1918 and 1928.

   Kamil Krofta, *Narodnostni Vyvoj Zemi Ceskoslovenskych* (*The Nationalities Development of the Czechoslovak Lands*) (Prague: Orbis, 1934). A scholarly treatise on the foundation and development of nationalism in the Czech lands.

   Thomas G. Masaryk, *Svetova Revoluce* (*World Revolution*) (Prague, 1925). President Masaryk's wartime reminiscences. A larger and more detailed version of his *The Making of a State*.

   J. O. Opocensky, *Politicke Dejiny Povalecne* (*The Political History of the Postwar Era*) (Prague, 1933). A thorough political history of the postwar era.

   Ferdinand Peroutka, *Budovani Statu* (*The Building of the State*) (4 vols.; Prague: Borovy, 1933–36). A monumental study of the formative years of the Republic, 1918–21.

   Additional works dealing more specifically with salient aspects of Czechoslovakia's evolution touched on in this chapter will be indicated at appropriate places in the text.

2. Thomas G. Masaryk, *The Making of a State* (London: George Allen and Unwin, 1927), p. 436.

3. See, for example, *At the Crossroads of Europe, An Historical Outline of the Democratic Idea in Czechoslovakia* (Prague: Pen Club, 1938). This is a symposium to which a number of prominent Czech writers and scholars, including Karel Capek and Albert Prazak, contributed.

4. The only serious attempt at analyzing Czech national character known to me is Ferdinand Peroutka's *Jaci Jsme* (*As We Are*) (Prague, 1924). Although this is a tentative sociological analysis, it is well worth reading.

5. Curiously, no good study of the Czechoslovak party system and of the parties themselves exists. There are, of course, Josef Chmelar's *Political Parties in Czechoslovakia* (Prague, 1926), and Charles Hoch's *The Political*

Parties in Czechoslovakia (Prague, 1936), as well as a chapter on political parties by Malbone H. Graham, in Robert J. Kerner, ed., *Czechoslovakia* (Berkeley, Calif.: University of California Press, 1944). None of these, however, qualify as more than superficial summary treatments of the subject.

6. Of the many books written by Masaryk, and about him, the reader might want to consult Karel Capek, *The President Masaryk Tells His Story* (New York: G. P. Putnam's Sons, 1938), as the best single volume in English, revealing Masaryk's character and the substance of his thought.

7. Masaryk, *The Making of a State*, p. 304.

8. See, for example, Compton Mackenzie, *Dr. Benes* (London: George Allen and Unwin, 1946), p. 46.

9. The reader with more than cursory interest in the subject might want to consult the following books for a more complete, if not altogether balanced, presentation of this complicated problem:

    R. W. Seton-Watson, *The New Slovakia* (Prague, 1924).

    R. W. Seton-Watson, *Slovakia Then and Now* (London, 1931).

    Ivan Derer, *Slovensky Vyvoj a Ludacka Zrada (The Development of Slovakia and the Betrayal of the Slovak Populists)* (Prague, 1946).

    Karol Sidor, *Slovenska Politika na Pode Prazskeho Snemu (Slovak Politics in the Prague Parliament)* (Bratislava, 1943).

    Alexander Kunosi, *The Basis of Czechoslovak Unity* (London: Dakers, 1944).

    Josef Rotnagl, *Cesi a Slovaci (Czechs and Slovaks)* (Prague: Vilimek, 1945).

    Josef Lettrich, *History of Modern Slovakia* (New York: Frederick A. Praeger, 1955).

10. Seton-Watson, *Slovakia Then and Now.*

11. See Karel Niģrin, *Cech a Slovak Pocas Republiky (Czechs and Slovaks under the Republic)* (London, 1944), p. 10.

12. Two general works of considerable merit are Elizabeth Wiskeman, *Czechs and Germans* (London and New York: Oxford University Press, 1938), and C. A. Macartney, *Hungary and Her Successors* (New York: Oxford University Press, 1937).

13. Czechoslovakia's foreign policy is best treated in Benes' own writings. See, for example, his *Problemy Nove Evropy (Problems of the New Europe)* (Prague, 1924), and *Boj o Mir a Bezpecnost Statu (The Struggle for the Peace and Security of the State)* (Prague, 1934). A good general work in English, summarizing Czechoslovak foreign policy, is Felix J. Vondracek, *The Foreign Policy of Czechoslovakia 1918–1935* (New York, 1937). The reader might also wish to consult my vignette of Benes and the policies he pursued in *The Diplomats, 1919–1939* (Princeton: Princeton University Press, 1953).

14. Eduard Taborsky, *Nase Nova Ustava (Our New Constitution)* (Prague, 1948), p. 35.

15. *Ibid.*, p. 83.

16. For a discussion of developments in the Czech lands after Munich, see:

    Adolf Zeman, *Ceskoslovenska Golgota (Czechoslovak Calvary)* (Prague, 1946).

    Emil Sobota, *Co To Byl Protektorat (What Was the Protectorate)* (Prague, 1946).

    Sheila G. Duff, *A German Protectorate, the Czechs under Nazi Rule* (London: The Macmillan Company, 1942).

Ladislav K. Feierabend, *Ve Vladach Druhe Republiky (In the Governments of the Second Republic)* (New York: Universum Press, 1961).

Chapter 2: The Origins of the Communist Party

1. Ferdinand Peroutka, *Budovani Statu*, I, 478.
2. *Ibid.*, p. 485.
3. *Ibid.*, p. 481.
4. *Ibid.*, p. 480.
5. *Ibid.*
6. P. Reimann, *Geschichte der Kommunistischen Partei der Tschechoslovakei* (Hamburg and Berlin: Carl Hoym, 1931), pp. 68–77; also Peroutka, pp. 561 ff.
7. Peroutka, p. 563. On the foundation of the Czechoslovak Communist Party in Russia, see Jindrich Vesely, *Cesi a Slovaci v Revolucnim Rusku, 1917–1920 (Czechs and Slovaks in Revolutionary Russia, 1917–1920)* (Prague: SNPL, 1954), pp. 105 ff. See also Stefan Stvrtecky, "Sjazd Ceskoslovenskych Komunistov v Moskve v Maji 1918" ("The Congress of Czechoslovak Communists in Moscow in May, 1918"), *Prispevky k Dejinam KSC*, V (1958), 131–51.
8. Peroutka, pp. 569 ff.
9. *Ibid.*, p. 574.
10. *Ibid.*, p. 576.
11. *Ibid.*, p. 577.
12. *Ibid.*, *pp.* 496–517.
13. *Ibid.*, pp. 1812 ff.
14. Reimann, *Geschichte*, p. 95. See also more recent Communist publications on the December strike, Ustav Dejin KSC, *Sbornik Dokumentu k Prosincove Stavce (Collection of Documents on the December Strike)* (Prague: SNPL, 1954); Jan Mlynarik, *Generalny Decembrovy Strajk 1920 na Slovensku (The General Strike of December 1920 in Slovakia)* (Bratislava: SVPL, 1960); and Irena Mala and Frantisek Stepan, eds., *Prosincova Generalni Stavka*, Prameny k Ohlasu Velke Rijnove Socialisticke Revoluce a Vzniku CSR *(The General Strike of December 1920*, a volume in the series of Sources on the Influence of the Great October Revolution and the Foundation of the Czechoslovak Republic) (Prague: CSAV, 1961).
15. *Kommunisticheskii Internatsional* II, No. 13 (1920), 2622.
16. Peroutka, p. 1962.
17. Hula, "Razkol v Chekho-Slovatskoi Sotsial Demokratii," *Kommunisticheskii Internatsional* II, No. 15 (1920), 3206 ff. Also Peroutka, pp. 1968 ff.
18. See Peroutka, pp. 2091 ff. Also Jaroslav Salat and Eduard Brenner, "Bor'ba za Kommunizm v Chekho-Slovakii," *Kommunisticheskii Internatsional* III, No. 17 (1921), 4187–4207.
19. Reimann, *Geschichte*, p. 124.
20. See Ustav Dejin KSS, *Slovenska Republika Rad (The Slovak Soviet Republic)* (Bratislava: SVPL, 1960), and also Peter Toma, "The Slovak Soviet Republic," *The American Slavic and East European Review*, XVII, No. 2 (April, 1958), 203–15.
21. *Rude Pravo*, January 14, 1951.
22. *Kommunisticheskii Internatsional* II, No. 16 (1920), 3882.
23. *Ibid.*, III, No. 17 (1921), 4318.

24. *Protokoll des III Kongresses der Kommunistischen Internationale* (Hamburg, 1921), p. 12.
25. *Ibid.*, p. 1070.
26. *Ibid.*, pp. 199–207. See also G. Zinoviev, "The Report of the Executive Committee of the Comintern for 1920–1921," published by the *Press Bureau of the Communist International* (Moscow, 1921), pp. 47, and 64–68.
27. This was a vastly exaggerated estimate. The figure was probably nearer 250,000. See Jindrich Vesely, *Z Prvnich Boju KSC, 1921–1924 (From the First Struggles of the Communist Party of Czechoslovakia)* (Prague: SNPL, 1958), pp. 91–92.
28. *Protokoll des III Kongresses*, pp. 504, 589.
29. *Ibid.*, p. 756.
30. *Ibid.*, pp. 543–48.

Chapter 3: The Bolshevization of the Communist Party

1. *International Press Correspondence (Inprecorr)*, V, No. 36 (April 23, 1925), 478 ff. Also *Pravda*, No. 72, March 29, 1925.
2. *Inprecorr*, V, No. 39 (April 28, 1925), 508–12.
3. *The Communist International*, VI, Nos. 11, 12, 13 combined (May, 1929), 540 ff.
4. *Inprecorr*, III, No. 46 (June 28, 1923), 44.
5. Reimann, *Geschichte*, p. 191.
6. *Ibid.*, p. 202.
7. *Inprecorr*, IV, No. 41 (July 16, 1924), 404.
8. *Ibid.*, V, No. 22 (March 30, 1925), 310.
9. *Ibid.*
10. *Ibid.*, V, No. 32 (April 16, 1925), 421.
11. *Ibid.*, IV, No. 81 (November 27, 1923), 923.
12. *Ibid.*
13. *Ibid.*, IV, No. 66 (September 18, 1924), 723.
14. *Ibid.*, V, No. 18 (March 5, 1925), 263.
15. Reimann, *Geschichte*, pp. 208–9.
16. *Inprecorr*, V, No. 19 (March 12, 1925), 279. Also Reimann, *Geschichte*, pp. 218–25.
17. *Inprecorr*, V, No. 19 (March 12, 1925), 279.
18. *Ibid.*, V, No. 39 (April 28, 1925), 508–12.
19. Reimann, *Geschichte*, pp. 240 ff.
20. *Inprecorr*, VI, No. 28 (April 15, 1926), 437.
21. *Protokoll 10. Plenum des Exekutivkomitees der Kommunistischen Internationale* (Hamburg, 1929), p. 455.
22. Reimann, "Opportunism in Czechoslovakia," *The Communist International*, VI, No. 5 (1929), 150 ff.
23. *Ibid.*
24. Reimann, *Geschichte*, pp. 286 ff.
25. *The Communist International*, VI, No. 8 (1929), 228.
26. *Ibid.*
27. For an account of the Fifth Congress of the Party see *Inprecorr*, IX, No. 15 (March 22, 1929), 304; IX, No. 17 (March 29, 1929), 327 ff, and also Reimann, *Geschichte*, pp. 358–68.
28. *Inprecorr*, V, No. 58 (July 23, 1925), 801.

29. Josef Stalin, *Sochineniia*, 10, 250.
30. *The Communist International*, VI, Nos. 11, 12, 13 (May, 1929), 540 ff.
31. Reimann, *Geschichte*, pp. 251–60.
32. *Inprecorr*, VIII, No. 69 (October 5, 1928), 1260.
33. *Ibid.*, IV, No. 41 (July 16, 1924), 404.
34. *Ibid.*, VI, No. 34 (April 29, 1926), 516.
35. *Ibid.*, II, No. 111 (December 13, 1922), 915.
36. *Ibid.*, V, No. 22 (March 30, 1925), 318.
37. *Fifth Congress of the Communist International*, pp. 248 ff.
38. *Inprecorr*, VI, No. 37 (May 5, 1926), 555.
39. Reimann, *Geschichte*, p. 282.
40. Kellermann, "The Strike Movement in Czechoslovakia," *The Communist International*, VI, No. 7 (1929), 205.
41. Reimann, *Geschichte*, p. 284.
42. *Inprecorr*, IX, No. 15 (March 22, 1929), 304.
43. *Ibid.*
44. *Ibid.*, IX, No. 58 (October 11, 1929), 1240.
45. *Ceskoslovenska Vlastiveda*, V, 493. Also *Ottuv Slovnik Naucny, Dodatky*, (Supplements) III, No. 1 (1934), 690–91.
46. G. Smolyansky, "The Chief Obstacles to the Work of the Communist Party of Czechoslovakia," *The Communist International*, X, No. 16 (August 15, 1933).
47. *Ibid.*
48. *Inprecorr*, XIV, No. 15 (March 5, 1934), 369.
49. *Ibid.*, XIV, No. 25 (April 23, 1934), 657.
50. *Ibid.*, IX, No. 45 (August 30, 1929), 959.
51. *Protokoll des VI Ordentlichen Parteitages der KPTsch*, p. 42.
52. *Inprecorr*, XIV, No. 2 (January 12, 1934), 50.
53. *Ibid.*, XIV, No. 7 (February 6, 1934), 127.
54. *Ibid.*, XVI, No. 12 (March 7, 1936), 336.
55. *Ibid.*
56. *Protokoll des VI Ordentlichen Parteitages der KPTsch* (Prague, 1931), pp. 252, and 292 ff.
57. *Die Kommunistische Internationale vor dem VII Weltkongress*, pp. 141–61.
58. *Rude Pravo*, January 15, 1951.
59. *Inprecorr*, XI, No. 17 (March 26, 1931), 342.
60. *Ibid.*, XVI, No. 21 (May 2, 1936), 583.
61. *Ibid.*
62. *Ibid.*, XVI, No. 21 (May 2, 1936), 583. Also Klement Gottwald, *Deset Let (Ten Years)* (Prague: Svoboda, 1947), pp. 22 ff.
63. *Inprecorr*, XVI, No. 10 (February 27, 1936), 279.
64. *Nase Doba*, XLIII, No. 6 (March, 1936), 361, and XLIII, No. 8 (May, 1936), 483.
65. *Inprecorr*, XV, No. 47 (September 21, 1935), 1204.
66. Gottwald, *Deset Let*, p. 29.
67. *Ibid.*, p. 57.
68. *Ibid.*, p. 88.
69. See the comments on this speech in Adolf Zeman, *Ceskoslovenska Golgota*, pp. 242–43.
70. Gottwald, *Deset Let*, pp. 126–27.
71. *Inprecorr*, XVIII, No. 31 (June 18, 1938), 723–24.

Chapter 4: The Party and the Masses

1. Gottwald, *Spisy* (*Collected Works*) (Prague, 1953), I, 109.
2. *Ibid.*
3. See, for example, *Inprekorr* (German edition), XI, No. 63 (June 30, 1931), 1434 ff.
4. *Protokoll 10. Plenum Des Exekutivkomitees der Kommunistischen Internationale,* p. 248.
5. "Les Elections à L'Assemblée Nationale en Avril 1920," *La Statistique Tchecoslovaque* (Prague, 1922), p. 69.
6. Peroutka, *Budovani Statu,* p. 1707.
7. *Ceskoslovenska Vlastiveda,* V, 493.

Chapter 5: Communist Strategy at Home and Abroad

1. *Rude Pravo,* March 28, 1946.
2. I. I. Udaltsev, ed., *Kommunisticheskaia Partiia Chekhoslovakii v Bor'be za Svobodu* (*The Communist Party of Czechoslovakia in the Struggle for Freedom*) (Moscow, 1951), pp. 78–79.
3. Vaclav Kopecky, *CSR a KSC* (*The Czechoslovak Republic and the Czechoslovak Communist Party*) (Prague: SNPL, 1960), p. 301.
4. Sixteen years after the end of World War II, there still is no comprehensive work dealing with the activities of the Communist Party in Bohemia and Moravia. The authoritative Party history, *Dejiny KSC* (*The History of the Czechoslovak Communist Party*) (Prague; SNPL, 1961) passes over the activities of the Czech underground perfunctorily, and the only serious work on the partisan movement, *Partyzanske Hnuti v Ceskoslovensku* (*The Partisan Movement in Czechoslovakia*) (Prague: Nase Vojsko, 1961), treats primarily the events in Slovakia, giving mute testimony to the passivity that characterized the resistance of the Czechs to the German occupation.
5. See Jaroslav Jelinek, *Politicke Ustredi Domaciho Odboje* (*The Political Center of the Domestic Resistance*) (Prague: Kvasnicka a Hampl, 1947), *passim.* This is one of the few accounts of the nature and organization of the non-Communist underground in the Czech lands, written by an unusually objective "rightist" journalist. See also references in Hubert Ripka, *Munich, Before and After* (London: Gollancz, 1939).
6. Vaclav Kopecky, "On the Death of Karel Capek," *World News and Views,* I, No. 19 (January 7, 1939), 8.
7. See the references to the Communist attitude toward him in Eduard Benes, *Pameti* (Memoirs) (Prague: Orbis, 1947), pp. 213 ff.
8. *Rude Pravo,* March 28, 1946.
9. E. Benes, *Pameti,* pp. 218–22.
10. J. Jelinek, *Politicke Ustredi,* pp. 171, 191, 196–98.
11. From 1939 to 1945, 24,920 Communists were reported to have "lost their lives." Of these, 3,649 were executed and 5,687 died in concentration camps. Milos Klimes and Marcel Zachoval, "Prispevek k Problematice Unorovych Udalosti v Ceskoslovensku v Unoru 1948" ("A Contribution to the Analysis of Problems Related to the February Events in Czechoslovakia in February, 1948"), *Ceskoslovensky Casopis Historicky,* VI, No. 2 (1958), 191.
12. *Dejiny KSC,* p. 399.

13. I. I. Udaltsev, *Kommunisticheskaia Partiia*, p. 118.
14. *Ibid.*, p. 186.
15. Stanislav Matousek, *Slovenske Narodne Organy (The Slovak National Organs)* (Bratislava: VSAV, 1960), pp. 83–104; also Josef Lettrich, *History of Modern Slovakia*, pp. 198–208.
16. Zdenek Fierlinger, *Ve Sluzbach CSR (In the Service of the Czechoslovak Republic)* (Prague: Svoboda, 1948), II, 330 ff., and V. Kopecky, *CSR a KSC*, pp. 348–51.
17. I. I. Udaltsev, *Kommunisticheskaia Partiia*, p. 198.
18. See, for example, Oto Krajnak, *Komunisti Bratislavskej Oblasti v Boji Proti Fasizmu v Rokoch 1938-1942 (The Communists of the Bratislava Region in the Struggle Against Fascism, 1938-1942)* (Bratislava: SVPL, 1959), pp. 104–5.
19. E. Benes, *Pameti*, pp. 208 ff.
20. *Ibid.*, p. 144.
21. Z. Fierlinger, *Ve Sluzbach CSR* (Prague: Svoboda, 1947), I, *passim.*
22. E. Benes, *Pameti*, pp. 358 ff.
23. *Ibid.*, p. 362.
24. *Loc. cit.*
25. E. Benes, *Pameti*, pp. 405 ff.
26. *Ibid.*, p. 408.
27. *Loc. cit.*
28. E. Benes, *Pameti*, p. 409.
29. *Loc. cit.*
30. E. Benes, *Pameti*, p. 410.
31. *Ibid.*, p. 413.
32. Z. Fierlinger, *Ve Sluzbach* CSR, II, 200–202.
33. The history of the Czechoslovak Social Democratic movement from 1938 to 1945 is comprehensively treated in a doctoral dissertation prepared under my supervision by Jiri Horak, "The Czechoslovak Social Democratic Party, 1938–1945," Columbia University, 1960.
34. See, for example, Frantisek Klatil, *Pohledy v Zitrek (Glimpses of Tomorrow)* (London, 1944), pp. 13 ff.
35. Klement Gottwald, "O Nekterych Otazkach Politickeho Vedeni Naseho Narodniho Odboje" ("Some Questions Concerning the Leadership of Our National Resistance Movement"), *Ceskoslovenske Listy*, (Moscow), No. 2, February 1, 1944.
36. *Loc. cit.*
37. Klement Gottwald, "O Nekterych Opatrenich Na Osvobozenem Uzemi Republiky" ("About Some Measures to be Taken in Liberated Areas of the Republic"), *Ceskoslovenske Listy*, No. 9, May 15, 1944.
38. I. I. Udaltsev, *Kommunisticheskaia Partiia*, p. 232.
39. See, for example, Kartel Bertelmann, "Vznik Narodnich Vyboru" ("The Origins of the National Committee"), in *Otazky Narodni a Demokraticke Revoluce v CSR (Questions of the National and Democratic Revolution in Czechoslovakia)* (Prague: NCSAV, 1955), pp. 113–38. The formation of National Committees is exhaustively analyzed in a master's essay prepared under my direction by Bohuslav Kymlicka, "The Origins and Establishment of National Committees in Czechoslovakia, 1943–1945," Columbia University, 1961.
40. *Ceskoslovenske Listy*, No. 10, June 1, 1944.
41. *Ibid.*, No. 8, May 1, 1944.

42. *Ibid.*, No. 2, February 1, 1944; and No. 3, February 15, 1944.
43. Jan Sverma, "Slovanska Myslenka v Nasi Ceske Politice," ("The Slavic Idea in Our Czech Politics"), *Ceskoslovenske Listy*, No. 3, September 15, 1943.
44. Vilem Bernard, "O Novou Cestu Socialni Demokracie," ("About the New Path of Social Democracy"), *Ceskoslovenske Listy*, No. 3, February 15, 1944.
45. A documented account of the exchange of views between London and Moscow on this subject will be found in Z. Fierlinger, *Ve Sluzbach CSR*, II, 334 ff.
46. *Cechoslovak* (London), December 15, 1944.
47. *Ibid.*, July 7, 1944.
48. The jockeying for position between the London government and the Communists is described in considerable detail in Z. Fierlinger, *Ve Sluzbach CSR*, II, 567–75.
49. See H. Ripka, *Le Coup de Prague* (Paris: Plon, 1948), p. 16.
50. For an account of the events that took place in the Carpatho-Ukraine see Ivo Duchacek, *The Strategy of Communist Infiltration: The Case of Czechoslovakia* (New Haven: Yale Institute of International Affairs, 1949), pp. 9–15. This subject is also exhaustively treated in Z. Fierlinger, *Ve Sluzbach CSR*, II, 386–90, 397–401, 405–10, 446–55, 462–504, 548–67, and in F. Nemec and V. Moudry, *The Soviet Seizure of Subcarpathian Ruthenia* (Toronto, 1955).
51. Z. Fierlinger, *Ve Sluzbach CSR*, II, 592.
52. I. I. Udaltsev, *Kommunisticheskaia Partiia*, p. 235.
53. *Ibid.*, p. 233.
54. See *Cechoslovak*, April 21, 1945.
55. K. Gottwald, *Deset Let*, p. 284.
56. *Nova Svoboda* (Moravska Ostrava), March 19, 1946.
57. References to this issue can be found in E. Benes, *Pameti*, pp. 33–34. See also Compton Mackenzie, *Dr. Benes*, pp. 184–85.
58. Commentaries on Benes' journeys to Moscow and on his reactions to his dealings with Stalin and the Czechoslovak Communists are provided by the President's wartime secretary, Eduard Taborsky. See his "Benes and Stalin—Moscow 1943 and 1945," *Journal of Central European Affairs*, XIII, No. 2 (July, 1953), 154–81; "Benes and the Soviets," *Foreign Affairs*, XXVII, No. 2 (January, 1949), 302–13; and "Benesovy Moskevske Cesty" ("Benes' Journeys to Moscow"), *Svedectvi*, (New York), I, Nos. 3–4 (1957), 193–214.

Chapter 6: The Setting

1. An account of popular reaction to the Red Army can be found in Jan Stransky, *East Wind over Prague* (New York: Random House, 1951), *passim.*
2. See, for example, I. Duchacek, *The Strategy of Communist Infiltration, passim.*
3. Interview with visiting Czech journalists, *San Francisco Chronicle*, July 6, 1946.
4. A succinct treatment of the underlying principles can be found in G. Craig and Felix Gilbert, eds., *The Diplomats, 1919–1939.*

5. See, for example, Hubert Ripka, *The Czechoslovak-Soviet Treaty* (London, 1943), p. 12.

6. Frantisek Uhlir, *O Nove Ceskoslovensko (For a New Czechoslovakia)* (London, 1944), *passim*.

7. Eduard Taborsky, *Pravda Zvitezila (The Truth Prevailed)* (Prague: Druzstevni Prace, 1947), pp. 411 and 419.

8. Eduard Taborsky, *Nase Nova Ustava (Our New Constitution)* (Prague: CIN, 1948), p. 9.

9. These views were expressed by Benes in one form or another on a number of occasions both before and after the liberation of Czechoslovakia. The quotations here are from a speech Benes delivered in the fall of 1945, upon being accorded an honorary doctorate by Charles University at Prague. The speech was subsequently published under the title E. Benes, *Svetova Krise, Kontinuita Prava a Nove Pravo Revolucni (The World Crisis, Continuity of Law and New Revolutionary Law)* (Prague, 1946).

10. Quoted in *The Marxian Way* (a non-Stalinist Marxist journal edited by the late M. N. Roy, Calcutta, India), 3, 4, (1947), pp. 306 ff.

11. *Ibid.*

12. *Ibid.*

13. Vladimir Kubes, *O Novou Ustavu (For a New Constitution)* (Prague: Melantrich, 1948), p. 38.

14. E. Benes, *Svetova Krise*, p. 22.

15. *Ibid.*

16. *Einheit* (London), VI, No. 12, June 16, 1945 (journal of the German Social Democrats from Czechoslovakia, who remained loyal to the Benes government).

17. I. Duchacek, *The Strategy of Communist Infiltration*, p. 22.

18. E. Benes, "Postwar Czechoslovakia," *Foreign Affairs*, XXIV, No. 3 (April, 1945), 408.

19. Estimate from *Einheit*, VI, No. 1 (January 13, 1945).

20. *Ceskoslovensky Prumysl*, II, No. 12 (December, 1946). (Official journal of the Ministry of Industry.)

21. A good, concise discussion of some aspects of the Czech-Slovak issue can be found in Samuel L. Sharp, "The Czechs and Slovaks: New Aspects of an Old Problem," *American Perspective*, I, No. 5 (October, 1947), 311–22. For a documented account of the evolution of Slovakia's constitutional status in the Republic (including the texts of political agreements) the reader is referred to Jaroslav Moravek, *Ustavni Pomer Cesko-Slovensky (Constitutional Relations between Czechs and Slovaks)* (Prague: V. Tomsa, 1947).

22. See, for example, J. Stransky, *East Wind over Prague*, *passim.*, S.G.D. "Czechoslovakia Revisited," *The World Today*, III, No. 1 (January, 1947), 6–18, and *Rude Pravo*, June 29, 1945.

23. R. R. Betts, *Central and South East Europe, 1945–1948* (London: Royal Institute of International Affairs, 1950), p. 165.

24. Josef Dvorak, *Slovenska Politika Vcera a Dnes (Slovak Politics Yesterday and Today)* (Prague, 1947), p. 118.

25. *Ibid.*, p. 116.

26. *Nase Doba*, LII, No. 8 (June, 1946), 365.

Chapter 7: The Communist Party: Policy, Composition, and Leadership

1. K. Gottwald, *Deset Let*, pp. 274–89.
2. For Rakosi's speech, see *Nepi Demokraciank Utja* (*The Road of Our People's Democracy*) (Budapest: Szikra, 1952).
3. K. Gottwald, *Deset Let*, p. 282.
4. *Loc. cit.*
5. *Loc. cit.*
6. *Loc. cit.*
7. *Loc. cit.*
8. *Ibid.*, p. 285.
9. *Ibid.*, p. 284.
10. *Ibid.*, p. 285.
11. *Ibid.*, pp. 288–89.
12. *Ibid.*, p. 284.
13. *Ibid.*, p. 285.
14. *Ibid.*, pp. 286–87.
15. See Adam Ulam, *Titoism and the Cominform* (Cambridge: Harvard University Press, 1952), p. 58.
16. *Protokol IX Sjezdu KSC* (*Protocol of the Ninth Congress of the Communist Party of Czechoslovakia*) (Prague, 1949), pp. 148–49. The figure for the Czech lands is given as 1,081,544 in *Dejiny KSC*, p. 498.
17. *Protokol IX Sjezdu*, p. 149; and Klimes and Zachoval, *Prispevek k Problematice*, p. 220.
18. *Rude Pravo*, November 30, 1948.
19. Klimes and Zachoval, *Prispevek k Problematice*, p. 220.
20. *Rude Pravo*, November 30, 1948.
21. *Ibid.*, March 31, 1946.
22. *Ibid.*
23. Identical figures are given in *Dejiny KSC* (p. 498), but Klimes and Zachoval, *Prispevek k Problematice* (p. 220), give an entirely different breakdown. According to these authors, workers constituted only 43 per cent of the Communist membership, agricultural workers accounted for 4 per cent, state employees 11.6 per cent, farmers 7.4 per cent, private employees 4.4 per cent, artisans 4.1 per cent, professional people and students 1.4 per cent, soldiers and policemen 1.1 per cent, housewives 19.1 per cent, and pensioners 3.8 per cent.
24. *Rude Pravo*, March 31, 1946.
25. L. Frejka, *26. Unor*, p. 44; also *Rude Pravo*, November 19, 1948.
26. *Ibid.*
27. *Rude Pravo*, February 25, 1949.
28. *Ibid.*, May 22, 1946. (See this issue for a short biography of Svermova and other leading women members of the Communist Party.)
29. For this information on Kolman, see *Tvorba* (the Czech Communist literary weekly) XIV, No. 17 (December 12, 1945).
30. Gustav Beuer, *New Czechoslovakia and her Historical Background* (London: Lawrence and Wishart, 1947).
31. See Karl Gorovsky, *Der Heutige Stand der KP der Tschechoslovakei!* (Prague, 1928). This is a highly polemical and personally vituperative little pamphlet, recording some aspects of the Bolshevization of the Czech Communist Party and giving vignettes of a few Communist leaders.
32. *New York Times*, July 15, 1952.

33. *Funkcionar* (the Party journal for functionaries), IV No. 23, December 7, 1949.
34. *Rude Pravo,* November 23, 1946.
35. These disclosures were made in November, 1952, at the trial of 14 Communist leaders, of whom one was Geminder. See *Rude Pravo,* November 22, 1952.
36. Vltavsky is identified as "one of the oldest and best known militants, who was a confidant of Lenin's in Switzerland . . . and who knew all the secrets of the Third International. He was . . . a confidant of Stalin's . . . Gottwald's shadow, who in the final analysis decided everything [in the Czechoslovak Communist Party]." E. Reale, *Avec Jacques Duclos au Banc des Accuses* (Paris: Plon, 1958), pp. 12–13. See also the reference to Geminder as "one of the most senior and important Party officials," in Wolfgang Leonhard, *Child of the Revolution* (Chicago: Henry Regnery, 1958), p. 249.
37. *Rude Pravo,* November 18, 1948.

Chapter 8: The Conquest of Political Institutions

1. See V. I. Lenin, *State and Revolution* (New York: International Publishers, 1932), p. 33.
2. Eduard Taborsky, *Czechoslovak Democracy at Work* (London: George Allen and Unwin, 1945), p. 102.
3. E. Taborsky, *Nase Nova Ustava,* p. 23.
4. I. Duchacek, *The Strategy of Communist Infiltration,* p. 22.
5. *Ibid.,* p. 25.
6. *Rude Pravo,* November 15, 1945.
7. For statistics and information concerning the Provisional Assembly, see *Rocenka Prozatimniho Narodniho Shromazdeni Republiky Ceskoslovenske, 1945–1946 (Yearbook of the Provisional National Assembly)* (Prague: Ministry of Information, 1946).
8. I. Duchacek, *The Strategy of Communist Infiltration,* p. 15.
9. For a thorough discussion of the legal history of National Committees see Adolf Stafl, *Narodni Vybory* (National Committees: Prague, 1951).
10. *Rude Pravo,* May 20, 1945.
11. A. Stafl, *Narodni Vybory,* pp. 42 ff.
12. I. Duchacek, *The Strategy of Communist Infiltration,* p. 16.
13. N. P. Farberov, *Gosudarstvennoe Pravo Stran Narodnoi Demokratii* (Moscow, 1949), p. 175; *Dejiny KSC,* p. 505; and Klimes and Zachoval, *Prispevek k Problematice,* p. 197.
14. *Czechoslovakia on the Road to Socialism* (Prague, 1949), p. 189.
15. See Sbornik Lidove Spravy, *Rukovet Pro Funkcionare Narodnich Vyboru (Handbook for Officials of National Committees)* (Prague, 1947).
16. See, for example, Adolf Prochazka, *Lidova Strana v Narodni Fronte (The People's Party in the National Front)* (Prague, 1946), p. 8.
17. *Pravo Lidu,* May 12, 1945.
18. Hubert Ripka, *Czechoslovakia Enslaved: The Story of the Communist Coup d'État* (London: Gollancz, 1950), p. 19.
19. *Sbirka Zakonu a Narizeni (Collection of Laws and Statutes),* No. 149 (1947).
20. For a more detailed treatment of the evolution of the Czechoslovak military from 1945 to 1952, the reader might consult Ithiel de Sola Pool,

Satellite Generals, A Study of Military Elites in the Soviet Sphere (Stanford, Calif.: Stanford University Press, 1955), pp. 28–54.

21. Jaromir Navratil, "K Otazce Boje o Politicky Character CS. Armady v Predunorovem Obdobi" ("On the Struggle for the Political Character of the Czechoslovak Armed Forces in the Period before February"), *Historie a Vojenstvi,* III (1958), p. 425. According to this Communist source, 10,000 officers, "the overwhelming majority of the pre-Munich officer corps," were reinstated in 1945 alone. In Slovakia, only 87 of 1,530 applicants for reinstatement were rejected. Meanwhile, only a few partisans secured rapid promotion in the armed forces.

22. *Ibid.,* p. 426.

23. *Ibid.,* pp. 413–15.

24. Ludvik Svoboda, *Z Buzuluku do Prahy (From Buzuluk to Prague)* (Prague: Mlada Fronta, 1960), p. 305. See also Jaroslav Prochazka, "Prispevek k Historii Stranicke Organisace KSC v Cs. Vojenskych Jednotkach v SSSR" ("A Contribution to the History of the Communist Party's Organization in the Czechoslovak Army Units in the USSR), *Historie a Vojenstvi,* IV (1957), p. 562.

Chapter 9: Social Organizations, the Economy, and Mass Communications

1. *Prace,* December 14, 1949.

2. *Sbirka,* No. 144 (May 16, 1946).

3. *Ibid.*

4. *Rude Pravo,* July 4, 1945.

5. *Sbirka,* No. 104 (October 24, 1945).

6. See Government Ordinance in *Sbirka,* No. 216 (November 5, 1946), amending some sections of the Works-Council Decree.

7. *Rude Pravo,* April 24, 1946.

8. *Prace,* March 1, 1947, and December 2, 1949.

9. The date set by law for the termination of automatic exemption from prosecution for acts of violence committed on behalf of the "public good" (i.e., the liberation of Czechoslovakia) was October 28, 1945.

10. *Svobodne Slovo,* May 12, 1946.

11. For a general discussion of the political and economic aspects of land reform, see Jiri Kotatko, *Land Reform in Czechoslovakia* (Prague: Orbis, 1948).

12. See the article giving the Communist version of the "struggle for nationalization" in *Tvorba,* XIX, No. 43 (October 15, 1950), and XIX, No. 44 (November 1, 1950).

13. *Ceskoslovensky Prumysl,* I, No. 2 (August, 1945).

14. *Ibid.*

15. *Ibid.*

16. *Tvorba,* XIX, No. 43 (October 15, 1950).

17. *Ceskoslovensky Prumysl,* II, No. 6 (June, 1946), 202.

18. See *Statement of Policy of Mr. Gottwald's Government* (Prague: Orbis, 1946), p. 12.

19. See Josef Goldmann, *Czechoslovakia, Test Case of Nationalisation* (Prague: Orbis, 1947); and also *Zaklady Ceskoslovenske Dvouletky (Foundations of the Czechoslovak Two-Year Plan)* (Prague: Ministry of Information, 1946).

20. Klimes and Zachoval, *Prispevek k Problematice,* p. 195.

21. *Svobodne Noviny,* December 2, 1945, and *Rude Pravo,* December 22, 1945.

22. *Rude Pravo*, October 2, 1947.
23. For example, see *Tvorba* XV, No. 20 (May 25, 1946).
24. K. Gottwald, *Deset Let*, p. 348.
25. *Loc. cit.;* also *Prace*, March 11, 1947, and many other places.
26. *Rude Pravo*, March 31, 1946.
27. *Ibid.*
28. *Tvorba*, XV, No. 14 (April 3, 1946).
29. *Ibid.*, XV, No. 10 (March 10, 1946).
30. See *Rude Pravo*, March 28, 1946.
31. *Ibid.*, May 20, 1946.
32. *Ibid.*, April 3, 1946.
33. See, for example, *Rude Pravo*, April 5, 1946, and May 20, 1946.
34. *Ibid.*, April 3, 1946.
35. *Ibid.*, April 4, 1946.
36. K. Gottwald, *Deset Let*, p. 300; Antonin Zapotocky, *Po Staru Se Zit Neda (It is Impossible to Live in the Old Way)* (Prague: Prace, 1949), p. 49; Antonin Zmrhal, *Ceskoslovensky Vnitrni Obchod (Domestic Commerce in Czechoslovakia)* (Prague: Ustredni Svaz Obchodu, 1947), *passim.*
37. Vincenc Kramar, *Kulturne Politicky Program KSC a Vytvarne Umeni (The Cultural-Political Program of the Communist Party of Czechoslovakia and Creative Art)* (Prague, 1946), *passim.*
38. *Rude Pravo*, March 31, 1946.
39. *Ibid.*, May 23, 1946.
40. See, for example, *Lidova Demokracie*, May 27, 1946.

Chapter 10: The Revolution in the Balance: The General Election and Political Skirmishing

1. *Protokol IX Sjezdu KSC*, p. 361.
2. *Rude Pravo*, November 19, 1948.
3. The entire history of the activities of the extraordinary People's Courts and of the National Tribunal charged with trying the cases of top collaborationists is aptly summarized in *Na Soudu Naroda (Before the Nation's Tribunal)*, (Prague: Ministry of Justice, 1947.) The pamphlet contains three speeches of Prokop Drtina, the Minister of Justice.
4. *Rude Pravo*, November 19, 1948.
5. For an illuminating comment on the Czech view on collaboration see an editorial by E. Bass in *Svobodne Noviny*, September 23, 1945.
6. Hubert Ripka, *Czechoslovakia Enslaved*, pp. 56 ff.
7. See *Pravo Lidu*, November 14–18, 1947.
8. *Pravda* (Bratislava), November 20, 1947.
9. E. Reale, *Avec Jacques Duclos au Banc des Accuses, passim.*
10. *Rude Pravo*, November 17, 1947.

Chapter 11: The Coup d'État and Its Antecedents

1. *Rude Pravo*, November 30, 1947.
2. *Ibid.*
3. *Ibid.*
4. *Ibid.*, February 18, 1948.
5. L. Frejka, *26. Unor*, p. 42.

6. See *What is Your Opinion? A Year's Survey of Public Opinion in Czecho-slovakia* (Prague: Orbis, 1947).
7. Hubert Ripka, *Le Coup de Prague*, p. 190.
8. *Pravo Lidu,* February 6, 1948.
9. *Svobodne Slovo,* February 6, 1948.
10. *Ibid.,* February 7, 1948.
11. *Rude Pravo,* February 11, 1948.
12. *Ibid.,* February 14, 1948.
13. *Ibid.,* February 13, 1948.
14. *Ibid.,* February 15, 1948.
15. *Ibid.*
16. *Ibid.,* February 19, 1948.
17. *Svobodne Slovo,* February 13, 1948.
18. *Ibid.,* February 18, 1948.
19. *Ibid.,* February 19, 1948.
20. L. Frejka, *26. Unor,* p. 42.
21. *Loc. cit.*
22. *Rude Pravo,* February 18, 1948.
23. *Ibid.*
24. Miroslav Boucek, "Vznik a Uloha Lidovych Milici v Unoru 1948" ("The Origin and the Part Played by the People's Militia in 1948"), *Prispevky k Dejinam KSC,* VIII (1959), p. 72. This article comprehensively reviews the formation of the workers' militia and the uses to which it was put, revealing some previously unknown information.
25. The events of the coup d'état have been commented upon in a number of publications by democrats who fled Czechoslovakia after 1948. This documentary record fails to clear up controversial questions concerning the democrats' motives, plans, and expectations, and it does not offer any convincing excuse for their ineptness.
26. Anonymous, *What Happened in Czechoslovakia?* (Prague: Orbis, 1948), pp. 76–78. A Communist-inspired account of the February coup which, aside from recounting the Communist version of some critical developments, contains a helpful English text of several key speeches and documents. Later Communist accounts, such as Jindrich Vesely's *Kronika Unorovych Dnu 1948 (Chronicle of the Days of February 1948)* (Prague: SNPL, 1959), and *Vitezny Unor 1948 (The Victorious February of 1948; a book of reminiscences)* (Prague: SNPL, 1959), contain many useful details, although they also include distortions, made necessary by retrospective corrections of historical interpretations and omissions of Communist personalities who were purged from the Party after 1948. These volumes add little substantive information to what is known about the coup d'état.
27. M. Boucek, *Vznik a Uloha Lidovych Milici,* pp. 78–79.
28. Walter Storm, *The Crisis in Czechoslovakia* (Prague: Orbis, 1948), p. 52. Another pro-Communist version of the coup d'état.
29. *Pravo Lidu,* February 21, 1948.
30. L. Frejka, *26. Unor,* p. 44.
31. *Loc. cit.*
32. *Ibid.,* p. 50.
33. Walter Storm, *The Crisis,* p. 31.
34. M. Boucek, *Vznik a Uloha Lidovych Milici,* p. 78.
35. W. Storm, *The Crisis,* p. 31.

36. Anon., *What Happened in Czechoslovakia*, pp. 53–57.
37. W. Storm, *The Crisis*, pp. 30–38.
38. *Prace*, February 24, 1948.
39. See Josef Plojhar, *Vitezny Unor 1948 a CS. Strana Lidova (The Victorious February of 1948 and the Czechoslovak People's Party)* (Prague: NLD, 1958), p. 57.
40. Anon., *What Happened in Czechoslovakia*, p. 48.
41. *Loc. cit.*
42. L. Frejka, *26. Unor*, p. 46.
43. *Rude Pravo*, February 24, 1948.
44. Anon., *What Happened*, pp. 40–46.
45. W. Storm, *The Crisis*, p. 46.
46. *Rude Pravo*, November 19, 1948.
47. *Ibid.*, February 20, 1948.
48. *Ibid.*, February 27, 1948.
49. W. Storm, *The Crisis*, p. 37.
50. *Ibid.*, p. 31.
51. H. Ripka, *Czechoslovakia Enslaved*, pp. 208–20.
52. *Ibid.*, p. 287.
53. L. Frejka, *26. Unor*, p. 50.
54. *Ibid.*, p. 47.

Epilogue

1. L. Frejka, *26. Unor*, p. 36.
2. *Ibid.*, p. 44.
3. Josef Goldmann *et al.*, *Planned Economy in Czechoslovakia* (Prague: Orbis, 1949), pp. 107–9.
4. *Prvni Ceskoslovensky Petilety Plan (The First Czechoslovak Five-Year Plan)* (Prague: Ministerstvo Informaci a Osvety, 1948).
5. Leo Gruliow (ed.), *Current Soviet Policies II: The Documentary Record of the 20th Communist Party Congress and Its Aftermath* (New York: Frederick A. Praeger, 1957), p. 85. The Czechoslovak Communists themselves, especially in the years following Stalin's death, published a number of tracts dealing with the theoretical aspects of the national and democratic revolution and reviewing the grand strategy of the Party from 1945 to 1948. Aside from works already cited, the following contain useful information:
   Otazky Narodni a Demokraticke Revoluce v CSR (Questions of the National and Democratic Revolution in Czechoslovakia) (Prague: CSAV, 1955), a symposium on the tenth anniversary of the liberation of Czechoslovakia.
   Jaroslav Houska and Karel Kara, *Otazky Lidove Demokracie (Questions of People's Democracy)* (Prague: SNPL, 1955), especially pp. 66–177.
   Jan Kozak, *K Nekterym Otazkam Strategie a Taktiky KSC v Obdobi Prerustani Narodni a Demokraticke Revoluce v Revoluci Socialistickou: 1945–1948 (About Several Questions of Strategy and Tactics of the KSC in the Period of Transition from the National Democratic to the Socialist Revolution: 1945–1948)* (Prague, 1956).
   Ivan Bystrina, *Lidova Demokracie (People's Democracy)* (Prague: CSAV, 1957).

Michal Lakatos, *Otazky Lidove Demokracie v Ceskoslovensku (Questions of People's Democracy in Czechoslovakia)* (Prague: CSAV, 1957).

Jaroslav Opat, *Generalni Linie Vystavby Socialismu v CSR (The General Line of Construction of Socialism in the Czechoslovak Republic)* (Prague: SNPL, 1957).

Jan Kozak, "K Objasneni Postupu UV KSC v Boji za Ziskani Vetsiny Naroda v Obdobi pred Unorem 1948," ("For the Clarification of the Policies of the Central Committee of the KSC in the Struggle for Gaining a Majority of the Nation in the Period Before February, 1948"), *Prispevky k Dejinam KSC,* II (1958), 3–38.

Jaroslav Opat, "K Zakladnim Problemum Tridnich Vztahu a Politiky KSC v Dobe Upevnovani Unoroveho Vitezstvi" ("About Basic Problems of Class Relations and the Policy of the KSC in the Period of Consolidation of the February Victory"), *Prispevky k Dejinam KSC,* VI (1959), 3–70.

Gottwald's speech before the Prague regional conference of Communists on March 28, 1948, printed in full for the first time in *Prispevky k Dejinam KSC,* VIII (1959), 108–29.

Jan Kozak, "Vyznam Vnitrostranicke Diskuse Pred VIII. Sjezdem" ("The Significance of Intraparty Discussions before the VIII Congress [of the KSC, in March, 1946]"), *Prispevky k Dejinam KSC,* XII (1960), 21–47.

6. Karl Marx and Friedrich Engels, "Address of the Central Council to the Communist League," *Karl Marx: Selected Works* (New York: International Publishers, n.d.), II, 160–61.

Tables

TABLE 1

Communist Party Membership, 1921–38*

Year	Number of Members
1921	350,000
1922	170,000
1923	132,000[a]
1924	138,996[b]
	99,700[c]
1925	93,220[b]
1926	92,818[b]
1927	138,000[b]
1928	150,000[b]
1929	81,432[b]
1930:	
Spring	30,212[d]
Winter	37,998[d]
1931:	
Spring	40,000[d]
Fall	35,000[e]
1932:	
Fall	72,000[e]
1933:	
Spring	75,000[f]
1936	70,000[g]
1938	50,000[h]

*All figures are from Communist sources.

[a] *Dejiny KSC*, p. 194.

[b] *Protokoll 10. Plenum des Exekutivkomitees der Kommunistischen Internationale, 3 Juli 1929 bis 19 Juli 1929*, pp. 50 ff.

[c] *Dejiny KSC*, p. 213.

[d] *Internationale Presse Korrespondenz*, XI, 63 (June 30, 1931), 1434.

[e] *International Press Correspondence*, XII, 53 (December 1, 1932), 1151.

[f] *International Press Correspondence*, XIII, 16 (April 7, 1933), 370.

[g] *Dejiny KSC*, p. 349.

[h] Estimate based on postwar membership figures released by the Czechoslovak Communist Party.

TABLE 2

Communist Trade-Union Strength, 1922–37*

Year	Membership of Communist unions	Total number of union members
1922	89,941	1,712,934
1923	168,542	1,629,939
1924	210,611	1,690,584
1925	201,035	1,710,857
1926	196,509	1,671,382
1927	179,993	1,681,054
1928	165,780	1,733,979
1929	164,563	1,715,193
1930	113,702	1,730,494
1931	130,498	1,821,292
1932	167,535	1,974,527
1933	157,489	1,914,591
1934	172,681	1,994,236
1935	178,867	2,107,721
1936	152,295	2,219,059
1937	136,204	2,387,090

*Source: *Zpravy Statniho Uradu Statistickeho,* XIX (1938), 104–7, 701.

TABLE 3

Communist Trade-Union Strength Compared with
Social Democratic Trade-Union Strength, 1937*

(*by type of occupation*)

Industry or Occupation	Number of members in Communist union	Number of members in Social Democratic union
Mining	10,556	23,382
Iron and steel	18,033	97,819
Leather	2,377	6,275
Glass and ceramics	13,040	10,124
Independent trades	2,476	71,787
Building trades	31,662	42,274
Textile	32,377	31,260
White collar	1,024	20,350
Agriculture	19,127	27,559
Transportation	5,532	55,222

*Source: *Zpravy Statniho Uradu Statistickeho,* XIX (1938), 104–7, 797, 804.

TABLE 4

Communist Trade-Union Strength, 1937*
(*by area and nationality distribution*)

Area	Number of members	Percentage of gainfully employed persons
Bohemia	70,081	2.81
Moravia-Silesia	29,845	2.65
Slovakia	29,764	4.20
Ruthenia	6,514	5.64
Total	136,204	3.06

Nationality	Number of members	Percentage of total Communist union members	Percentage of total union members in given national group
Czech and Slovak	71,558	52.54	4.09
German	42,728	31.37	7.41
Hungarian	15,534	11.41	46.92
Other	6,384	4.68	

*Source: *Zpravy Statniho Uradu Statistickeho,* XIX (1938), 104–7, 794 ff.

TABLE 5

Comparative Electoral Strength of Social Democratic and
Communist Parties, 1920–35*

Province	Year	Total number of votes	Social Democratic Party	Communist Party	Total Social Democrats and Communists
Bohemia	1920	3,412,452	762,092		762,092
	1925	3,704,468	385,968	468,182	854,150
	1929	3,867,981	535,263	398,351	933,614
	1935	4,270,905	551,579	384,756	936,329
Moravia-Silesia	1920	1,446,389	318,087		318,087
	1925	1,729,777	166,141	191,850	357,991
	1929	1,822,749	269,631	162,125	431,756
	1935	2,024,968	269,089	174,574	443,663
Slovakia	1920	1,341,191	510,341		510,341
	1925	1,425,288	60,602	198,010	258,612
	1929	1,428,030	135,496	152,385	287,885
	1935	1,625,549	184,389	210,785	395,174
Ruthenia	1920	No elections			
	1925	245,743	18,183	75,669	93,852
	1929	266,324	22,922	40,583	63,505
	1935	309,990	29,717	79,400	109,117

*Source: 1920 elections from *Zpravy Statniho Uradu Statistickeho*, II (1921),
2; 1925 elections, *ibid.*, VI (1925), 76; 1929 elections, *ibid.*, X (1929), 87, series
b; 1935 elections, *ibid.*, XVI (1935).

253

TABLE 6

Election Returns in the Czech Lands, 1935 and 1946*

District	Year	Total number of votes	Communist Party		National Socialist Party		People's Party		Social Democratic Party		Other, right-wing parties[b]	
			number	percentage	number	percentage	number	percentage	number	percentage	number	percentage
Prague	1946	661,901	239,059	36.1	221,099	33.3	105,252	15.9	96,491	14.5*		
	1935•	489,055	69,762	14.3	107,200	21.9	29,767	6.1	77,773	15.9	204,553	41.8
Kladno	1946	239,299	128,619	53.6	55,186	23.0	20,540	8.6	34,954	14.6		
	1935	224,757	50,350	22.4	31,723	14.2	9,189	4.1	45,365	20.1	88,125	39.2
Mlada Boleslav	1946	212,551	93,128	43.7	62,679	29.4	30,349	14.2	26,395	12.4		
	1935	191,427	18,815	9.8	33,685	17.8	15,659	8.4	26,035	13.5	97,233	50.5
Prague rural districts, south	1946	308,825	145,437	47.2	76,436	24.7	42,225	13.6	44,727	14.4		
	1935	265,967	48,863	18.4	45,203	16.9	19,475	7.2	49,687	18.8	102,739	38.7
Plzen	1946	356,281	160,124	44.9	78,904	22.1	50,434	14.1	66,819	18.7		
	1935	308,580	14,403	4.7	50,735	16.5	17,732	5.7	108,251	35.1	117,459	38.0
Karlovy Vary	1946	83,937	44,063	52.2	19,460	23.1	6,173	7.3	14,241	16.9		
	1935	38,648	20,761	53.8	4,979	12.9	483	1.2	4,821	12.5	7,604	19.6
Usti nad Labem	1946	243,169	137,936	56.5	48,008	19.7	10,665	4.4	46,560	19.1		
	1935	125,410	30,903	24.6	35,197	28.1	2,642	2.1	30,279	24.1	26,389	21.1
Liberec	1946	206,280	100,110	48.3	52,271	25.3	21,983	10.6	31,916	15.4		
	1935	144,301	35,673	24.9	28,573	20.0	8,433	5.4	24,540	17.2	47,082	32.5
Hradec Kralove	1946	313,835	124,236	39.5	81,325	25.8	61,208	19.4	47,066	15.0		
	1935	272,279	25,501	9.4	45,471	16.7	35,467	13.0	42,914	15.8	122,926	45.1
Pardubice	1946	263,039	94,031	35.7	57,775	22.0	63,605	24.2	46,786	17.8		
	1935	236,250	16,601	7.0	35,223	14.9	35,968	15.2	46,369	19.6	102,089	43.3

	Year											
Havlickuv Brod	1946	216,217	89,924	41.5	46,927	21.7	52,258	24.1	27,108	12.6	100,183	48.8
	1935	205,560	18,787	9.1	24,256	11.8	27,026	13.1	35,308	17.2		
Tabor	1946	183,436	73,164	39.7	42,005	22.9	50,284	27.3	17,983	9.8	95,969	54.5
	1935	175,944	13,943	7.9	19,962	11.4	26,980	15.3	19,090	10.9		
Ceske Budejovice	1946	265,382	112,021	42.1	56,350	21.2	65,028	24.4	31,983	12.0	126,096	52.3
	1935	241,038	16,009	6.6	32,069	13.3	26,653	11.1	40,211	16.7		
Jihlava	1946	217,317	84,286	38.6	37,382	17.2	69,892	32.0	25,757	11.8	80,269	46.6
	1935	172,236	12,182	7.0	17,007	9.8	38,903	22.8	23,875	13.8		
Brno	1946	514,389	174,518	33.8	127,243	24.7	138,405	26.8	74,223	14.4	142,459	35.3
	1935	403,725	43,468	10.8	73,990	18.3	82,947	20.5	60,861	15.1		
Olomouc	1946	396,011	128,852	32.4	83,528	21.1	110,596	27.8	73,035	18.4	124,320	39.2
	1935	317,141	29,640	9.3	32,154	10.1	69,717	22.0	61,310	19.3		
Zlin	1946	278,490	86,279	30.9	50,616	18.2	101,719	36.4	39,876	14.2	91,577	39.8
	1935	230,205	21,480	9.3	21,826	9.5	63,474	27.6	31,848	13.8		
Moravska Ostrava	1946	396,680	151,668	37.9	78,968	19.7	79,789	19.9	86,255	21.6	98,308	30.4
	1935	323,528	61,173	18.9	41,569	12.8	46,814	14.5	75,664	23.4		
Opava	1946	115,027	38,242	33.1	22,818	19.8	30,604	26.5	23,363	20.2	17,989	27.5
	1935	65,414	6,631	10.1	11,551	17.7	13,712	21.0	15,531	23.7		

*Source: 1946 figures from *Statistical Bulletin of Czechoslovakia*, I, Nos. 2–3 (1946), 9; 1935 figures from *Zpravy Statniho Uradu Statistickeho*, XVI (1935).

a The 1935 percentages are figured in terms of the approximate total of Czech votes, discounting the positively identifiable "minority vote," in order to provide a basis for comparison with the relative standing of the Czech parties in 1946. For the purpose of this table, the 1935 Communist vote is included under the heading of Czech votes, although in several districts, with a heavy concentration of Germans, it is significantly inflated by the electoral support of this nationality and is not properly comparable with the other Czech parties.

b Under this heading are included all "right wing" Czech parties that participated in the 1935 elections, but were outlawed after the war. For this reason, no figures appear in the column for 1946.

c Where the percentages do not equal 100 per cent, the difference is accounted for by the so-called "blank ballots," which voters were permitted to cast if they did not approve of the slates presented.

TABLE 7

1946 Election Returns in Slovakia*

District	Democratic Party		Communist Party		Freedom Party		Labor Party	
	number	percent-age	number	percent-age	number	percent-age	number	percent-age
Bratislava	132,912	60.16	66,792	30.23	8,705	3.94	10,057	4.55
Trnava	108,486	56.93	62,962	33.04	11,790	6.19	5,655	2.97
Trencin	98,446	60.38	55,535	34.06	4,033	2.47	3,864	2.37
Nitra	93,073	58.79	45,867	28.97	13,994	8.84	4,226	2.67
Zilina	91,588	60.49	52,527	34.69	2,690	1.78	3,492	2.31
Liptovsky Sv. Mikulas	123,861	68.36	49,230	27.17	2,411	1.33	4,378	2.42
Banska Bystrica	104,271	52.71	77,671	39.27	7,042	3.56	7,358	3.72
Presov	96,377	68.12	39,610	28.00	2,362	1.67	2,401	1.70
Kosice	150,543	72.55	39,336	18.96	7,173	3.46	8,783	4.23

*Source: *Statistical Bulletin of Czechoslovakia*, I, Nos. 2–3 (1946), 9. No comparison with 1935 is possible, because electoral districts were substantially changed.

TABLE 8

Distribution of Votes Between the Left and the Right in the
General Election of 1946*

(figures denote percentages of total vote[a])

Province	Left[c]	Right[d]
Bohemia	58.2	41.5
District		
Prague	50.6	49.2
Kladno	68.2	31.6
Mlada Boleslav	56.1	43.6
Prague (rural)	61.6	38.3
Plzen[b]	63.6	36.2
Karlovy Vary[b]	69.1	30.4
Usti nad Labem[b]	75.6	24.1
Liberec[b]	63.7	35.9
Hradec Kralove	54.5	45.2
Pardubice	53.5	46.2
Havlickuv Brod	54.1	45.8
Tabor	49.5	50.2
Ceske Budejovice	54.1	45.6
Moravia-Silesia	51.2	48.4
Jihlava	50.4	49.2
Brno	48.2	51.5
Olomouc	50.8	48.9
Zlin	45.1	54.6
Moravska Ostrava	59.5	39.6
Opava[b]	53.3	46.3
Slovakia	33.5	65.7
Bratislava	34.8	64.1
Trnava	36.0	63.1
Trencin	36.4	62.9
Nitra	31.7	67.7
Zilina	37.0	62.3
Liptovsky Sv. Mikulas	29.6	69.7
Banska Bystrica	43.0	56.3
Presov	29.7	69.7
Kosice	23.2	76.1
Czechoslovakia (Parliament)	50.7	48.9

*Figures computed from data in the *Statistical Bulletin of Czechoslovakia*, I, Nos. 2–3 (1946), 9.

[a] Where the percentages do not equal 100 per cent, the difference is accounted for by the so-called "blank ballots," which voters were permitted to cast if they did not approve of the slates presented.

[b] Border districts from which Germans were expelled and into which there has been intensive immigration of Czechs.

[c] Includes Communists and Social Democrats in the Czech lands, and Communists and the Labor Party in Slovakia.

[d] Includes the National Socialist and People's parties in the Czech lands, and the Democratic and Freedom parties in Slovakia.

TABLE 9

Summary of 1946 Election Returns*

Party	Bohemia		Moravia		Slovakia		Czechoslovakia	
	number of votes	percentage	number of votes	percentage	number of votes	percentage	number of votes	percentage
Communist	1,541,852	43.3	663,845	34.5	489,530	30.4	2,695,227	38.0
National Socialist	898,425	25.2	400,555	20.8			1,299,980	18.3
People's	580,004	16.3	531,005	27.6			1,111,009	15.6
Social Democratic	533,029	14.9	322,509	16.7			855,538	12.1
Democratic					999,557	62.0	999,557	14.1
Freedom					60,200	3.7	60,200	.9
Labor					50,214	3.1	50,214	.7
"Blank ballots"	10,969	.3	8,484	.4	12,711	.8	32,164	.3
Total	3,564,279	100	1,926,398	100	1,612,212	100	7,102,889	100

* Source: *Statistical Bulletin of Czechoslovakia*, I, Nos. 2–3 (1946), 10.

INDEX